P9-DYJ-643

Insightful.
Inspiring.
Full of knowledge.
You just can't
put a good
bookseller down.

Waterstones

ADAM FOULDS

'Intensely pleasurable to read'

Observer

DAVID SZALAY

'A texture of truthfuln
quite unlike that of an
other fiction'

Evening Standard

ADAM
THIRLWELL

'A craftsman –
a master builder –
hugely entertaining'

Scotsman

BRITISH NOVELISTS

EVIE WYLD

'So complete, so compelling and potent, that you are fearful of breaking its hold'
Daily Mail

XIAOLU GUO

'It is impossible not to be charmed'
Sunday Times

GRANTA

12 Addison Avenue, London W11 4QR | email editorial@granta.com
To subscribe go to www.granta.com, or call 845-267-3031 (toll-free 866-438-6150)
in the United States, 020 8955 7011 in the United Kingdom

ISSUE 123: SPRING 2013

EDITOR	John Freeman
DEPUTY EDITOR	Ellah Allfrey
ARTISTIC DIRECTOR	Michael Salu
ASSOCIATE EDITOR	Patrick Ryan
ONLINE EDITOR	Ted Hodgkinson
EDITORIAL ASSISTANT	Yuka Igarashi
PUBLICITY	Saskia Vogel
ASSISTANT DESIGNER	Daniela Silva
FINANCE	Geoffrey Gordon, Morgan Graver, Craig Nicholson
MARKETING AND SUBSCRIPTIONS	David Robinson
SALES DIRECTOR	Brigid Macleod
SALES MANAGER	Sharon Murphy
TO ADVERTISE CONTACT	Kate Rochester, katerochester@granta.com
IT MANAGER	Mark Williams
PRODUCTION ASSOCIATE	Sarah Wasley
PROOFS	David Atkinson, Sarah Barlow, Katherine Fry, Jessica Rawlinson, Vimbai Shire
PUBLISHER	Sigrid Rausing
CONTRIBUTING EDITORS	Daniel Alarcón, Diana Athill, Peter Carey, Mohsin Hamid, Sophie Harrison, Isabel Hilton, Blake Morrison, John Ryle, Edmund White

Congratulations to two of our Picador authors

Sunjeev Sahota

© Simon Revill

picador.com/oursarethestreets

Helen Oyeyemi

To pre-order a signed first edition of Helen's new book coming in 2014 visit: Panmacmillan.com/helen

© Saneesh Sukumaran

Faber and Faber congratulates

SARAH HALL
BENJAMIN MARKOVITS
JOANNA KAVENNA

2013 *Granta* Best of Young British Novelists

CONTENTS

11 **Introduction**
    John Freeman

19 **Vipers**
    Kamila Shamsie

39 **Glow**
    Ned Beauman

53 **Anwar Gets Everything**
    Tahmima Anam

67 **Soon and in Our Days**
    Naomi Alderman

83 **Filsan**
    Nadifa Mohamed

103 **Europa**
    David Szalay

127 **After the Hedland**
    Evie Wyld

147 **Driver**
    Taiye Selasi

165 **Slow Motion**
    Adam Thirlwell

185 **The End of Endings**
    Steven Hall

211 **A World Intact**
    Adam Foulds

CONTENTS

225 **The Best of Young British Novelists**
Nadav Kander

257 **You Don't Have to Live Like This**
Benjamin Markovits

283 **Tomorrow**
Joanna Kavenna

295 **Just Right**
Zadie Smith

311 **The Reservation**
Sarah Hall

329 **Interim Zone**
Xiaolu Guo

335 **Boy, Snow, Bird**
Helen Oyeyemi

351 **Zephyrs**
Jenni Fagan

359 **Arrivals**
Sunjeev Sahota

383 **Submersion**
Ross Raisin

LONDON LITERATURE FESTIVAL /

20 MAY – 5 JUNE 2013

Literary stars join us at Southbank Centre for the London Literature Festival. The festival includes two prize-reading events – the 2013 Man International Booker Prize Readings and the Women's Prize for Fiction Readings.

William Dalrymple
Barbara Kingsolver
Audrey Niffenegger
Lionel Shriver
Rebecca Solnit
Claire Tomalin
Gavin Turk & Jarvis Cocker

Tom Dixon
AC Grayling
Ute Lemper Sings Pablo Neruda
Rachel Lichtenstein
Man International Booker Prize Readings
China Miéville
Cornelia Parker
Sylvia Plath's *Ariel*
Polari
James Salter
George Saunders
Richard Sennett
Craig Taylor's One Million Tiny Plays About London
Paul Theroux
Women's Prize for Fiction Readings
& many more

TICKETS: 0844 847 9910
londonlitfest.com

Part of Southbank Centre's
Festival of Neighbourhood
with MasterCard

SOUTHBANK CENTRE

Supporting using public funding by
ARTS COUNCIL ENGLAND
LOTTERY FUNDED

BATH
SPA
UNIVERSITY

WRITE HERE

Join a thriving community of writers in and around the beautiful city of Bath. Work with our award-winning staff including new professors Naomi Alderman, David Almond, Aminatta Forna, Maggie Gee, Tessa Hadley, David Harsent, Philip Hensher, Kate Pullinger and Fay Weldon.

Small groups, specialist workshops, passionate staff and students working in close collaboration: it's no wonder so many of our graduates see their work published by companies such as Random House, Oxford University Press, Hodder & Stoughton, Bloomsbury and HarperCollins.

MA CREATIVE WRITING
MA WRITING FOR YOUNG PEOPLE
MA TRAVEL AND NATURE WRITING
PHD CREATIVE WRITING

admissions@bathspa.ac.uk
www.bathspa.ac.uk

Introduction

I am an American, Cleveland born – Cleveland, that river-saddened city – and became a reader when my family moved to California. Bit by bit I began discovering British writers, climbing onto our low, sloped rooftop in Sacramento with its view of a single ivy-bearded palm tree, with novels by Jane Austen, the Brontë sisters and George Orwell in my backpack. I didn't then, and do not now, think of these writers as exclusively British. Of course I knew their lives bracketed the heyday of the Empire. But the fact of their Britishness was less important to me than how reliably they took me somewhere else – an elsewhere defined less by a place than by a consciousness alive on the page. This is what makes novels last. To borrow a phrase from an essay by Jonathan Franzen, reading taught me how to be alone. If I could register the spooky flexion of Virginia Woolf's or Charles Dickens's mind at work, thinking of love or betrayal, madness or suffering, a half or full century after their books were published, then my inner world could become as important – in some cases far richer – as the outer one, which in California was swimming pools and heatwaves and pickup trucks. I still believe that the moment you recognize the inner life is when you become a reader.

Granta's Best of Young British Novelists, now in its fourth incarnation, arrives once a decade with the newspapery whiff of zeitgeist prediction and socio-literary importance. Not just: Who will we be reading in the future? But also: What do these writers say about the state of or the future of Britain? On the first score, the list has, to date, been startlingly accurate. From the inaugural group of 1983, including Ian McEwan, Pat Barker, Salman Rushdie, Graham Swift, Kazuo Ishiguro, Julian Barnes, Rose Tremain and Martin Amis to Alan Hollinghurst, Will Self, Helen Simpson and Jeanette Winterson in 1993. The most recent list, in 2003, picked out David Mitchell, David Peace, Hari Kunzru and Monica Ali before their books were widely read. Historically, the judges of this series have got it right. If they were stock pickers they would have their own global funds.

But what did these writers' books say of Thatcherite Britain? Or of London's rise as a centre of global capital? England in its nervous post-riot ruptures? Even if you could read these writers' work in such a manner, why in the world would you want to?

What is exciting about a novel is not what it tells us about reality, but how it uses the tools of literature – language and structure, time and voice – to create an alternative world that feels as real and as urgent as reality, a world against which even realistic novels scratch. The way a book does this is a form of political alchemy. Literature exists, after all, not just for escape, but to speak truth to power, and it does so by asserting that the world as it is imagined is every bit as important as the world as it exists. In this way literature creates a new reality, drip by drip, in the lives of its readers. It changes the way people imagine, which alters how they think, and expands what they believe is possible. It tells stories of grief and longing, of ordinary lives, but also of power and oppression. It is not an accident that writers are persecuted where there is no freedom. If they are good enough, novelists are dangerous individuals.

It was with all this in mind that I assembled the judges to select *Granta*'s Best of Young British Novelists for 2013. Britain is obviously a free state, but it is hardly an ideal one, and surely novelists exist to fill in the gaps where stone-cold reality fails. So I wanted readers with strong, idiosyncratic tastes, people who read literature imaginatively, rather than as a social document. They had to be people without an axe to grind or a set of friends to promote, people with an ability to articulate why a book or a writer was good without reaching for the props of reputation or acclaim, or gender and ethnic balance, to support their assessments. In short, I wanted a band of outsider minds that worked inside the system of publishing. In April of last year, they began to come together.

I knew from the beginning that Sigrid Rausing, the publisher of this magazine, and Ellah Allfrey, its deputy, needed to be on board. The library they have read between them is vast, and their record of spotting something good in a large pile is extraordinary. Gaby Wood, the literary editor of the *Telegraph*, joined us last spring, bringing to the committee a decade and a half at the coalface of literature and reporting desks on both sides of the Atlantic. A.L. Kennedy, who has twice been selected as a *Granta* Best Young British Novelist, in 1993 and 2003, signed on early, and brought a hilarious seriousness to the proceedings. The novelist Romesh Gunesekera joined us early too, with his elegant and thoughtful mind, and finally we had Stuart Kelly, literary critic for the *Scotsman*, who seems to have read every book that was ever published, as well as some that weren't.

And then the books started coming.

Over one hundred and fifty authors applied for this distinction. To be considered they had to be forty or under at the time of our publication, hold a British passport and have published, or have a contract to publish, at least one work of fiction. Our sifting system was simple. Between the two of us, Ellah and I would read everything: I would read all – or around in – the backlist titles of the authors, and Ellah would focus on reading all the pieces that the writers submitted with their entries. This latter task was important, and a new addition to the process. We wanted this issue to be not just a list of names but a representative selection of their best fiction, and previous experience taught that writers needed lead time to produce something strong. So all the writers were told they had to submit a new story or part of a new novel by the middle of October 2012. *Granta* staff – Patrick Ryan, Ted Hodgkinson, Yuka Igarashi, Michael Salu, Saskia Vogel, David Robinson, Kate Rochester and Daniela Silva – also read and filed insightful and informative reports on the writers as they came in.

We met for the first time at a bistro in Soho in May, after the *Independent* Foreign Fiction Prize, to discuss books together well before the debates kicked off. We began sending writers to the judges in July when the submission trickle turned into a slow-moving creek. As it quickened and deepened, we forwarded the judges three or four, sometimes five writers a week. The eerie silence into which they disappeared was hard to interpret at first. It was either the sound of people reading, or the politeness of a group unimpressed. As it turns out, it was a bit of both. A.L. Kennedy sent along her enthusiasm for Jenni Fagan, Ross Raisin and Joanna Kavenna, but bemoaned the feel of 'lots of wine-bar show-offs' and 'shake-and-bake first novels'. Gaby Wood was more upbeat, but wondered if novelists at age forty-one or forty-two had been cut off on the wrong side of an arbitrary line. Stuart Kelly echoed this point over the telephone, as we professed our mutual frustration that Rana Dasgupta and China Miéville and Tom McCarthy would be too old this time round. I also lamented Mohsin Hamid's 1971 birthdate.

We met two more times in 2012, first in mid-October at *Granta*'s company flat in Holland Park, stoked by Lebanese takeaway and a feeling that we had to do better. Out of this meeting developed a discussion about what we were looking for in young novelists. Romesh asked for 'an engagement with language', 'a feeling for the form', 'writing that absorbs the reader' and 'something distinctive', to which Ellah added 'control and energy' as well as 'the sense that this is a writer whose overall "project" has a future'. For Stuart, the highest consideration was: 'Does this expand what it is possible for the novel to do?' He also admitted, 'I think we should remember that we are reading in somewhat unideal conditions, since no reader outside the critical community would ever undertake such a task – and that memory is perhaps the best guide. I'm sure my opinions about some books will change since they may have managed to create that snag in the brain that even a superabundance of other novels layered over will not dim.'

Stuart's prediction came true. By late November, when we met at the Hospital Club over tea in a room that looked like it belonged in an Amsterdam canal-front window, enthusiasms had developed, and corresponding antipathies, too. We spent the first half of the meeting talking about the writers each of us wanted on the list, and the second half annotating the culled list that the judges had been sent – sixty-five or so writers in all. After five or six hours, there was a list of thirty-five we would focus on reading (and rereading) for the final meeting in January, which took place at Sigrid's home in Holland Park. That discussion stretched from lunchtime until early evening, some six hours, over which time unexpected realignments occurred. One author who had seemed to have strong, almost universal support, Edward Hogan, didn't make it to the final list; neither did Jon McGregor and Peter Hobbs and Cynan Jones, all of whom had been contenders. A groundswell was felt for Tom Rachman, who is easily one of the funniest novelists in Britain – in the end, though, he did not make the list either. There was a near-consensus about the first seven writers to include, but it took us another five hours to fill out the list.

So who are the twenty? For those who are counting, there are twelve women and eight men, the first time one of these lists has had more female than male writers. There are three writers with African backgrounds; one who was born in China and began only recently to write in English; another brought up on her parents' sugar-cane farm in New South Wales; one from Pakistan, another from Bangladesh, a third a second-generation Indian from Derbyshire. Four Jewish writers, one born in Canada of Hungarian descent, and another who was partially raised in Texas. This background snapshot caught us off guard when the list was completed because not once during our proceedings did we talk about the need for diversity, or gender balance, or a multiplicity of background. What we kept coming back to was the necessary snap of a bold style, the confident sweep of storytelling ability and the sense that the writers were in dialogue with the novel as a form.

On this last point, Stuart's criteria were easily met. Zadie Smith and Adam Thirlwell, both of whom were on our 2003 list, are having a debate in their work about the nature of the novel. In her recent *NW*, Smith collapses the social-realist style she perfected in *On Beauty* with a more fragmentary narrative voice that recalls the short stories of David Foster Wallace. Thirlwell's books, notably *The Escape*, erect elaborate scaffolding to support their mysterious inner workings and then magic out their central concerns. This intricate engineering makes him a keen humorist, which his piece in this issue reveals. Helen Oyeyemi began publishing at a very young age, but even in her first book, *The Icarus Girl*, she turned the coming-of-age story inside out by giving it an unreliable narrator reminiscent of Patricia Highsmith's best work.

The writers we were drawn to dazzled with narrative intelligence, but never at the expense of story. Steven Hall is probably the most fantastical narrative architect on this list. His *Raw Shark Texts* is part textual art piece, but also part romance, and although this is his only novel, its success in melding these unlikely elements made us willing to believe he would do something even better. Taiye Selasi, whose debut, *Ghana Must Go*, will just be published when this issue is out, is beginning her career, but the mindfulness with which she re-envisions how an 'African novel' can sound, and who it can talk about, impressed all of us. Naomi Alderman's novels never try to tell us what she knows, but rather, gently, sometimes hilariously, rewrites the myths of faith. Her most recent novel, *The Liars' Gospel*, takes her writing to a new level.

Several writers here have already demonstrated their ability to speak in many tongues. Ross Raisin's first novel, *God's Own Country*, invented a northern sociopath and gave him a language that felt like sprung rhyme, while his second, *Waterline*, found a whole other gravelled voice for a Glaswegian man who ends up homeless. In his three books, especially *The Broken Word*, a long narrative poem about the Mau Mau revolt in Kenya, Adam Foulds has shown an electrifying talent for building a story from the sound of its language. Sarah Hall's five books leapfrog from a Cumbrian landscape to Coney Island to vacation spots in the Caribbean, sinister occurrences seething through her ferocious sentences. Joanna Kavenna has written travelogue, farce and one of the most perceptive novels on motherhood many of us had read in some time. Ned Beauman's two novels are like Rube Goldberg machines that take history and scramble its lethal logic. In the short story we publish here, though, he takes us to the Burmese–Thai border and tells the tale of a drug worker who is having an affair with an American contractor.

We weren't looking for novelists to retell history, but we admired those who captured its refractive power in the lives of their characters. Nadifa Mohamed's *Black Mamba Boy* is a modern-day Odysseus yarn about a boy trying to make his way across the African continent in the post-war period. Tahmima Anam's two novels straddle the liberation war of Bangladesh, a conflict that throws her characters into anguished moral dilemmas and challenges their loyalties. In his series of novels about Lord Byron, Benjamin Markovits takes a prismatic view of the poet's inner life, his work and the bargains made by characters who dedicate their days to understanding him. David Szalay's work, which stretches from the very funny *London and the South-East* to the more sombre *Spring*, a portrait of a marriage unravelled, investigates a culture in which more is never enough.

Our happiness as readers in this process increased greatly when we stopped looking for the next Will Self, the next David Mitchell, the next whoever, for these writers were original in their own way when they emerged. This generation of Best Young Novelists, more than any we've collected to date, appear to have ripped up the moorings and set off on their own. Or they point their compasses elsewhere. The film-maker and writer Xiaolu Guo modelled one of her books, *A Concise Chinese–English Dictionary for Lovers*, on Roland Barthes's *A Lover's Discourse*, and her next book will meld ancient Chinese myths with the life of an imagined pop star. Evie Wyld, who grew up in Australia, has clearly learned from the American short-story writer Raymond Carver but has made a voice all her own. In *The Panopticon*, Jenni Fagan gave her narrator, trapped in a care home, a voice that is unstable, knowing and yet vulnerable, and feels entirely fresh.

Sunjeev Sahota's outstanding novel *Ours are the Streets* was a discovery for all of us. Sahota, a mathematics graduate who didn't begin writing until his mid-twenties, said Salman Rushdie turned him first into a reader and then a writer. His next novel, *The Year of the*

Runaways, is a huge, thrilling epic set in a Sheffield home where twelve men live in fear of the immigration services catching them. Rushdie's influence can also be felt in the novels of Kamila Shamsie, whose work beautifully infuses Pakistani history with human narratives, especially of love. Shamsie is not yet a British citizen, but on her way to becoming one. If *Granta* had not previously included Yiyun Li, a Chinese green-card holder who only last year became a fully fledged American, on our 2007 Best of Young American Novelists list, we might not have bent our rules. But exceptional writers call for exceptions.

We live in unreaderly times, but our belief is that these novelists will be exceptions to the general rule of irrelevance faced by writers today. I would like to thank the writers, agents and publishers who were involved in this selection. I would also like to thank the judges, whose humour and diligence and passion in this task was, for me, unmatched in any experience of reading collectively. They proved, each time we met, that reading is not just a way to be alone, but a way to connect, something each one of these novelists has done with language that is beautiful and urgent and all their own. ■

John Freeman

GRANTA

VIPERS

Kamila Shamsie

KAMILA SHAMSIE

1973

Kamila Shamsie is the author of five novels. The first, *In the City by the Sea*, was published by Granta Books in 1998 and shortlisted for the John Llewellyn Rhys Prize. Her most recent novel, *Burnt Shadows*, was shortlisted for the Orange Prize for Fiction and translated into more than twenty languages. She grew up in Karachi and now lives in London. She is a Fellow of the Royal Society of Literature, a trustee of English PEN and a member of the Authors Cricket Club. 'Vipers' is an excerpt from a forthcoming novel.

I

Qayyum raised the buttered bread to his nose, the scent of it a confirmation that Allah himself loved the French more than the Pashtun. Beside him, Kalam Khan, impatient for the taste of fruit, bit right through the skin of an orange to get to the flesh beneath, eyes closed in pleasure as his jaws worked their way around the peel.

– How is it?

– Tasteless.

Kalam wiped a smear of butter off Qayyum's nose and spat a mix of peel and rind onto the train tracks, grinning – a boy who grew up in fruit orchards delighted to discover that his father's produce in the Peshawar Valley was superior to anything France could grow in her soil. No matter that everything else here was better than the world they'd left behind – the cows sleeker, the buildings grander, the men more dignified, the women . . . what to think about the women? One of the men coming out of the station made a gesture as if holding two plump melons against his chest and there was a rush of men towards the doorway just as Lieutenant Bonham-Carter stepped out, followed by a Frenchman and a woman whose dress was cut to display her breasts as if they were wares for sale. 'Whore,' Kalam said cheerfully, but Qayyum looked away when he saw how the woman first crossed her hands in front of her chest and then, raising her head to stare down the men, lowered them to her hips.

Lieutenant Bonham-Carter asked for the regimental band to gather together. The Frenchman refused to take any money for the cigarettes, coffee, oranges and bread the men had purchased, and asked instead for the band to play the Marseillaise, as it had when the 40th Pathans disembarked at the port of that city and processed through town. Lieutenant Bonham-Carter smiled as he said it – he'd been the one to teach the dhol and shehnai band how to play the French tune on the journey from Alexandria. The brilliance of the English was to understand all the races of the world; how the French had cheered the 40th Pathans as they made their way from

the docks to the racecourse in Marseilles. *Les Indiens! Les Indiens!*
A cry of welcome that made the men heroes before they had even
stepped onto the battlefield. How much finer this was than Qayyum's
first deployment to Calcutta where the Bengali babus were trying to
cause trouble for the Raj and required a few Pashtun in their midst to
instruct them how to behave.

The band followed up the Marseillaise with their regimental song,
'Zakhmi Dil', all the men joining in, including most of the English
officers. Kalam turned to Qayyum, arms spread in resignation as
he sang the opening words on a platform in rural France where the
Pashto language might never have been heard before: 'There's a
boy across the river / With a bottom like a peach / But alas! I cannot
swim.' When the song ended, the Frenchman, for whom none of
the officers had provided a translation, declared: *Magnifique!* And
the woman rested both elbows on the back of a bench and leaned
forward, looking straight at Qayyum. *Magnifique*, she echoed.

Embarrassed at himself for wondering if she wasn't talking about
the song, Qayyum looked away and around the platform; how proud
they were – Punjabis, Dogras, Pashtun, all! – to be received with such
warmth by these strangers. The generosity of the Frenchman was all
it had taken to allow them to set aside the disgruntlement they had
been carrying around since Marseilles, where they were told they
had to give up their turbans and drab-and-green regimental wear in
favour of balaclavas and badly fitting, prickly uniforms of grey that
were better suited to the climate. And their guns, too, had been taken
away because they weren't right for the French ammunition; the new
rifles were unfamiliar, the weight, the shape of them not yet a natural
extension of the soldiers' bodies.

But a few minutes later, in the storage room where the smell of coffee
beans soon fused with an even earthier scent, the French girl showed
Qayyum how quickly an unknown body could become joined to yours.
He was tentative until that became impossible. His only previous
experience had been in Kowloon, the night before the 40th shipped off
to France, with a woman who didn't pretend he was giving her anything

she wanted other than the money he'd been told to place on the table before they started. That had been less troubling in some way than the responses of this girl who seemed to derive pleasure from things that made him worry he was hurting her. Would a Pashtun woman react this way? he wondered, almost as soon as it was over, the thought making him feel ashamed for both himself and the French girl, who kissed him on the mouth and said something he couldn't understand. It was only then he realized they hadn't said a word to each other, and when he spoke to her in his broken English she shook her head and laughed. He had assumed all white people could understand each other's language in the way all the Indians in the army had at least one tongue in common.

Kalam was watching for him when he stepped out of the storage room, his expression mocking, slightly hurt.

– Watch out, brother. You are too much in love with these people already.

– Salute your officers, sepoy.

– Yes, sir, Lance-Naik, sir!

His salute was so sharp it meant to draw blood. Qayyum – his promotion from sepoy just days old – dismissed him with a lazy wave of his hand, refusing to take the challenge. Yes, he was in love with these people, this world. The shame had passed as quickly as it had arrived, and he drew himself up to his full height as the train whistled its arrival, understanding at that moment what it was to be a man – the wonder, the beauty of it.

They arrived in Ouderdom in the rain, Kalam hobbling on the ankle he had twisted when he had slipped on a slick cobblestone. The fall had been a bad one, and Qayyum fell out to help him up, putting Kalam's arm around his own shoulders, prepared to support him for as long as they needed to keep marching. But a Belgian woman had come out of her house, put salve on Kalam's ankle, bound his foot in a bandage and disappeared back inside without a word. Kalam had felt shamed by that and hadn't said a word since, except to tell Qayyum that he could walk on his own feet.

But now Kalam looked up across the farmland and smiled – there, walking across the field, were men whose faces were known to the 40th, not personally but in the set of their features, their expression. The soldiers of the Lahore Division, the first of the Indian Army to arrive in France. Above the howl of the wind a voice called out in Pashto: What took you so long? Too many peach bottoms distracting you along the way?

– We thought we'd give you some chance at glory before taking it all for ourselves!

Kalam, restored to good humour. Qayyum looked over his shoulder at the men of the 40th grinning, name-calling, all around him. Not just the Pashtun, but also the Dogras, the Punjabis. Brothers recognizing brothers with a jolt of love, a shot of competition. What Qayyum felt on seeing battalion after battalion of Indian soldiers bivouacked on the farmland was something quite different – a deep, inexplicable relief.

The havildar-naik of 57th Wilde's Rifle fell into step with Qayyum as he walked across the moonlit stretch of grass. No sound except that of snoring soldiers and the call of a solitary night bird.

– Worrying about tomorrow, Lance-Naik?

– Sir, no, sir.

– I don't want to be 'sir' just now. Mohammad Khan Afridi, from Landi Kotal.

– Qayyum Gul. Peshawar.

– Do you think one day they'll tell stories about us in the Street of Storytellers?

The Afridi lit a cigarette, handed it to Qayyum and lit another one for himself. Qayyum's shoes squeaked on the wet grass as he rocked back on his heels, blowing smoke up into the air, watching the ghostly trail of it ascend and dissipate.

– Did you hear about the 5th Light Infantry? the Afridi asked.

– No, sir. What? Are they here also?

– No, Singapore. On trial for mutiny. Not all of them, but many.

– Pashtun?

– Pashtun and Rajput Muslims. They heard a rumour they would be sent to Turkey to fight fellow Muslims, so they mutinied. Killed their officers.

Qayyum swore loudly, and the older man nodded his head, held the tip of his cigarette against an oak leaf and burned a circle into it. The smell carried a hint of winter fires.

– They join an army formed to fight fellow Pashtun in the tribal areas, but they'll mutiny at the thought of taking up arms against Turks. That's our people for you, Lance-Naik.

– The British Indian Army was formed to fight the Pashtun?

– Yes, of course. You didn't know that?

Qayyum shook his head, looked over the encampment. At five thirty tomorrow morning they'd be on the march again. He cleared his throat, moistened his lips.

– What's it really like? Fighting the Germans?

– Go and sleep now, Lance-Naik. Dream of Peshawar. That's an order. You'll have the answer to your question tomorrow, at Vipers.

Again and again the pain plunged him into oblivion and a fresh burst of gunfire pulled him out. Then there was silence, and he waited for the darkness to claim him, but there was only fire racing along his face, licking deep into his eye socket. An ant climbed a blade of grass and his laboured breath blew it off in the direction of the stream, a few feet away, unreachable; the sun that made the fire burn more fiercely on his face turned playful as it dipped into the balm of the water. I will die here, Qayyum thought and waited for Allah or his family or the mountains of Peshawar to take hold of his heart. But there was only the fire, and the blood drowning his eye and the stench of dead men. Was he the only man alive, or were there others like him who knew the gunners would find them if they twitched a limb?

Perhaps he was dead already, and this was hell. The eternal fires, yes. It must have happened just as they ascended the slopes – the Germans were right on the other side of it, just over the crest of the hill. But the first round of bullets must have killed him and flung him into this devil-made world in which men had to run across a field without cover, stumbling over the corpses of their brothers, and when the tattered remnants of one division reached the enemy lines on the slope across the field, a yellow mist entered their bodies and made them fall, foam at their mouths. Cover your nose and mouth, the order came, swift and useless; if they'd had their turbans they would have wound them around their faces but there were only the balaclavas. Qayyum remembered the handkerchief in his pocket, the one Captain Dalmohy had instructed him to dip into the buckets of liquid they passed, and he held it up against his face even as he watched the breeze move the yellow mist eastward. So this wasn't hell. The mist would have leapt into his lungs if it were.

The emerald green of the grass turned to pine green; the sun sank entirely into the water. His hand had gone to sleep but he was afraid to shake it awake even though the numbness was moving up his arm. There had been a sepoy sitting upright in the field as men advanced around him, one arm ending at the wrist. Qayyum picked up the severed hand he'd almost trodden on, and passed it to the man who thanked him, very politely, and tried to join the hand in place. I think there's a piece missing. Can you look? he said, and died. Qayyum had forgotten this, though it had happened only hours earlier.

Qayyum tried to pray, but the Merciful, the Beneficent, had abandoned this field and the men within it. Something was moving along the ground, a heavy weight; a starving animal, wolf or jackal, with its belly pressed against the ground, smelling meat; a German with a knife between his teeth. Grass flattened, the thing entered the space between Qayyum and the stream. Any movement was pain, any movement was target practice to the gunners. And then a whisper, his name.

– Kalam, stay there. They'll shoot you.

– Lance-Naik, sir. Shut up.

One afternoon in the Street of Moneychangers, Qayyum and his brother Najeeb had stumbled on an object in the road – a dead rabbit with its lips sewn together, foam at its mouth. A man walked past a hundred cruelties in Peshawar every day, and nothing about the rabbit made him slow his stride, but Najeeb knelt on the street and carefully cut away the thread, the animal's fur-and-mud-caked head in his palm. When Qayyum put a hand on the boy's shoulder, Najeeb looked up and asked, do you think its family was nearby and it tried to call out to them? As if that were the real reason for distress, not the needle lancing the animal's lips, the hand which would have stopped the breath at its nose. Oh Allah, the cruelty of the world. How had Najeeb known this terror, this loneliness of dying alone? Kalam's hand clasped his ankle and he felt tears dislodge the blood in his eye, which he couldn't touch without feeling as if he were wiping off his whole face.

– Don't leave me.

– Brainless Pashtun, do you think I came all this way just to smell your socks?

Time had never moved more slowly than in those minutes – or was it hours? – in which Kalam inched himself along the ground until his face was level with Qayyum's, and he could see what the fire had done.

– Tell me. How bad is it?

– Don't worry, Yousuf, all Zuleikhas will still want to seduce you and so will the Potiphars.

– Kalam, don't joke.

– It's this or tears. Just be patient, we'll retreat when it's dark.

– The sun has gone.

– My friend, you've forgotten the moon, large and white as your Frenchwoman's breast and climbing through the sky. Still a few more hours. But I'm here, don't worry. Your Kalam is here.

The end of his sentence disappeared in gunfire. Qayyum's body jerked in anticipation of the bullets that would rip through him, but Kalam had a hand on his chest, telling him to hold still, the gunners were aiming at something else. You stay still too, Qayyum said, but

Kalam braced on his elbows and used them as a pivot for his arms, the rest of his body motionless as – again and again – he lowered his palms into the stream and slowly, hardly spilling a drop, brought them to Qayyum's parched mouth, washed the blood from his face and tried to clean the mess that was his eye. With the stink of blood all around, the only light in the world came from those cupped palms, the shifting water within them.

2

I'm sorry, no, it won't recover like a knife-cut on your arm. We must remove it.

The Indian doctor stepped back and switched off a torch which Qayyum didn't realize he'd been holding. When the doctor patted his shoulder and moved to the next bed, the white-skinned woman, grey-haired, with lines all around her mouth, stayed to replace his bandages, her touch impersonal in a way he'd never imagined a woman's touch could be. Where was it they had brought him? Brighton, they said, but all he knew of it was the pebbled beach, the damp smell of the ambulance, and then this place, this page out of a book of djinn stories into which they'd carried him. Everything ever seen or imagined painted upon its walls, its ceilings – dragons and trees and birds and men from Tashkent or Farghana like those in the Street of Storytellers. Such colour, such richness. More than a single eye could hold. He was floating above it all, beside the gilded dragons on the leather canopy of the ceiling. England had made the pain stop. But the woman was speaking to him, he must return to the bed to hear what she was saying.

– We'll fit you up with a glass eye, and you'll be breaking hearts again in no time.

– I don't want to break hearts.

– Oh, love.

He didn't know why she looked at him in that way, or what a woman was doing among all these men, but when she said 'love' in that sad tone of voice he understood, even through the glow of painlessness, that he was maimed now, a partial man, and from here on he would never be admired, only pitied.

He used to be a man who climbed trees just to see the view from the top, one who entered a new city and sought out its densest alleys, a man who strode towards clamour. Now he couldn't think of a branch without imagining the tip of it entering his remaining eye. Everything, everywhere, was a threat. Every branch, every ball arcing through the air, every gust of wind, every sharp sound, every darkened room, every night, every day. The elbows of a woman; her sudden movements towards him in desire; her hands searching his face for those expressions that only revealed themselves in the dark. He traced the skin around his bandaged eye. Who was he now, this man who saw proximity as danger?

A warning, brother, if you see me walking through the streets, stay far from me. What I want I will have – women or men, wine or gold. A blade through the heart of anyone who tries to stop me. This is how it is when a man walks into hell and survives it. When you return to Peshawar, tell my father he was right. I should have stayed in the orchards.

Qayyum looked up from the letter. Through the mist, the arched gateway and green dome of the Pavilion entrance seemed insubstantial, a fantasy thrown up against the English sky by the force of the soldiers' homesickness. He wound his blanket tighter around his shoulders, his eye aching from the strain of reading only a few sentences. Was there a taunt in the letter beneath the rage directed at the world, or did this unease all come from within himself? One day at Vipers, and his war ended. Now here he was in the grounds of a palace in Brighton while Sepoy Kalam Khan wrote to him from the trenches at Aubers Ridge.

He raised his hand to his eyelid, permanently closed, and pressed down gently, feeling no resistance. There were men here who envied him this, his ticket home. *When you return to Peshawar.* But he wanted neither Peshawar nor Aubers Ridge – wanted only this domed pavilion by the sea, this place which did all that human hands could do to repair broken men and asked nothing about a soldier's caste or religion to make him feel inferior but understood enough about these things to have nine different kitchens where food could be prepared separately for each group, and where the meat for Muslims was plentiful and halal. The King-Emperor himself had sent strict instructions that no one should treat a black – and this word included Pashtun – soldier as a lesser man. The thought of the King-Emperor made Qayyum rest a hand against his chest and bow his head. He had given his own palace to wounded Indian soldiers. What nawab or maharaja would do as much?

This thought first came to him when he looked at the great chandelier in Ward 1, which was once the banqueting room, its immensity hanging from the claw of a silver dragon; the long-tongued beast descended from copper banana leaves that seemed to grow straight out of the painted foliage on the ceiling. Was it beautiful or ugly? He couldn't decide. But he knew that this one chandelier had more grandeur than all of Peshawar. In time, he came to see the chandelier as Empire – the King was the silver dragon, one single claw bearing the weight of smaller dragons, glass lotus flowers, a star of mirrors. He repeated this to one of the English doctors, and thereafter he was called upon whenever there were important visitors to explain that when he looked at the chandelier he gazed upon the glory of the King. What he said was a source of marvel equalled, if not exceeded, by the fact that he said it in English. When the supervising nurse was there to hear the compliment she'd wink at Qayyum and place a finger on her lips – she was the one who had taught him the English words he hadn't known, polished the grammar of his sentences, explained that the glass objects were lotus flowers and not replicas of the dusters which the staff used to clean the chandelier.

It was astonishing how easy the nurses here made it to be in the presence of a woman who wasn't mother or sister or wife. In the wards the soldiers talked endlessly about white women – not just the nurses but also the French farm girls some of them had bivouacked with and the female aviator who one of them swore he'd met (no one believed him, but everyone asked him to tell the story over and over). Nothing about France or England was more different from India than the women – and from here it was a step some of the soldiers made to declare that if India's women changed then India too would become prosperous like the white nations, and everything from the livestock to the people would have a gleam to it. Qayyum listened to them and tried to imagine telling his mother she should be more like the women of Europe – she'd hit him about the ears with a shoe as if he were still a child.

Without warning, the air became driving rain, and Kalam's words smeared across the page. Qayyum ducked his head and, as quickly as his fumbling hands could manage, threw the blanket over his head, covering it completely. The day his youngest sister put on a burqa for the first time she wore it backwards, no face mesh for sight or breath, and she had burst into tears until Qayyum lifted it off and put it on the right way round; she was still young enough to throw her arms around him and say, Lala, forget the army, stay here and defend us from our mistakes. Even the lost eye didn't make him wish he'd listened. Here he was, in the King's own palace.

But there was another side to this world and Kalam Khan was in it, regretting his soldier's uniform, the brotherhood of the 40th, the honour of service. Qayyum wondered who had written Kalam's words for him now that he wasn't there to do it, and if the letter writer had left anything out. Qayyum recognized a process of selection as part of his own duty as letter writer to the wounded, unlettered men at the Pavilion. So many of them asked him to write home *For God's sake don't don't don't allow my brother my cousin anyone from our village to sign up*. Such words would never get past the censors, and they would reflect poorly on the Indian troops who had been trusted to come halfway round the world to fight for their King though there were many in England who thought their loyalty would fail the challenge.

Any doubts about you are held only by those who've never had the honour of serving beside you. That was the only thing the English officers said, or needed to say, when the 40th set sail for France.

The rain was knocking on the blanket and pain was responding, yes, yes, I'm here, I haven't really gone away. He peeled the wet wool away from his face and held it above his head like a canopy; the relief of emerging from the clinging fabric was immense. Across the garden he saw a limping figure. It was the sepoy whose ankle had been shattered by a bullet and whose lungs were weakened by chlorine gas; soon he would be sent back to France. His letter had been addressed to the King-Emperor himself, complaining that wounded Indians were sent back into the field with injuries that would allow an English soldier to return home. Qayyum wrote down every word the man said, knowing it would never reach the palace. The letter ended: *If a man is to die defending a field, let the field be his field, the land his land, the people his people.*

Two nurses approached, umbrellas held above their heads. Flanking Qayyum like bodyguards, they each placed a hand on his upper arms and guided him back to the ward, his one remaining eye closed to protect it from the piercing rain.

He saw the supervising nurse approach when he was in the Pavilion garden reading aloud a letter that one of the sepoys had received from his wife. The sepoy wept in his wheelchair, knowing that his wife's dreams of the children they would have together when he returned would never be realized. Qayyum thought the nurse was there to let him know that the car was ready to take him to the glass-maker's to be measured for an eye but, despite his eagerness to walk through the world with the semblance of a whole man, he finished reading the letter and sat with his hand on the sepoy's shoulder for a period of time until the man's sobbing quietened, before walking over to where she stood beneath a tree.

– You are very kind with the men, Lance-Naik. I think you must spend half your day reading or writing letters for your fellows.

– It helps the day become night.

–Yes. Well, I wanted to say goodbye, and good luck.

– I am going?

– Not you.

She glanced over her shoulder, and spoke to the Englishman in civilian clothes who had approached unobserved.

– Put this in your report. Tell them a fifty-six-year-old widow was seen giving signs of favour to a Pathan boy. Let the Empire tremble at that.

Turning back to Qayyum, she pressed her handkerchief into his hands.

–When you have your new eye, you may want something to wrap it in at night.

He didn't immediately understand. Not that day or the one after, not even when he realized all the female nurses had left. But later in the week, on an excursion to the pebbled seafront, he met two fellow NCOs of the Lahore Division – a Sikh and a Rajput – who said all the women had been removed from York Place Hospital as well.

– Have the English decided women shouldn't see wounded men? Qayyum asked.

The Sikh merely grunted, picking up a pebble with the hand that remained – his left – and concentrating all his attention on readying to throw, the sleeve on his right side flapping. It was early in the morning, the sun had barely risen; the hour when disfigured men went out into the emptied world.

But the Rajput with half a face in bandages and the rasping voice of one who has swallowed gas made a sound of derision.

–They haven't removed them from all hospitals. Just the ones with Indian patients.

–Why?

–Why do you think? Why do you think the Englishwomen who come to visit you in the wards and tell you how much the Empire owes you are never young and never out of sight of an Englishman?

The Sikh flung the pebble, his entire body pivoting. Qayyum

stepped away from him, shielding his good eye. If the Rajput hadn't been there to steady the Sikh he would have fallen to the ground. The pebble landed on another pebble – a sharp clinking sound – and the sea rushed in to cover it. The Sikh pushed the Rajput away, tottered, regained his balance, and when he spoke his face was a snarl.

– They're right to worry. I'm going to find every Englishwoman whose husband is at war and quench her thirst for a man.

– Watch what you say. You Sikhs have to be twice as loyal as the rest of us now.

The Rajput spoke with sympathy, but his words were met with a string of curses. In Lahore, a conspiracy trial was underway for almost 300 men – most of them Sikhs – accused of trying to start a rebellion in the British Indian Army, backed by the Germans. The supervising nurse had said to Qayyum, if a whisper of doubt should attach itself to any of the soldiers here because of this wicked plot I'll go to Lahore, and hang the conspirators myself. He had found himself imagining an embrace with the old lady. The conspiracy itself, which never had any real chance of success, wasn't as unsettling for Qayyum as was the fact that some of the sepoys in the Pavilion had already started to use the name 'Kirpal Singh' to mean an informer, a double-dealer, one who couldn't be trusted. Kirpal Singh, the man who had informed the British of the plot and sent his fellow Sikhs to prison and soon – it was inevitable – the firing squad.

One of the Indian doctors from the Pavilion, the one on the night shift, was walking towards them along the seafront. Qayyum called him over, and asked about the nurses. The doctor spread his hands to indicate the strange workings of the English and said their withdrawal had followed the outrage created in official circles by a newspaper photograph of a nurse standing beside the bed of Khudadad Khan, the first Indian to receive a Victoria Cross.

Neither the Rajput nor Qayyum knew what to say about that. All three men stood silently watching the Sikh, who had the end of his empty sleeve between his teeth, pulling it taut, and was dragging the sharp point of a pebble back and forth against the fabric just below the stump of his arm. The word 'dishonour' entered Qayyum's mind and would not be dislodged.

Qayyum, I am here, in Brighton. At Kitchener Hospital. Don't worry, it is bullet wounds in places where the flesh will heal and soon they will send me back to France. But I am here now, in Brighton. I pray to Allah you haven't left for Peshawar yet. Kalam Khan, Sepoy.

He walked through Brighton's streets, the sunshine sharp. Previously he had only walked the short distance from the Pavilion to the seafront in the early morning. Now he gathered a group of curious children who followed after him whistling 'It's a Long Way to Tipperary' until he turned round and, expression blank, mimed playing a flute. One of the nurses had told him this was a useful way to make a crowd of children disperse and, astonishingly, it worked, though why they screamed and ran he didn't know. On Queen's Park Road a car stopped and the driver offered to take him to the hospital, but he was enjoying the grand houses and the quiet street and the feeling of anticipation with which he was walking towards Kalam, so he thanked the man and continued on. Further along the road an Englishman with large whiskers tipped his hat to Qayyum, and his wife murmured 'Thank you'. His strides lengthened, the sun flung its warmth at him, extravagantly. He was still Qayyum Gul, despite everything.

Kitchener Hospital was a vast building, four storeys high with a clock tower against which Qayyum checked his wristwatch, stopping to wind it up and move the minute hand forward by a tiny degree. One of the doctors on the hospital ship to Brighton had strapped it onto his wrist, and no explanation was asked for or received. He would give it to Kalam, he decided, as he slowly approached the gate, squinting at every open window to see if a familiar form might be leaning out of it, waiting. With his attention on the upper storeys he didn't see the man in the sentry box and would have walked right through the open gate if the man – a military policeman – hadn't commanded him to stop, and asked what he wanted.

– Lance-Naik Qayyum Gul. Here to see Sepoy Kalam Khan.

– No visitors allowed.

–What time I should come back?

– No visitors allowed.

– Because today is Sunday?

– No, because no visitors are allowed. Any day. Any time.

– My friend is in there. We were at Vipers. 40th Pathans.

– No. Visitors. Allowed.

– I am a lance-naik. 40th Pathans.

–That won't stop me from arresting you if you don't move along.

A car, with three Indians and an Englishman in it, drove out of the open gate and stopped next to the sentry box. What's going on? the English officer said in Urdu, and Qayyum, immeasurably relieved, saluted and said there was some miscommunication, his English wasn't very good, could the officer please tell the MP he was here to visit one of the sepoys under his command.

– Sorry, Lance-Naik, hospital rules. No visitors.

– Can you find out if he's well enough to come out? I don't know how bad the injuries are but maybe he can walk, or use a wheelchair.

– No Indian personnel, except NCOs, are allowed out of the hospital grounds. Except on supervised marches.

– Sir?

– Look, Lance-Naik, I didn't make the rules.

– But how do I see him?

– I'm afraid you don't.

– But we were at Vipers together. Sir? We fought at Vipers. He was at Aubers Ridge. He was under my command. 40th Pathans.

– I understand what you're trying to say. I'm extremely sorry, there's nothing I can do, not even for men who were at Ypres.

Qayyum looked frantically at the three Indian NCOs in the car, two of whom had their heads turned away from him. The third – with the insignia of a naik – reached out of the car and touched his arm. Tell me his name, the naik said. I'll make sure he knows you were here.

Qayyum tilted his head back, cupped his hands around his mouth and called out through the hospital gates as loudly as his lungs would allow:
– Kalam Khan!

His voice was cut off by the hand at his throat. The military policeman brought his face close to Qayyum, who could see the man's eyeball, the yellowish tint of it, the blood vessels. What was he doing, this Englishman, young and able-bodied, standing outside a hospital keeping one soldier away from another?

–You are no one, Qayyum heard himself tell the Englishman.

–What did you just say?

The MP's hand closed around Qayyum's throat and Qayyum knew he could do it – he could strike an Englishman. But before that 'could' became 'would', the naik who had reached out towards him jumped out of the car, interposing himself between Qayyum and the MP, one hand on Qayyum's chest.

– He's only obeying rules, Lance-Naik. You need to leave.

The waves crashed over pebbles again – no, it was the gate closing, scraping the gravel beneath. The MP slid the bolt in place, and stood in front of it, arms crossed.

– Rules? Are there rules against saying a friend's name?

Again he raised his voice, drawing it out from deep in his belly:
– Kalam! It's me, it's Qayyum. Kalam!

The naik rested a finger just beneath Qayyum's good eye, the pad of his finger caressing the skin. Qayyum's voice stilled.

– Good man. Don't cause any trouble now.

Leaning in closer, he whispered: Even I can't go out unsupervised. We are prisoners here. You will make it worse for your friend.

That last sentence made it impossible to do anything but leave. When Qayyum returned to the Pavilion he saw, as if for the first time, the barbed wire around the walls, the sentries at the gate, the boarded-up gaps in the hedge. For the briefest of moments he believed he was in a German prisoner-of-war camp, with English-speaking men and women all around – an elaborate plan to turn the Indian soldiers against their King-Emperor.

But no, this was England and Kalam Khan was locked up in a hospital waiting for Qayyum to come to him as he had gone to Qayyum across a field of moonlight and dead men and German gunners. Tomorrow, Qayyum would find a way to see him, even if it meant petitioning the King-Emperor himself.

The next morning came a note from the naik at Kitchener to say Kalam would soon recover, and in the meantime he had been transferred to Barton-on-Sea. And that afternoon Qayyum's glass eye arrived from the glass-maker and the doctor said he could return to India.

On the last day in Brighton, Qayyum stood for a very long time near the doorway of Ward 3, formerly the saloon. Along the length of the walls were paintings of slim-trunked trees. A caged bird and an uncaged bird looked at each other, their gazes undeflected by the black-and-white butterflies flitting between them. The caged bird was the same muted orange as the door to its prison; the uncaged bird was the brown of the branch on which it stood, the tips of its wings the green and red of surrounding leaves and flowers. Qayyum took a step back – the birds, the flowers, the butterflies and the tree itself were enclosed in a gold frame, its shape that of a cage.

It wasn't until he was on the hospital ship, on his way back to India, that Qayyum realized the reason he hadn't received any response to the letters sent to Barton-on-Sea was that the message from the naik was a lie. He rushed out onto the deck, prepared to leap into the cold waters of the Atlantic, but it was too late, Britain was just a pinprick – such a small, small island. ■

GLOW

Ned Beauman

NED BEAUMAN

1985

Ned Beauman was born in London. His debut novel, *Boxer, Beetle*, won the Goldberg Prize for Outstanding Debut Fiction and the Writers' Guild Award for Best Fiction Book. His second novel, *The Teleportation Accident*, was longlisted for the Man Booker Prize. His third novel, *Glow*, from which this excerpt is taken, is published in 2014 by Sceptre in the UK.

The drug might never have come to exist if Win hadn't wandered into a bar in Gandayaw one muggy, sour night in 2007 to watch a Muay Thai match they were screening. One of the fighters was getting ground up like fish paste by the other, and the picture on the old TV set was flopping and wincing as if the satellite dish on the roof could feel the punches all the way from Bangkok. The only other customers that night were a handsome white guy in a sweat-soaked shirt and three drunken Burmese boys whom Win had seen around town several times already in the month or so since he came to Gandayaw. About ten minutes after Win bought a bottle of beer and took a seat in front of the television, he became aware of angry voices behind him. Evidently the three boys were determined to sell the white guy a carton of cigarettes but their English was so bad that the sales pitch just involved snarling 'Cig-et! Cig-et!' The white guy thought they were asking him to give them some cigarettes, and he kept pointing at the carton as if they might have forgotten about it. 'But you already have all those,' he was saying. 'There must be ten packs in there.' By now they'd decided he was being deliberately obstructive and one of them had just taken out a flick knife.

Win got up and walked over to the white guy's table. 'They want to sell you the box. Just give them five dollar and they leave you alone.' His English wasn't quite as good back then.

'Oh,' said the white guy, and laughed. 'Shit. OK.' He found a five-dollar note in his wallet – holding the wallet under the table like a poker hand in that tourist way that's supposed to stop anyone from seeing that you have a lot of cash on you but in fact just makes it immediately obvious that you do – and passed it across. The boys sneered at him and walked out. 'Thanks,' said the white guy, looking up at Win. 'Do you want . . . uh . . . do you want some money too? Or a drink?' They held eye contact for a waxy second before Win called to the barman for a glass of Johnnie Walker Red and Coca-Cola, which was the most expensive thing you could order in this bar. The white guy turned the carton of cigarettes upside down so that all the individual packs fell out onto the table. 'There are only four in here,' he said, and laughed again.

Win knew that if they went back to the white guy's hotel room later, the white guy would probably offer him cash again at some point, and he wasn't sure whether he'd take it. He had never quite decided whether it was more gangster to turn down money for sex, because a gangster couldn't be bought and sold, or more gangster never to turn down money for anything, because a gangster was always on his grind. Anyway, tonight it didn't really matter, because he genuinely wanted to fuck this guy. It had been a long while since he'd had sex with anyone but Hseng, and sex with Hseng was like having ten thousand scalding-hot pork dumplings shot at you point-blank out of a greasy mortar cannon.

'You Lacebark?' Win said.

'Yeah. Just arrived yesterday from Jakarta. But I live in North Carolina.' There was a wasp in the ashtray, almost dead, shivering in small circles like a mobile phone left to vibrate on a table. After a long pause, as if he was so surprised to be having this kind of conversation that he'd lost track of the rules of banality, the white guy said, 'Are you from around here?'

'No. From Mong La.'

'Oh. I haven't heard of it.'

Mong La was a town on the Chinese border where the United Wa State Army made such extraordinary profits from opium that one year they whimsically used some of the surplus to construct a Museum of Drug Eradication. Win's aunt had sent him to work in Hseng's small *yaba* factory when he was fifteen years old. The pay was low and the hours were long and the fumes gave him headaches, but at least he knew it was gangster to be so close to the drugs and so close to the money. Also, he was captivated by the chemistry: the magic and odorous grammar of the catalytic reactions, the precursor's ascension to new forms like a soul moving through the thirty-one planes of existence, the idealistic, asymptotic pursuit of absolute purity. He even loved to watch the last fastidious hesitation of the electronic scales before they settled on a count, the polar shimmer of the crystallized product in the first few seconds after it was sifted out of the evaporator. His boss, Hseng, was an obese, mottled Chinese guy with a big appetite for boys. Once or twice a week, Hseng would bring Win into the back office, lock the door and undo his fake designer belt. But Hseng had what Win would later come to identify as a rare disability among males: he couldn't seem to turn himself on by the use of force. Hseng was happy to let Win suck his cock for the price of a bowl of soup, but if Win ever started trying to fight him off, Hseng would immediately forfeit his erection. This left Win with some bargaining power. And quite soon he asked to be allowed to take some lessons from Hseng's chemists and to spend a few hours a week in the Internet cafe on the corner browsing websites like Lotophage.

Within two years, he was running the factory for Hseng, and its output had never been higher.

For a while, everything was pretty good. Hseng paid Win quadruple his old wage, and even bashfully presented him with a gift: a shoddy Chinese-made portable CD player so he could take his hip hop with him wherever he went. He took to wearing a home-made necklace based on the hexagonal benzene ring common to all amphetamines. Then, late one night towards the end of the rainy season, Hseng came to Win's aunt's house and told her to wake him up because he was needed at the factory. Win blearily followed Hseng outside, and they stood in the damp shadows under a banyan tree while Hseng explained that a colonel in the United Wa State Army was planning to murder him and steal his business. 'We have to leave Mong La. I have a cousin in a town called Gandayaw about a hundred miles west of here. He'll set us up. We'll start a bigger factory. You can oversee everything.'

'Why would I leave?' said Win. 'My aunt is my only family.'

Hseng looked hurt. 'You have to come with me. They'll kill you too. They'll gut you with hooks.' Later Win would realize that Hseng had been lying about this – if anything, the colonel probably would have given Win a better job. And it was almost certain that Hseng had done something idiotic to provoke the colonel, because his second-rate business alone would scarcely have been worth killing for. But at the time Win wasn't savvy enough to understand any of that, so he packed a bag, said an inadequate goodbye to his aunt and set off west with Hseng.

When they got to Gandayaw, however, it was obvious at once that although the town had a lot of drug addicts and a lot of drug dealers it had no place for a drug factory. The Tatmadaw and the Lacebark security force had never been on such spiteful terms with each other, so even if one had tolerated a factory, that would have been reason enough for the other to shut it down. Also, Hseng's legendary cousin turned out to have left for Thailand almost a year earlier. So Hseng decided he was going to start a casino. He used most of the cash he'd brought with him from Mong La to buy an old brothel that had closed after an electrical fire, with the intention of installing baccarat and blackjack tables. (Also he wouldn't shut up about his idea for a fish tank full of turtles whose shells would be encrusted with tiny mirrors, like autonomous disco balls.) But Hseng didn't have any connections here, plus no one trusted the Chinese, so he ended up paying for most of the materials and labour in advance, and in Gandayaw paying for anything in advance was like giving alms to a monastery: you certainly wouldn't expect to see any direct benefit in your current lifetime. After a month, the former brothel looked even more dilapidated than when he'd bought it. One morning Hseng decreed that Win should start helping out with the refurbishment, but Win deliberately hammered enough holes in the walls that by lunchtime Hseng changed his mind and banned him from the project. So now he just mooched around Gandayaw, pining for his reactor and his drying oven and his rotary tablet press.

The white guy's name turned out to be Craig. He was an 'internal management consultant' at Lacebark specializing in 'process efficiency optimization', and he'd been sent to Gandayaw for three months to find out how to boost the productivity of the mine workers in the Concession. Modern efficiency consulting, he told Win, was all about neuroscience: the old, loose terms like 'alertness' and 'initiative' and 'morale' just gestured at specific brain states that could now be described much more precisely in empirical language. When Win started posing questions about dopamine and norepinephrine, Craig asked him how he already knew so much about all that stuff.

'Back in Mong La, I run factory for *yaba* pills,' Win said.

'What's *yaba*?'

'Mix of methamphetamine and caffeine.'

'Really?' said Craig. 'You were in the drug trade?' His hair was dark but there was both ginger and grey in his stubble.

Win nodded and clenched a fist over his heart. 'For life.' He rapped a few lines: '*The chemist is brolic, Pyrex scholars, professors at war over raw, killing partners for a million dollars.*'

'Did you do much business with sweatshops in Thailand? They get through amphetamine like it's powdered milk. You can't knock it from an efficiency point of view. But we've done a couple of studies and in the long run we think it works best for small, repetitive, seated tasks. Not so much for heavy resource extraction . . . Goddammit, sorry, I've got to stop talking about work.'

Three drinks later, they walked back to Craig's room in the Lacebark-owned hotel on the north side of town, where the American turned out to have the biggest penis Win had ever seen outside porn videos. Afterwards, as Win lay dreamy and exhausted, Craig got up and started rummaging through his suitcase. Even though the windows were wide open, the air in the room was still fuggy and ammoniac, as if within the valvular manifold of their connected bodies they had synthesized a molecule so complex it couldn't filter out through the mosquito screens. Craig held up a bag of coffee beans. 'You ever had this? Civet coffee. I got it in Jakarta. The civet eats the coffee berries, softens them up in its stomach and craps them out. Then you make coffee with the roasted beans. Tastes amazing – like cherries. The Indonesians came up with it in the eighteenth century because the Dutch wouldn't let them pick coffee berries from the plantations but they couldn't stop them scooping up the civet crap.' He started fiddling with some sort of expensive-looking black appliance on the desk. 'I got the company to send this here before I arrived. I'm a coffee nerd, obviously, and there was no way I was going to live in a hotel for three months without my own grinder. You know, back in the States, you can't use the coffee pots in hotels, because people like you use them to brew meth. Even in the good hotels, I heard. Do you want a cup?'

'No,' said Win.

Craig pursed his lips apologetically. 'I'd rather come back to bed but it's still the afternoon in North Carolina and I'm going to have a million emails. It's like they've never heard of time zones.'

Later, Win walked home to the brothel. Craig hadn't offered him money and Win was glad that he hadn't. The room at the back was dark when he came in but Hseng was still awake. 'Where have you been?' he said.

Win lay down beside Hseng on the psoriatic foam mattress. 'I was at a bar watching videos.'

'You don't smell right.'

Win realized he should have just rinsed his cock and arse before he left the hotel instead of taking a long, soapy shower – this was the cleanest he'd been in weeks, and Hseng could tell. 'I swam in the stream on the way home.' He spat on his hand and reached under the sheet for the chubby radish between Hseng's legs. If he surprised him with a handjob right away, it would both etherize Hseng's suspicions and pre-empt any larger demands that Win was still too sore to satisfy.

Win started meeting Craig at the bar about every other evening while Hseng was back at the brothel accomplishing nothing much. Even apart from the diverse pleasures of Craig's company, he found that simply to carry with him a pleasant secret was in itself enjoyable. Growing up, you got so used to all your secrets being sad or shameful that you came to assume they were, like alkyl halides, intrinsically neurotoxic, and now he had learned for the first time that they weren't. One night, after they'd gone at each other like Muay Thai fighters for a couple of hours, Craig got up to work on his laptop as usual, but instead of brewing a pot of coffee he took from his holdall a small clear plastic bag full of what looked like white petals.

'What's that?' said Win.

'It's just a flower that grows out in the forest. Most of the Myanmar guys I've interviewed in the Concession say they don't like our polyphasic sleep schedule, but if they eat this, it makes everything a little easier. I tried it yesterday. It works. I mean, it's no Adderall, but it's better than a cup of coffee if you want to get a whole draft report done in one night, and the really special thing is, you can still get to sleep afterwards without any trouble. We might start prescribing it officially, after a few tests.' He tossed the bag onto the bed. 'Want to try some? You just chew and swallow with some water.'

The effect was mild, as Craig had said, but Win was certain that he could perceive something more in this drug, an incandescence blotted out, an urgent thought left unspoken. It was there in the smallest seams of his awareness, in the instants of absent-mindedness or blurred concentration, when he turned his head or licked his lips or scratched his neck in the first sixty minutes after eating the petals. What had set him apart from the older chemists at Hseng's factory wasn't just that he could pick up chemistry so easily, it was also that he seemed to have powers of introspection that they entirely lacked, as if his eyeballs could swivel all the way round to focus on his own frontal lobes. And he'd tried enough different batches of *yaba* back in Mong La to know when a phenethylamine's real potential was still unborn.

'I can make this better for you,' he said to Craig.

'What do you mean?'

'I just need some equipment and some lab chemicals and I can make this a better drug for you to give to your workers.' In fact, what he anticipated from a more potent formulation of glo wasn't the boring and reliable concentration and wakefulness that were needed at Lacebark's mines – it was the lawless, luminous core that he'd already sensed. But he couldn't admit that yet.

Craig was bemused. 'How the hell would I get you equipment and lab chemicals?'

'Same way you got your coffee grinder,' said Win, who could feel his English improving with every night he spent in this room.

'Oh. Right.' Craig admitted that it might not be that hard to put in an order with Lacebark's procurement department and make it look as if it was all needed at the mine. He'd heard rumours and jokes about the Lacebark executive – no one seemed to agree on who he was or whether he was still at the firm – who'd managed to use corporate money to set up his Burmese mistress and love child in a beach house in Los Angeles five or six years earlier.

When the supplies finally arrived, Win installed them in one of the two defunct indoor toilets in the brothel, telling Hseng that he'd scavenged them from a dump out of sheer boredom. Hseng, who by now had been obliged to sell off all his gold jewellery, accepted this explanation with his usual sceptical silence. Craig started bringing back several bags of glo a week from the Concession for Win to use in his experiments. At first Win tried to get something out of glo the same way you might get morphine out of a poppy or cocaine out of a coca leaf or ephedrine out of a joint fir. But he had no luck with oxidation or isolation or acid-base extraction or any of the other documented methods. There was something evasive, almost coquettish, about the alkaloids in the flower. It was as if the skin of the ripening molecule couldn't be peeled away without pulping the flesh inside.

Then one day he came into his toilet laboratory to find that all his bags of glo had been ripped up. He accused Hseng, of course, because he knew that Hseng had some suspicions now, and this was just the sort of pathetic, thuggish way that Hseng might express his jealousy. But Hseng insisted he didn't know anything about it. It happened twice more, and Win was baffled, until at last he happened to catch the perpetrators in the act.

Two foxes stared back at him as he came in, their jaws still working the petals like cud. He'd never seen a live fox before. Unhurriedly, one of them bent its hind legs and shat on the floor, as if that was the only comment it wanted to make. Then they darted out past him down the corridor.

There were at least three new smells in the small room: dung, and fox musk, just as he would have expected, but also a third that stood in some cognatic relation to the aftertaste of glo petals. Remembering Craig's civet coffee, he pulled on a pair of latex gloves, picked the turd up off the floor, and began another experiment.

A fortnight later he brought an eighth of a gram of white powder with him to Craig's hotel room. 'Do we snort it?' Craig asked.

'No, it really stings.'

Win poured out two small glasses of Coke and dissolved half the dose into each glass. After they'd both gulped down their drinks, Craig kissed him and then looked around the room. 'I can't believe how long I've been living here. I never thought I'd miss my ugly condo in Charlotte.'

On the Internet Win had seen PDFs of the laboratory notebooks that the chemist Alexander Shulgin had maintained in the 1960s when, out of gratitude for his invention of a new pesticide called Zectran, his employer Dow Chemical had funded his experiments with drugs like MDMA and mescalin, and during those experiments Shulgin had made continuous painstaking observations on 'visual distortion', 'mental coordination', 'mental attitude' and so on, sometimes interspersed with hand-drawn graphs. Despite its complexity, the chemistry was often much easier for Win to follow than some of Shulgin's other references. Win had planned to imitate Shulgin's methods, even his irritatingly precise time measurements – why should anyone care about the exact minute that something happened? – and he persuaded Craig to take notes too. But when they checked the next morning, Craig had written only a few lines:

12.30 a.m.   *Nothing so far.*
12.50 a.m.   *OK, quite tingly now – reminds me of that*
             one time I took ecstasy in NY.
1.10 a.m.   *No, this is much better than ecstasy.*

Then:

LIGHTS!!!

And Win had written nothing at all.

'Did I say anything really schmaltzy to you last night?' asked Craig. When they hadn't been flipping the fluorescent light above the bathroom mirror on and off or gazing at the red neon across the road, they had mostly been having meandering, slithery sex, any possibility of orgasm suspended several miles out of reach.

'About what?' said Win.

Craig smiled and looked away.

There was nobody at the brothel when Win got home around noon. This was the first time he'd ever stayed out past dawn, and he wondered if Hseng had noticed. Too tired and stiff to work in his laboratory, with raw patches all over his body where he'd rubbed himself against Craig for too long without any feeling of pain to tell him to stop, he lay in bed eating a couple of poppy-seed cakes in such tiny rodent mouthfuls that they lasted the whole afternoon. When Hseng still wasn't back by dusk, he began to wonder if something might have happened, and he put his flip-flops back on to go outside. Blue and gold and pink were piled up on the horizon like bolts of silk on a dressmaker's shelf. Outside the bar where he'd first met Craig, he saw the same three boys who'd wanted to sell their carton of cigarettes.

'Are you looking for your fat Chink boyfriend?' said one. Win, who couldn't be bothered to start a fight, just nodded. 'Try the dump.'

For a while Win knelt watching two black cats gnawing at Hseng's fingertips. A small landslide further up this hillock of rotten cardboard and burned plastic had already covered parts of the corpse, so it looked more like an old buried thing exposed by erosion than a recent delivery from a van or a pickup truck. In its back were three exit wounds, not too bloody, the bullets perhaps exhausted by the long slog through Hseng's blubber.

Maybe Hseng had tried to default on a loan, or maybe an old enemy of his cousin's had come back to Gandayaw; either way, it was a reasonably gangster way to die. Those were Win's suppositions until he talked to a bald ragpicker at the edge of the dump who told him that the shooting had happened that afternoon outside the Lacebark hotel. The sight of Hseng's body had only given him a gentle churn in his bowels, but as soon as he heard that he was really anxious. He ran all the way there, but he couldn't see anything out of the ordinary, so he asked a woman selling biryani from a cart. She'd seen the whole thing, she explained excitedly. An American had been on his way out of the hotel when a fat Chinese man had rushed out of an alley and run him through the belly with a samurai sword. Then a Lacebark security guard who was smoking a cigarette nearby had opened fire on the Chinese man with his AK-47. Win asked about the American's body, and she said it had been wrapped up in a plastic sheet and taken back inside the hotel. After she wheeled her cart on down the street, Win just stood there staring up at the hotel, trying to find the window of his lover's room. ■

ARVON

**GROW
YOUR
OWN**

STORIES

IDEAS

POETRY

**RESIDENTIAL
CREATIVE WRITING
COURSES 2013**

Come to an Arvon centre, and grow your own story. Fiction. Non-fiction. Poetry. Drama. Songwriting. Comedy. Memoir. Text and image. For children. For radio. For film and TV. You name it. All varieties are here. We also have a programme of courses for schools and community groups.

Find out more, support our work, apply for a grant to help with fees, or book a course at:

www.arvon.org

@arvonfoundation

Supported using public funding by Arts Council England

ANWAR GETS EVERYTHING

Tahmima Anam

TAHMIMA ANAM

1975

Tahmima Anam is the author of the Bengal Trilogy, which chronicles three generations of the Haque family from the Bangladesh war of independence to the present day. Her debut novel, *A Golden Age,* was awarded the Commonwealth Writers' Prize for Best First Book. It was followed in 2011 by *The Good Muslim.* 'Anwar Gets Everything' is an excerpt from the final instalment of the trilogy, *Shipbreaker,* published in 2014 by Canongate in the UK and HarperCollins in the US. She lives in Hackney, east London, with her husband, the musician and inventor Roland Lamb.

Foreman likes to hoist the new ones up, see what they're made of. Some of them have never climbed higher than a tree in their village. Back home the place is flat, flat. I'm here nine years, I know what's what, so I tell them, don't look, don't look. Hold the torch in one hand, like this, and keep your eye on one screw at a time. From here to here, I show them, holding my fingers apart an inch, maybe an inch and a half. Your eye will see this much, no more. Understand?

I don't tell them the whole story. Whole story is this: you look down, you die. You see the world has shrunk below you. You call God but no one answers. You recite the kalma. You see God is not there. You piss your pants. No one is watching. No one cares about your shitty speck of a life. The people below are specks and you are a speck. God looks down and sees nothing but tiny ants below Him. You choke. You move your legs. You scream. The building shifts, it moves, it throws you up, it throws you over. You're done for, a chapatti. They scrape you off the pavement; they don't even write to your family. Months later, someone will go to your village and tell the news to your people. And that will be the end of your life.

All this I don't say. I say only what is useful.

This new kid won't listen. Came in with a swagger – I spotted it right away, the way he moved his legs and his trousers hanging, his head loose on his shoulder, nodding, doesn't look down when Foreman is talking, raises his head and gives two eyes to the boss. Eye for an eye. Foreman smiles. I know that smile; it means I'll take that two-eyed look right out of your skull. Soon you'll be like the rest of them, giving me the top of your head and mumbling into your shirt.

I have schooling, sir, the kid says. Intermediate pass.

Foreman says, Crane will take you to the top. And the kid says *yessir* as if he's been given a gift. All that school, he doesn't even know when his ass is being strung up.

Later I ask the kid where his people are. We're on the same sleeping shift, starts two in the afternoon, the shed hot as an animal's mouth. You can't touch the metal rails on the bunk, you just jump onto the mattress and pray for a breeze.

TAHMIMA ANAM

He says he's a Pahari, says it with a little edge, like I'm a Pahari, you gonna fuck with me? I've never seen such pride in a tribal, and I say, so what, no one cares here.

Army took our village, so I had to come here, make some money. He shrugs like he doesn't mind but I can see when he closes his eyes he is going to dream about college, hearing his name in the roll-call, getting his degree and spending his life in a shirt with buttons and getting some respect. Some day, someone might even call him sir. Buy a scooter and get himself a salty wife.

But now he is here. Shit, he says, it's like a fry pan inside.

It's only March. Wait a few months, I tell him. Then you'll see what hell feels like. Then I give him my two paisa little bit of advice. I tell him, stay away from Foreman and keep your mouth shut. And when he hauls you up, whatever you do, don't look down. The kid nods, but I know what he's thinking, thinking it's not going to be him at the end of a rope.

I go to my bunk and try to sleep. This month I'm in the middle. We take turns, Hameed, Malek and me. Top bunk is hottest, but there's a breeze, if you can catch it, from a small window out of the side of the shed. Bottom bunk is cooler, but closer to the ground and the toilet stink is strong. Middle is the worst, like being sandwiched between two asses, especially because this month I've got Malek on top. He makes the springs creak as he pleasures himself to sleep. I'm used to the steady rhythm of it, I don't say anything. A man has his needs, out here in the desert. Myself, I can't do it. I reach down and Megna's face comes into my head. She won't let me sleep. I see her little tears and she's asking me to stay – what will I do when the baby comes? And I'm saying no, I'm shrugging. I'm calling her a slut, even though I know it was her first time, and I'd told her I loved her and meant it, except my uncle is there too, and he's telling me Dubai, Dubai, son, it's like paradise, shopping malls and television and air con. Marry my daughter and the ticket is in your hand. You're a slut, I tell Megna, and I swivel around and leave her there, except I don't leave her because whenever I try to get myself a little something, like a piece of sleep

56

or a full stomach, she comes out and she comes out strong. I want to know what she did to the little seed I planted in her, where does it live, does it know me, and does it have the eyes of its mother. I'm in the dark and I can't sleep. Malek sighs, rolls over, and the room gets hotter and the stink rises.

Too quickly the sleep shift is over and it's time to get back to the site. Pahari kid is about to get his first kick in the head, but he doesn't know it, he just pulls on his uniform like he's the Sheikh himself. I have to throw water on Malek's face to wake him up. He curses me and jumps down. The floor vibrates. How the man stays fat with hardly any rice in his stomach is beyond me. Next shift is already waiting outside – it's dark, and starting to cool down, the lucky bastards.

The bus drops us at the canteen. Hameed sits at the end of the table so people can bring him the letters. He's the only one who can read. We pay him a few dirhams to tell us the news from home. He reads me letters from my darkie wife, she says *take care don't forget to eat and does it get cold do you have a shawl?* The others are always laughing, she's going to tell you how to wipe the shit from your ass, they say. I laugh with them. Stupid girl. I don't write back.

Hameed says sometimes he changes the letters, because there's only so much a man can take. Last week he read that Chottu's mother had died. Poor bastard's only been here a month, still cries every time he has to stand out in the baking hot, carrying bricks on his head. So Hameed told him his mother was well, much better in fact, since he started sending money for her asthma medicine. Later, when Chottu gets hard like the rest of us, Hameed will tell him the truth. And by then he won't even stop to take a breath.

The canteen manager is Filipino, so stingy we get a piece of bread, dal and a few vegetables, and even that they cut from our pay. Eid comes he gives us meat, but only bones and fat. One thing my uncle said was true – as much Coke as we want, straight out of a spout.

Tareque Bhai, Hameed says, your sister has given birth to a healthy baby boy.

Mahshallah, Tareque Bhai says. Tareque has been here the longest
and he has gone the religious way. Two ways a man can go here, in
the direction of God or the direction of believing there is nothing up
there but a sun that will kill you whether you pray five times or not.

We wash our hands and head to the site. They've turned the lights
on, the buildings are winking. We come to the Mall of Dubai, which
Tareque Bhai remembers was only a few years ago a pile of rubble,
and Pahari kid says, why don't we walk through here? And we all look
at him like he was born yesterday. Even dumber than I thought.

You can't go in there, I say.

Why, is there a law?

Doesn't have to be a law.

I'm going in, he says, loose, like it's the easiest thing in the world.
Anyone coming with me?

I think Hameed's going – those book-learning types always stick
together – but it's Malek that breaks off and joins him and I'm cursing
myself for not grabbing him before it's too late, telling him, don't even
smell that, it'll kill you.

The rest of us make tracks, shaking our heads. This month,
Hameed and me are in the hole. Two buildings going up side by side,
facing each other. We call them Bride and Groom. Bride is almost
finished, Groom still in foundations. Fifty-fifty, they tell us, fifty
stories for Bride, fifty for Groom. Who knows what they'll name it
once it's finished. Burj-al-Arab-al-Sheikh-al-Maktoum-al-kiss-my-
ass. Shit, if I said that aloud I would be finished. I giggle to myself and
Hameed swings his arm around my shoulder, laughing with me even
though he hasn't heard the joke.

Bride and Groom makes me think of darkie wife. She was the
skinniest, ugliest girl I ever saw. I took one look at her and I swear
a few tears came to my eyes. To this girl I was going to be tied for
life? Just do it, my mother said, you won't even see her for years.
Who knows what will happen between now and then? But give us a
grandchild, something to keep us company while you're gone.

I did my duty. Girl started to cry and I even felt a little sorry for her though I was also thinking, two times I've done it and both times the girl has burst into tears – something wrong with me or what? Next day I took her to the cinema, but even Shah Rukh Khan couldn't wipe the sad from her face.

We climb down and the bright lights make the hole turn blue-grey. The diggers are awake and we start to haul the dirt around, everything dry and sucked of life.

I pick up a basket and start hauling the dirt. I wonder if Malek and Pahari have made it out of the mall without getting their eyes pulled out and just as I'm imagining what it must have looked like, two guys in their blue jumpsuits staring at those diamond-necked swans of Dubai, I feel a jab in my side, and there's Malek, laughing so hard I can see the gap where he lost a tooth last year after biting down on a piece of candy he bought from the Filipino. Worth it, he'd said, I never tasted anything so good. Now he's telling me about the mall, the cold air that made your sweat dry to salt, and the high ceilings, and the women, the women, didn't cover their legs, no, or even their breasts. Breasts, man, like you wouldn't believe. He slaps me hard on the back, shaking up my basket so I can taste the dirt. Go to work, I say, but he's too busy talking, and now some of the other boys, Hameed and even Tareque Bhai, have joined in, and I can see them all thinking it could be them next, them in the ice-cream cold of the mall, gaping and staring and taking a little slice of heaven back to the hole to chew over.

Worst of all, Pahari kid got hauled up to the top of Bride and nothing happened. Absolutely nothing. He swung like a monkey and laughed his way through the shift. Turns out those tribals like floating on top of buildings, hitched up so the whole world is spread below them.

For the next two weeks, every day, Malek and Pahari pass through the Mall of Dubai on their way to the site. They take their jumpsuits in a plastic bag and go in wearing trousers and T-shirts. One day Malek comes over to my bunk with a pair of sunglasses draped over his eyes. Look, he says, I'm James Bond now.

I keep my head down. I have debts to pay, I can't take the chance.

Once, only once, I am tempted. They are going to the cinema – not the cheap, rundown place by the camp, I'm talking a brand-new theatre, air con, seats like pillows. Pahari knows this guy at the ticket stall, been wooing him since day one, going up, talking about home, saying *yaar* this and *my friend* that. And finally the guy gave it up, late show on Monday nights usually empty, come in with the cleaning crew and sit at the back. Four people, max. Don't get me fired or I'll tell the cops everything, even about the girl.

Pahari has a girlfriend. Not even a darkie or a Chink, a proper fair-faced blondie, a shopgirl who sells perfume. He leans over the counter and she smiles like she's seen Shah Rukh Khan. We huddle close to Pahari, trying to catch a whisper of that girl's smell.

While we're heaving bags of sand to Groom, Pahari and Malek start arguing about what to see. Malek says it has to be the new *Dhoom!* but our boy wants to see an English film. What you're going to do with an English film, you little shit? But Pahari's not thinking about himself, he's thinking of his girl, moving his hand in the dark, cupping her knee, fingering the border of her skirt, and what's going to make her open up, a movie with mummy-daddy and fake kissing and chasing around trees, or real humpty-dumpty, tongues and blonde hair and New York City?

Pahari has a point, but I'm just hauling the sand, keeping my head low. Wife has sent another letter. April and the waters are going up, up. Last week my brother, who works at a weaving mill, came home with a bad leg. Needs an operation. Can I send money? I shove the letter under my mattress.

Send money, send money. All anyone ever wants. I have to ask for an advance, so I crawl to Foreman. He's got a toothpick hanging out from the side of his mouth, and he twirls it around and around. You Bangladeshis, he says, can't hold on to your money, *na*. Look at this. He points to a big black book, lines of names. Everyone borrowing, nobody saving. You're going to drown, all of you.

He opens his mouth, toothpick falls out, frayed and shining with spit. Should I pick it up? I stare at my feet.

How much you want?

I don't know why, but I don't say anything for a long time. Pahari and Malek are going to the movies tonight. He's going to lean back on that chair and swing his arm over his girl. He's going to sip Coke through a straw and the music will breeze through him, free and liquid.

Then I say, I have been loyal, sir.

Foreman leans back. Chair squeaks like a dying mouse.

Sure, you never stole.

Yes, sir. I always do what you say.

I lift my chin a little and he knows what I'm talking about, the little cover-ups, taking a few bags of cement off the truck, losing a little cash. The boss, the Sheikh with three wives, always wearing a prayer cap and telling us to call him Master Al-Haj because he goes to Saudi every year and kisses the prophet's grave – he wouldn't miss a few things here and there. A sack of rivets, a few pots of paint were nothing to him.

So you're telling me what, *na*, that I should be grateful? Fresh toothpick in his mouth. Now I'm thinking about Megna, her thick river of hair, how she smelled so good and told me I should be a proud man. Nothing to be proud of, I always said.

Yes, sir, I find myself saying. Loyalty like that, it doesn't come easy.

And I suppose you want something for your trouble? He's getting up, he's coming towards me, he's going to give me something, a little money and a slap on the shoulder, friendly like. You have to ask for it, I think. All you have to do is ask. Foreman's close now, he takes my chin in his hand, lifts me up so we're eye to eye, and for a minute I see him staring at my lips and I think he's going to kiss me. He opens his mouth. And then he spits, toothpick flying out of his mouth, right there on my face.

You stinking bitch, fuck off. You blackmailing me? He makes a fist, sends it to my cheek. I fall, cursing Megna, her hair and her stupid wisdom. I try to make myself small. He kicks me. I feel his shoe in my stomach. I double up, he kicks me again. My face explodes. I taste blood. A tooth comes loose.

Who pulled you out of the shithole you call a country?

You.

Louder!

You!

Who gave you a job when you came crawling back?

You.

Say it.

You!

And then I make the begging sounds, I tell him about my brother, about his leg, they make him sit in those clay pits, eighteen, twenty hours, feeding silk into the loom, the cold grabbing his thighs. Please, Foreman, I say, forgive me.

Piece of shit. Get out.

Pahari and Malek come back from the cinema with smiles so big I can see their back teeth. I show off my broken face.

What happened to you? Malek asks.

Foreman. What you get for thinking big thoughts.

You?

Ya, me. Surprise.

Pahari's looking at my face, my swollen eye.

Uglier than ever, I say, trying to laugh.

He's shaking his head. That's not right. They can't do that.

They can do whatever the fuck they like. It's their country.

We'll go to the police. He can't just beat you.

He makes me cheerful with his baby talk. It's nothing, I say. Sit. Tell me about the cinema. I pat the bunk. Come, Malek. But he's pacing the tiny corridor between our beds.

Bastard, bastard, he mutters.

I turn to Pahari. So what did you see?

English film, he says, raising his eyebrows. Lots of shooting.

Your girl enjoyed?

He lay back on the bunk, raised his hands to his face. Shit, man.

I could almost remember that feeling, the first time I tasted a woman's mouth.

Be careful, was all I could say. They put you under a spell and then you're finished.

So what you'll do about your brother? Malek is squeezing himself onto my bunk.

Brother will have to wait.

Let me give it to you.

What do you have?

I have, I have.

I can't help it, my tongue keeps going to the missing tooth, the gap made of jelly. Malek tries to press me but I won't eat his rice.

Oh, I almost forgot, brother. We brought you a gift. Pahari takes a packet of candy out of his pocket. I chew with my good side.

Sleep now, I say to them both. It will last longer if you dream about it.

Next day, Foreman comes to the camp. I have a job, he says. Bride is almost finished, she just needs her windows cleaned. Sheikh Abdullah Bin-Richistan is coming to cut a ribbon and everything has to be perfect. We're running out of time and job needs to be done in a hurry. I'll go, Pahari says, even though it's higher, much higher, than he's ever been, but he wants to take his girl out, proper restaurant this time, with people smiling and asking if he wants ice in his Coke and bringing plates to the table.

I want double overtime, he says. Foreman smiles and says, all right, and then, because I see something in the boss's eye, I raise my hand too, and before you know it, Malek is watching us drive off in a truck. Foreman takes us into Bride's lobby, empty and shining, and I give myself a little smile, because I know I put this thing together with my own hands, me and Malek and the other boys, working through the devil's breath of summer. Pahari is looking around, dreaming of when he's going to own the whole place. They've taken off the elevator on the outside, but there's another one at the back of the building, where all the cooks and cleaners and guards will come and go, and we're going up, up, all the way. Wear this, Foreman says, handing us a pair of hard hats. Then he slides open a big door, and we are on the roof of the building, flat and open to the sky. I wonder if Pahari's thinking it wasn't such a good idea after all, but he's not one to admit it. When I put my hand on his back he shrugs it away, moving with speed to where Foreman is pointing, to a little balcony hanging over the edge of the building.

Clips and ropes fix us to the sides of the balcony. I'm going to lower you all the way down, Foreman says. You do one floor at a time, slowly. Then you push the button, and you go up. He shows me how to work it. I see there isn't anything holding us to the side of the building; we're only attached at the top. It's going to sway. I look over at Pahari again, wondering if I should cut out of the whole thing, but he's grinning like it's Eid. Don't worry, Foreman says. And he winks.

On the way down Pahari hangs on the edge and makes a strange, low sound which I think maybe is panic but then he turns around and says, FLYING! The bastard is laughing, holding his arms out and shaking his shoulders around like he's hero in a *filmi* dance sequence. The windows are like mirrors, we can see our reflections. He puts his arm around me and we are floating down, angels from heaven, Superman and God and people who don't eat shit for a living.

Every window we clean, we go up one more flight. We're shining up that Bride and she's looking good. There's a wind up here, the balcony moves a little, then a bit more as we move higher. Now we're holding on with one hand and cleaning with another. We wash, I push the button, we go up, wind gets stronger.

I'm going to marry her, Pahari tells me.

A man marrying for love. Too good for me, but nothing's too good for Pahari. He wants everything.

Do it, I say. Is she going to convert?

I'm Christian, you idiot.

All this time, and I didn't even know. That was my problem. I thought everyone was the same, but it didn't have to be that way. Even I didn't have to be the same. I could be different. The wind dies down and we have a moment of quiet so I can think about all the ways

I could be different. And then, before my dreaming starts making me big, wind picks up again. This time, it comes with sand. Minute later the air is thick with it, so thick I can only just make out Pahari on the other side, holding on with both arms. It will pass, I shout, swallowing a mouthful of the desert. Don't worry. Hold on.

We wait, turning our backs to the wind, becoming small, small as we can. I crawl to Pahari and I grab his jumpsuit, put my arm through his arm. We groan as the sand comes into our ears, into our clothes, the devil's spit. The balcony lifts, higher on one side and then another. I pull the lever, but we can only go up, not down. Only one way, so I climb us up, slow as I can. Close to the top and suddenly it shudders to a stop, and I push and push but nothing happens. I crawl to the other side, see if I can make the ropes move. I can't. I ask myself if this is the time to start praying, but no God was going to hear me now, not after all the curses I had sent in His direction. It will pass, it will pass, I keep saying, but Pahari can't hear me now, he's on the other side, and the wind is too high, and before I know it, we're going back and forth like a swing, and it's everything I've got to keep my arm around the bars of the platform, and I do just like what I teach those boys when they first get here, just focus on a small piece of the building, not the tall of it falling away below me, just this little piece in front of me, and I will the moment to stand very still, and then I see Pahari, his arm has come loose, and the ropes that tie him to the machine, and the sound of him falling is swallowed by the hiss of the desert, that shape-shifting snake.

Now I'm home and I've got everything. Because Pahari's dead and they paid me off. I'm the greedy bastard now. I'm the one who isn't the same. The old me would've stayed, maybe made sure Pahari got his proper burial, maybe I wouldn't even have taken their dirty money, maybe I would've made a stink about it, but soon as they handed me that envelope I was gone. Malek told me the Sheikh was getting rid of Foreman. We shouldn't have been up there, not without better safety equipment. It's not something they can cover up, like the boys who jump because they miss their mamas and can't take another day. We were up there for over an hour; lots of people saw, real people who matter. We can make our demands, Malek said, ask for better pay, overtime and a good place to sleep.

But I didn't care about any of that. Because when I was going to die, when I was hanging up there with the storm in my face, all I could think about was my kid. My kid, walking around with no memory of a father, a kid who would look at himself in the mirror and not know where his face came from. Who knows what Megna had told him, though if she said bad, it would all be true, because I was a bastard for letting it come into the world without a name. Now I want it all, I want my fridge and my socks and my name and Megna, my little piece of heaven, and I'm coming to get it. ■

GRANTA

SOON AND IN OUR DAYS

Naomi Alderman

NAOMI ALDERMAN

1974

Naomi Alderman is the author of three novels: *Disobedience*, *The Lessons* and *The Liars' Gospel*. She writes and designs computer games and is co-creator of *Zombies, Run!*, the best-selling iPhone fitness game and audio adventure. A professor of creative writing at Bath Spa University, she has been paired with Margaret Atwood in the Rolex Mentor and Protégé Arts Initiative. She is currently working on her fourth novel. 'Soon and in Our Days' is a new story.

On the first night of Passover, the Prophet Elijah came to the house of Mr and Mrs Rosenbaum in Finchley Lane, Hendon.

Mrs Rosenbaum had opened the door as usual, after supper, at the point in the evening when one is supposed to anticipate the arrival of the Prophet Elijah, whose appearance will herald the beginning of the Messianic Age. Mr Rosenbaum, standing at the long dining table, began to recite the verses that accompany this moment: 'Pour out thy wrath upon the nations who know you not,' he declared.

The young Rosenbaums – ten-year-old Gerda, the teenagers Saul and Simon – sat, bored and moody, around the table. The magical Seder, with its many quaint rituals and little games, its traditional holiday cheer and special foods and gifts, no longer held for them the charm with which it had brimmed when they were small children. Even Gerda, this year, did not run to the door with their mother, eagerly looking out for Elijah. Thus it was that Mrs Rosenbaum alone, opening her door onto the cool night air of Hendon, witnessed the miracle of the prophet's arrival.

When Mrs Rosenbaum was a girl, her older cousins had sometimes played tricks on the women of the house when they opened the door for the prophet, sneaking around the side door to shout 'Boo!' in their faces, or even wearing a mask or a sheet to frighten them. So when she heard the windy clattering of hooves, and saw a fiery missile speeding towards her from the heavens, she wondered at first whether her sons had rigged up some elaborate prank.

'For they have consumed Jacob and laid waste his habitation,' her husband intoned in the dining room – he did have a good speaking voice; it was one of the things she'd noticed when they first met. The fiery object grew closer and began to resolve itself into moving shapes. She stood, mouth open, eyes wide, watching the thing draw nearer. It is not often, even in Hendon, that one witnesses a miracle.

'Pour out thy rage upon them,' read Mr Rosenbaum, with passion and gusto. Mrs Rosenbaum could see it quite clearly now. It was a chariot, just like the Roman chariots she'd seen in pictures at school or in *Ben-Hur*. It was pulled by four horses made of fire, the edges of their bodies dissolving and coalescing like swift clouds, as they galloped across the sodium-tinged sky. In the chariot was a man, sitting serenely in the heart of the fire.

'. . . from the Heavens of the Lord,' concluded Mr Rosenbaum in excellent declamatory style. Then, hearing that his wife had not yet closed the front door, he shouted more loudly, 'It's finished, Netta! Come back inside!'

Mrs Rosenbaum heard him but did not answer. She was looking at the burning chariot parked on the front driveway next to her Renault Espace. She was looking at the four fiery horses shaking their bridles and whinnying out small breaths of flame. She could not cease staring at the bearded man in the long robes who was stepping from the carriage and whose clothing, miraculously, was not even scorched.

'Happy Passover to you,' said Elijah. 'Have I missed much?'

Elijah was a gracious dinner guest. He appeared overjoyed to find that the Rosenbaum family had poured out a cup of wine in expectation of his arrival. He did not complain in the least that he had missed the meal, declaring that he was not hungry. When Mrs Rosenbaum insisted on placing before him a bowl of kneidlach soup, some chicken, roast potatoes, salad and a slice of her excellent apricot cake, he was voluble in his praise.

After Elijah had eaten, and the family was ready to begin the Seder again, Mr Rosenbaum asked, tentatively:

'Rabbi,' (he felt it was proper to address the prophet with some honorific, but 'Prophet' sat oddly in his mouth) 'does your arrival mean that the Messiah has arisen from the House of David? Is the world-to-come upon us?'

Elijah, pressing crumbs of cake into the plate with his index finger and then raising the digit to his mouth to lick it, blinked. He looked around the table at the expectant faces.

'Oh!' he said. 'Sorry. How silly of me. No. I didn't mean to get your hopes up. I just thought, you know, for a change it might be nice to come down. For Passover. To see how things are. It's been, literally, ages.'

The family stared at him. Even Old Mrs Rosenbaum, Mr Rosenbaum's mother, stopped stirring her tea and just looked at him.

'I thought maybe I could stay in the spare room,' said Elijah brightly. 'If it's not too much trouble.'

M r and Mrs Rosenbaum made up the spare bed together. 'It's your fault,' Mrs Rosenbaum said, plumping a pillow viciously. 'You and your learning and constant praying. That's what's caused this. Does it happen to the Krantzs? Does it happen to the Mulavnas?'

'I don't think,' said Mr Rosenbaum, shaking out a duvet, 'that we should be looking for reasons here. It's a miracle, a holy event. We should feel blessed. And besides' – he popped the poppers – 'you were the one who opened the door.'

'I opened the door,' whispered Mrs Rosenbaum, 'because *you* told me it was *your* family tradition when we were married. The man sits at the table and reads, the woman opens the door, that's what you said. *I* would have quite liked to be more modern, but you said no.'

They tucked the fresh sheet in together, making sure to keep it very tight at the corners.

'That's how we've always done it, Netta. I don't think I can be blamed for a family tradition. And it is a miracle, after all.'

'People will notice, that's all I'm saying,' she said. 'You can't expect a fiery chariot in the front garden to pass everyone by.'

D ownstairs in the lounge, Elijah had found an old Argos catalogue and leafed through it, making astonished faces at the huge variety of goods therein. Gerda, Saul and Simon were exchanging furtive glances, giggling and whispering behind their hands.

'The bed's ready,' Mrs Rosenbaum called down the stairs, 'if you're tired. Long journey!'

The Prophet Elijah got up. He almost took the Argos catalogue upstairs with him, but after an inward tussle left it, with evident regret, on the nested tables next to his half-drunk lemon tea.

There was the matter, the next morning, of what to feed the fiery horses drawing the fiery chariot. Mrs Rosenbaum was relieved to find that they hadn't scorched the Renault Espace, which, after all, she and Mr Rosenbaum had only just finished paying off. The horses weren't the slightest bit interested in the bucket of water she put down gingerly in front of them, stepping outside in the early morning in her dressing gown and slippers.

The children were fascinated by the animals and it was Simon who discovered, after some experimentation with roast potatoes and broccoli kugel, that they would deign to eat a matza cracker. They wolfed down a box each, in fact, and set fire to the cardboard as they did so, letting the wind carry a trail of sooty Rakusen's embers down the road. It wasn't clear that they needed to eat, but finding something to feed her guests made Mrs Rosenbaum feel more comfortable.

The Prophet Elijah slept late – it had been a long Seder and none of them had got to bed before 2 a.m.

At 10 a.m., Mrs Rosenbaum thought it would be right to wake him with a cup of tea. She opened the door and was surprised to find him fully dressed in his robes – the pyjamas Mr Rosenbaum had lent him were neatly folded at the end of the bed – and examining her bookshelves.

'No works of Torah?' He turned round with a quizzical air. 'No holy writings of the rabbis?'

Mrs Rosenbaum shrugged awkwardly.

'We . . . the holy books are downstairs?' She hoped he wouldn't look at the two meagre shelves of presentation prayer books the boys had received for their bar mitzvahs and barely looked at since.

'And what *is* "Yogacizing"? And "The 30-day Body Cleanse"? Some sort of ritual bath?'

After a whispered conversation between Mr and Mrs Rosenbaum, centring on the phrases 'You brought him here' and 'He's your friend', Mr Rosenbaum agreed to take him to synagogue.

There was, it must be admitted, a certain amount of surprise that the Prophet Elijah had come to synagogue with Mr Rosenbaum.

'Why the Rosenbaums?' muttered Levitt under his breath. 'We all know they eat vegetarian cheese.'

'If it were anyone, it should have been the Krantz family. With all they've been through,' rumbled Moskovitch, whose fridge had never been tarnished by a vegetarian cheese from a supermarket, and indeed only ever housed dairy products labelled with conspicuous emblems advertising the various rabbis who had pronounced them kosher.

'No, no, Moskovitch,' said Gold. 'We all know it should have been you. You've been a rock to this synagogue.' He nodded for emphasis. 'A rock.'

Moskovitch shrugged magnanimously. 'Maybe he chose a home where he could do some good. You know,' he mouthed, '*not very kosher.*'

And the men agreed that this must be the answer.

After the service was over, the rabbi hurried over to welcome the Prophet Elijah officially to the neighbourhood.

'I hope . . . ahahah . . .' said the rabbi, 'that you haven't come to warn us that the Lord will smite our vineyards and our fields. Aha. Ha.'

Elijah smiled warmly. 'Not unless you've turned your faces from the Lord and started to worship false gods – but everything looks very much in order.'

'Good, good,' said the rabbi, only slightly alarmed that smiting was not, apparently, entirely ruled out. 'Good,' he said again. And then, finding that he had nothing else to say, 'Good.'

'How is Ba'al getting along these days?' asked Elijah, in an apparent attempt to help. 'Get much trouble with Ba'al round these parts?'

'Oh, no,' said the rabbi. 'No, there hasn't been any . . . well, apart from that unfortunate business with Mr Bloom . . . No. We haven't had any Ba'al worship for quite some time.'

Elijah looked crestfallen.

'Not even a little bit? Ba'al's a tricky customer, you know, just when you think he's been rooted out, then he comes back –' he made a wiggly motion with his hand – 'worming his way back in. I could certainly sort out any Ba'al issues for you right away.'

'I think we'd have noticed is the thing,' said the rabbi, 'if there were any devotion to Ba'al still lingering. Although I do often say to the congregants that *money* is the modern Ba'al, since people devote so much attention to business . . . ?' He raised his eyebrows hopefully. 'Or computer games? Xbox, PlayStation, iPhones? It sometimes seems that our young people are worshipping those things instead of paying attention to God.' He frowned, still trying to raise the prophet's interest. 'Or . . . celebrity culture? Men and women worshipped as gods?'

'That sounds quite promising,' said Elijah, brightening considerably. 'I'm sure I can help out. Do tell me more.'

And the rabbi and Elijah spent much of the afternoon deep in conversation.

The first Mr and Mrs Rosenbaum saw of the trouble was when they came home the next day and found that the Prophet Elijah had erected a small altar in their front garden. Some stones, wood laid on top of it, the makings of a fire underneath.

'To contest with the idol-worshippers,' said Elijah cheerfully. 'See, what I do is, I have them come here and call on their god to send down fire from heaven upon their offerings . . . which they never do, obviously, and then I pour jugs and jugs of water on mine, and call on the Lord, who lights it for me, and clearly the Lord wins. It's super. Just a bit of fun. Gets them every time.'

Mr Rosenbaum frowned at the altar.

'You see,' he said, 'we don't –'

'Is that my coffee table?' said Mrs Rosenbaum.

'Perhaps I should make some sort of proclamation? That sort of thing? What do you think? I could go stand outside the ritual baths and tell people that I'm contesting the might of . . .' he looked upwards, trying to remember, 'Bee'Yon'Say? Or, the rabbi was telling me about a terrible cult of young women worshipping a Bee-Bear?'

Saul whispered something in Gerda's ear and she burst out laughing. The Prophet Elijah looked hurt. Mr Rosenbaum distracted him by asking about the relative dangers and iniquities of Moloch and Ashera while Mrs Rosenbaum rescued her coffee table from the threat of the Lord's holy fire and hid it in the garage.

M r and Mrs Rosenbaum tried to entertain Elijah. They felt it was their duty – the Lord commands us to welcome wayfarers into our homes. During the middle days of Passover, when the children went to revise for exams or play at their friends' houses, Mr Rosenbaum took Elijah on an open-topped bus tour around central London, but the prophet became distressed by the pictures of nearly naked men and women advertising yogurt and linoleum. Mrs Rosenbaum took him to a nice craft fair, but he wasn't able to accustom himself to the idea that, yes, many of these embroidered pincushions had probably been made on the Sabbath. Mr Rosenbaum took him ice skating, but although he tried to get into it, Elijah kept mentioning that skating would be, and he didn't mean to be rude, a totally useless skill when the Messiah called all the Jews home to the land of Israel.

To be honest, Mr Rosenbaum thought, it had got a bit much, having the Prophet Elijah around all the time. When he went to the bathroom, the Prophet Elijah would remind him to say the blessing on a speedy and painless defecation. When he read a novel, the Prophet Elijah would glance in his direction and shake his head ever so slightly, politely, as much as to say, 'This is time you could be using to study the Holy Scripture.'

Mr Rosenbaum asked Elijah if he had any thoughts, just any vague ideas, of how long he would be blessing their home with his holy presence.

Elijah beamed and said, 'Oh, I'm in no rush. Don't you trouble yourself about it.'

At last, feeling that all forms of culture and entertainment would be abhorrent to him, Mr and Mrs Rosenbaum decided to take the Prophet Elijah on a nice walk by the Welsh Harp reservoir with the children. This, as it transpired, was the worst idea of all.

There were families picnicking at the reservoir. Happy young families with small children, blankets spread out with Thermos flasks and sandwiches.

Elijah eyed the sandwiches.

'Those people are eating leavened bread,' he said. 'During Passover. Do you think they know that's not allowed? We should probably go and tell them.'

'I expect they're not Jewish,' said Mrs Rosenbaum. 'You remember we told you that most people around here aren't Jews?'

Simon whispered something to Saul, and Saul whispered something to Gerda.

'Some of them are Jews,' said Gerda loudly. 'That's Hannah Blatt, I know her from Brownies. But her family aren't religious. And she's gluten-intolerant, so she can't eat matza anyway. I expect it's her special bread.'

The children seemed to have tired of the Prophet Elijah.

Elijah looked at Gerda.

'Are you sure?' he said. 'After all, she is a child. But the punishment for eating bread on Passover is rather serious, you know.' He looked to Mr and Mrs Rosenbaum for support.

'We try to . . . live and let . . .'

But Elijah was already striding over to the picnicking family, shouting, 'Hello! Hello there! Just a quick word if I may?'

The Rosenbaums watched with alarm from a distance as Elijah spoke to the Blatts. He had a pleasant demeanour, open and apologetic, and yet, as he continued to speak, the father of the family grew increasingly tense, the mother upset, the child confused. The Prophet Elijah leaned forward, earnestly, to have a word with the child herself. She stared at her sandwich with dread, allowing the bite she'd just taken to fall from her mouth. Suddenly the father stood up and punched Elijah in the nose. It was a good solid blow. Elijah fell over.

'Should I . . . go and help him?' said Mr Rosenbaum.

Mrs Rosenbaum held tightly onto her husband's arm.

Eventually the Prophet Elijah scrambled unsteadily to his feet and made his way back over to them.

'Things with this generation,' he said, 'have reached a very serious level indeed.'

Elijah talked about it all that night, and all the next day. He had Mr Rosenbaum explain everything to him, from non-religious Jews to multi-faith or secular schools, to what went on in churches and how bacon wasn't even sold with a 'No Jews Allowed' warning label. Every piece of news made his frown deepen and his expression become more grim.

'Something must be done,' he said at last, 'regarding this generation.'

'Something . . .' Mr Rosenbaum was suddenly worried. 'You don't mean something apocalyptic? The end of days? Rains of fire and blood?'

'Oh no, no. I'm not authorized to set anything like that in motion. But, Rosenbaum, you must see that this generation has come to a terrible place. You need a leader. Yes, that's it. You called me here for a reason and the reason must be that I am needed to lead the people as once I did! Yes!'

'I *called* you?'

'Take me to the synagogue! I must speak to the people!'

It was, in fact, a little late when Elijah made this demand, but Mr Rosenbaum had no difficulty in arranging a gathering at the synagogue of the usual attendees the next day, to hear the Prophet Elijah speak. The crowd was not, perhaps, as large as Elijah might have wished but, after all, most of the synagogue-goers had already seen him before.

'Even the Chief Rabbi,' whispered the rabbi encouragingly, 'wouldn't get a big crowd if he'd been around all week.'

So Elijah spoke unto the people, saying: 'Well. It has been a terribly interesting visit. I've learned so much, and I've got some thoughts on how we might like to proceed. Churches, for example. Are you all familiar with churches?'

The people nodded.

'Well,' said Elijah. 'You know that *officially* we should be stoning those people to death. I mean, placing candles in front of statues? Praying to them? Now I know I've been away for a long time but . . . who's with me? A little stoning?'

The rabbi frowned.

'That's not possible, I'm afraid. You see, this isn't our country. We're subject to the same laws as everyone else and stoning – even just a few warning stones – well, it's just not allowed.'

There followed a brief conversation between Elijah and the rabbi.

'Ah,' said the Prophet Elijah, turning to the people. 'I see the problem now. Yes, quite right, not your country, quite right, quite right. There's only one solution.' Elijah drew breath. 'You all have to move. To the Promised Land, a land flowing with milk and honey.'

The people stared at him.

'Er,' said Simon Rosenbaum. 'No. We don't want to move. I've got GCSEs next year. Mum, we don't have to move, do we?'

His mother tried to reassure him at the same moment that the Prophet Elijah said, 'I'm afraid you do, yes. But do not fear. As the Lord said to Abraham: "Go to the land which I will show you and He will protect you and feed you with quails and fresh goat curds."'

Gerda began to cry, because it was all quite intense and she didn't understand most of it, and the one thing she did know was that she didn't like goat's cheese at all.

There was a muttering among the crowd, which grew louder and louder. And a great voice rose up from the people as if each were saying in their turn, 'We can't move, we've just put in a new kitchen and we're in negative equity, and besides we're in a good school district and we're very convenient for Waitrose.'

And a cloud crossed the face of Elijah. One could see, suddenly, why the Bible puts such an emphasis on the prophet having had a bit of a temper.

'The Lord speaks through me,' he thundered. 'Put your faith in the Lord and He will protect you! Come with me now to the Holy Land, and cast out foreign gods! We shall smite the idol-worshippers and the infidels! Leave your homes now, all you able-bodied men, and travel with me to the Holy Land, where we shall rejoice in the protection of the Lord God Almighty, the Lord of Hosts and we shall find a mighty victory!'

There was a long silence.

'But . . .' said the rabbi, in a small voice, 'isn't God the God of peace? Beating swords into ploughshares and, er, and so on?'

'Mighty are those who are zealous in the word of the Lord! He will pour out His wrath on the nations that know Him not!' shouted Elijah.

There was another long silence, and a sudden understanding slowly dawning. Mr Rosenbaum did always utter that particular passage at Seder night with uncommon conviction. He was a very good reader. So good, apparently, that he could pull down a prophet from the heavens.

'So you want us,' said Mr Rosenbaum quietly, 'to leave our homes and our neighbours and our, not to boast, but our thriving accountancy practices, and go to Israel to make war on everyone there who isn't Jewish?'

'The holy places of the Lord must be cleansed!'

Mr Rosenbaum shifted uncomfortably. 'Well. It's been tried before, you know. I mean, people seem to keep trying it. It's . . . it's a sort of long-running tragedy.'

Eljiah's vocal register was really very impressive. 'DOES NOT THE LORD ENJOIN US TO DESTROY UTTERLY THE TRIBE OF AMALEK WHOSE HOME IS MECCA? WE MUST WIPE THEM FROM THE EARTH.'

At this there was a certain change in the people. A stiff, uncomfortable, English wind seemed to blow through Hendon in that moment. It was a breath of custard and boiled swede, and the sort of persistent grey drizzling rain which is very far from the longed-for blessing of a desert nation. Perhaps this is the breath of the Lord. In England.

'No,' said the rabbi. 'No, that's not going to happen.'

And the people spoke in one voice, saying, 'Yeah, no.'

One by one the people began to walk away from the synagogue, towards their own homes, thanking Mrs Rosenbaum for providing the snacks on the side table, and shaking Mr Rosenbaum's hand and nudging Simon and joking with Saul, and comforting Gerda that no one was going to make her eat goat's cheese.

And when the people were all gone, Mr Rosenbaum let out a deep sigh and stretched his arms and said, 'Well, Elijah, it's been a lovely visit, but we really don't want to keep you. I'm sure you have things to be getting on with. In heaven. I expect.'

The miracle of Elijah's departure from Hendon in his fiery chariot was witnessed by a great many more people than his arrival. In fact, half of Hendon seemed to have turned out to make sure that the flaming steeds really had dragged him up towards the sky where he became merely a glowing speck, smaller and smaller until it disappeared completely.

He hadn't made a speech, exactly. He'd looked at them. They'd looked at him. Each, it seemed clear, was equally disappointed in the other.

'Look,' said Elijah, 'I really never meant to . . .'

'We know,' said Mrs Rosenbaum. 'Here. I packed you a snack for the trip.' She handed him a Sainsbury's bag, which he received with gratitude.

'Don't forget,' said Elijah, 'the messages I've brought you.'

The people looked at each other awkwardly. And waited. And eventually he was gone.

'Well,' said Mr Rosenbaum to the rabbi, 'I do think it's probably for the best if we try to forget all of that, really, don't you?'

And the rabbi agreed, with a sigh.

'Do you . . .' said Mr Rosenbaum, 'feel we should alter the prayers at all? In light of . . .'

The rabbi looked at him.

'Alter. The prayers?'

'Well, you know, how we pray for the arrival of Elijah, the coming of the Messiah . . .'

The rabbi nodded piously. 'Oh yes,' he said. 'We long for them soon, and in our days. And let us hope we will continue to long for many years to come.' ■

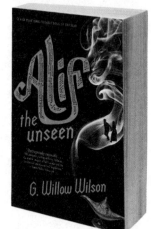

FILSAN

Nadifa Mohamed

NADIFA MOHAMED

1981

Nadifa Mohamed was born in Somalia and moved to Britain in 1986. Her first novel, *Black Mamba Boy*, published in 2010, was longlisted for the Orange Prize; shortlisted for the *Guardian* First Book Award, the Dylan Thomas Award, the John Llewellyn Rhys Prize and the PEN/Open Book Award; and won the Betty Trask Award. 'Filsan' is an excerpt from her new novel, *The Orchard of Lost Souls*, forthcoming from Simon & Schuster in the UK and Farrar, Straus and Giroux in the US.

Filsan rises and takes her uniform from the peg on the door; she is up ten minutes before the alarm but doesn't want to remain with her thoughts, simultaneously mulling over everything and nothing. She pulls her tunic over her head and her trousers over her legs. A quick visit to the bathroom and then she is beside the stove in the communal kitchen, the wall above her blackened with soot, the smell of meat and ghee still in the air from the previous night. Water boils in her saucepan, tea leaves, cardamom pods and cloves shivering on the surface of it. As it's about to bubble over, she grabs the handle and pours just enough to fill her enamel cup.

She drinks the tea immediately, its heat scorching her throat in a way she finds pleasant. This is the entirety of her breakfast. Back home, her housekeeper Intisaar would have covered the dining table with a vinyl sheet decorated with small yellow flowers and laid out a flask of black tea, a jug of orange juice, a fruit salad of mangoes, papayas and bananas, a plateful of *laxoox* hidden under a domed fly guard and, if her father had requested it the night before, scrambled eggs and lamb kidneys.

The other women – there are about fifty altogether in the barracks – drift into the kitchen while Filsan nurses her empty cup and gazes at the view beyond the window, a bare yard criss-crossed by poles and clothes lines with the two domes of the central mosque on the horizon. Breeze blocks abandoned when the nearly completed hotel was commandeered by the military have become another kind of barracks for cooing pigeons beneath the window. She ignores her comrades as they ignore her, but what would she say to them if she could? She would tell them that she has never been good at making friends, that Intisaar's children had seemed kind but hadn't been allowed inside the house by her father, that the neighbourhood kids had scorned her, that she found it easier to talk to her father's friends, that her face was closed because she didn't know how to open it. Silence takes the place of all these words and her loneliness remains as dense and close as a shadow.

Filsan rinses her cup, locks it away and returns to her room to make the bed before departing for the offices of the Mobile Military Court. She hears laughter from the kitchen as she turns the handle to her door, and knows it is aimed at her. As she enters she finds herself overwhelmed by an urge to wail, her blood suddenly darkening with self-loathing and anger that her life should be so small and inconsequential, that this two-metre-by-two-metre cell that is her room should be the span of her world.

The offices of the Mobile Military Court are in an old colonial complex. The brick chimney jutting out from one of the rooftops is something Filsan had never seen in Mogadishu, where the weather was never less than sultry, but here the wind is so cold and fierce at times that it is not hard to imagine an Englishman dozing by a fire with a long-haired dog at his feet. In her spartan office there are just two desks, one for Captain Yasin and a small, scratched one for her, Corporal Adan Ali.

She is an office worker, neither noticed nor commended by the uniformed men above her, and it galls her that despite two years of enlistment in the Women's Auxiliary Corps and five years working for the Victory Pioneers in Mogadishu her chief tasks are still those of a secretary. Had her father been dreaming or lying when he told her that she would make the ground shake in Hargeisa? Had he been drunk? Or just desperate to remove her from Mogadishu in case the suspicion around him became something more tangible and sinister? In the notes sent from the agents to her desk she sees how difficult it is to interpret someone's actions, intentions, words; if she had to create a dossier on her own unknowable father where would she even begin? He had shown her both tenderness and contempt, cruelty yet honour, a glimpse of the world through the bars of his love. She sees him now pacing the flat roof of their three-storey villa in Mogadishu, a strip of the Indian Ocean visible between two slender minarets, watching over the neighbourhood with binoculars, scanning east and west for the spies he believes watch him.

Captain Yasin arrives, tall and elegant in his black beret. With just the two of them in the office she cannot help but watch him all day: his regular strolls around the room and into the corridor, the private calls he makes on the only telephone line in their department, the menthol cigarette butts slowly filling his dark glass ashtray, the tin of mints he rattles absent-mindedly when frowning over some report.

Filsan stands up and salutes him but he waves her back to her chair.

'Now don't get too excited, Miss Corporal, but I spoke to Major Adow a few days ago and he asked me if I could recommend a graduate to go on a mission to the border. I looked high and low and then I remembered you, crouched over your little desk. Such efficiency! Such honesty!'

Filsan looks up at him, with half contempt, half desire.

'To Birjeeh with you, on the double!' He points dramatically to the door and she laughs despite herself. As she leaves the room, his eyes track her with an interest she doesn't find unwelcome.

Birjeeh Military HQ reminds Filsan of an illustration in one of the books she read as a child, something from the Brothers Grimm or Hans Christian Andersen. It has the presence of an enchanted castle perched on a hill, partially hidden behind high crenulated walls with watchtowers; its wide arched entrance only needs a portcullis and moat to finish the picture. Filsan has escorted prisoners to the concrete armoury that now functions as a detention room but can imagine long-forgotten prisoners with scraggly beards hidden in secret, underground cells.

The logistics officer, Lieutenant Hashi, ushers her to the Major's office with a scowl on his tight, fox-like face, already aggravated by something.

The room is crowded with around thirty bulky commandos from the locally garrisoned 26th Infantry Division. They stand in a crescent shape around Major Adow; between their bodies she can see snatches of the brown, khaki and gold of his jacket and a black pen held between his fingers like a wand.

'Come closer, comrades,' he says before standing up.

Lieutenant Hashi unrolls a map on the table and then pins its corners to the felt board behind the desk. It shows the north-western region of Somalia in minute detail: waterholes, reservoirs, dry riverbeds, dirt tracks. There are three blue circles on the map over villages near the Ethiopian border; enclosing the blue circles are red semicircles.

Major Adow points his pen at each blue circle and names it in turn.

'Salahley, Baha Dhamal, Ina Guuhaa. We have solid intelligence that NFM rebels are fed, watered and sheltered in these villages. Ever since the secessionists moved their headquarters from London to Ethiopia they have been bolder and bolder and it is places like these that allow them to think they stand a chance in hell of defeating us.'

Filsan stands at armpit height to the soldiers. She finds herself enjoying their smell, the musk of their sweat mixed with hair and gun oil.

Lieutenant Hashi catches her gaze, his bloodshot stare intended to intimidate her, but it is nothing in comparison to her father's.

'You are charged with demolishing the water reservoirs of Salahley. They have been building one every year for more than ten years now and have given some over to the rebels to use. Corporal Adan Ali! Where are you, my girl?' Major Adow shouts.

Filsan pushes forward until she is a metre away from the desk.

'It is your duty to communicate our anger and ensure that it is understood that further punitive measures can and will be enforced. We need an educated comrade who can articulate the principles of the revolution. That's you, isn't it?'

'Yes, Major,' Filsan replies quickly.

'They will have water trucked in monthly and they can use their traditional wells.'

'I will tell them, sir.'

'The exact date and time of the operation will be confirmed by Lieutenant Hashi. Baha Dhamal and Ina Guuhaa will be dealt with by the 4th and 18th sectors simultaneously. Are there any questions?'

The soldiers shift nervously but don't reply. Filsan clears her throat and all faces turn to her. 'Will we be taking prisoners?' she almost whispers.

Major Adow smiles broadly, the same kind of smile he would give a dog riding a bicycle. 'Good question, *jaalle*. We have yet to confirm that detail but well done for speaking up.'

Filsan sees the other soldiers smiling condescendingly, even though they were too cowardly to raise their own voices.

2

The call comes two days later. They are scheduled to leave Hargeisa the next day at five in the morning and to arrive in Salahley by 7 a.m. Filsan had hoped that her period would wait until after the operation but, as if to spite her, it comes early, blanching her face and nearly doubling her over with cramps. She gulps back cup after cup of black tea and avoids eating anything that might worsen her nausea but by the morning of the attack she is curled up, sobbing at how diminished she feels. Taking a deep breath she unfurls her limbs and forces herself through her morning routine. She arrives at Birjeeh before the others, the sky still dark but birds flapping and shaking one another awake in the branches. The compound looks even more imposing now, its walls blending into the darkness beyond to form a citadel of ether and stone.

The unit of thirty men and Filsan leave Birjeeh in a convoy of four large trucks of the type the locals called 'the fates' because of their role in dozens of fatal traffic accidents. Filsan rides in the passenger seat of the first truck, the pain in her abdomen and back lulled by the gentle reverberations of her seat. The driver had held out his arm as she struggled to clamber into the tall vehicle but apart from that there is no interaction between them.

'Morning, Corporal.' Lieutenant Afrah twists his neck into the cab from the bench behind.

'Good morning, sir.' Filsan salutes awkwardly. The Lieutenant has the strange-coloured eyes that some Somalis possess, brown around the pupil with a thick halo of blue as if he is going blind.

'Are you nervous?' He smiles and reveals the sweet gap between his teeth.

'No, I just want to do a decent job.'

'It will be easy, in and out before the engine's even cooled. I have a rifle here for you, an FAL automatic, the recoil isn't so bad on them, better for you than the Kalashnikov. Major Adow said you have had arms training?'

'With the Women's Auxiliary Corps, but that was some time ago, I don't know . . .'

'You won't need it. It will just be a deterrence if there are any troublemakers in the village.'

'Yes, Lieutenant.' Filsan takes the weapon from him; the stock is relatively short while the barrel scrapes the roof of the lorry. She holds it across her chest with the strap over her back. She had never hit the targets well during practice in Mogadishu but it feels good to hold a rifle again; a gun makes a soldier even out of a woman.

They sail through the last urban checkpoint and leave the messy, compacted town to shrink and disappear in the rear-view mirror. A rim of light is developing all around them, as blotchy and bright as overexposed film, the horizon broken up by lopsided pyramids of granite. It is a barren landscape, hard and dull, made for nothing other than mischief, as strange to her as any foreign country.

There are no signs or obvious landmarks; the driver seems to know by intuition which forks in the road to take.

Filsan asks how nomads navigate on moonless nights in these desolate areas, and he points up to the sky. 'Maybe God tells them or they still know the old maps of the stars and find their way like that.'

Her own ancestors were merchants on her father's side and sorghum farmers on her mother's; her people weren't wanderers but sedate accumulators of land and wealth. It seems as if this wild terrain had determined the character of the people or had attracted like-minded spirits to dwell upon it. As the lorry approaches the border with Ethiopia it begins to climb slowly but steadily, the air fresh and scented by the yellow flowers of gum arabic trees. A young shepherd hides behind a thicket of acacia as the convoy passes, his small figure just visible between the scrubby crowns, his black-headed sheep grazing across a vast distance.

It is a *tuulo*, barely even a village: a few beehive-shaped dwellings with old cloth hanging from their entrances, a tea shop with kettles resting on open fires, one solitary stone building with a tin roof, goats, stray children, a cleared space under a tall tree for religious lessons and clan meetings. The elders have been summoned and Filsan remembers her role in this theatre. She steps forward to intercept the three men but they ignore her, and carry on with their sticks and bandy legs to a conscript behind.

She grabs the man on the right by the arm, '*Jaalle*, it is me you need to speak with.'

He is a thin, wiry man but he shakes her off with surprising force. Filsan pursues, not willing to ask for anyone's assistance in dealing with him. She wants to drag him back by the long tufts of grey hair skirting his bald pate and make him kneel at her feet. She catches up with him and shoves the barrel of her gun in the small of his back. 'Stop!'

He freezes and turns slowly to face her.

She withdraws the rifle but holds it tightly, still aimed in his direction.

'My commander has delegated me to speak with you. We are here with the full authority of the revolutionary government. There is strong evidence that you have been assisting the outlawed National Freedom Movement, and to prevent further collaboration the *berkeds* surrounding this settlement will be destroyed.' Filsan speaks in a rush, not stopping to breathe. 'You are still entitled to use your traditional drop wells and will be supplied with supplementary water once a month by the local government.'

The whole village now seems to have crowded around her. The other soldiers have disappeared into the shacks.

'This is government land,' Filsan raises her voice and gestures to the expanse beyond them, 'and you do not even deny that you use the *berkeds* to support the terrorists.'

The third elder, younger than the other two and still possessing a full head of black hair, joins the conversation. '*Jaalle*,' he says mockingly, 'we use those *berkeds* to water our camels, our goats and sheep, to perform ablutions before prayers, for a cup of tea in the mornings. We have nothing to spare for anything else. We are in the middle of a long drought; do you think we would give water to rebels?'

And then a huge plume of water, mud and stone flies into the sky to the west of the village, the bellow of the dynamite echoing against the limestone hills. The villagers run towards the explosions, the elders in the lead, children yelping in excitement and fear behind them.

Filsan catches up with the crowd just as Lieutenant Afrah orders the final detonation. The rectangular cement walls of the nearest *berked* have been blown into fragments and fresh water glides over the parched, eroded earth and slips quietly into deep cracks on the surface.

The destruction silences the elders but she can sense their anger in the same way she had learned to read her father's; the set of their jaws, the tension in their shoulders, their bodies angled away from the subject of their hate.

The commandos begin to filter into view, smiling and relaxed, unconcerned by the reaction of the villagers. These kinds of raids are welcome to them, bringing minimal risk and potential loot. Filsan pants after her chase and presses her palm against the stitch in her ribs. The villagers are rooted to the soil, their heads turning from crater to crater, false rain dripping from the acacias. She marches towards the elders, intending to explain the necessity of the action, the benefits they could enjoy if they only shunned the rebels, the projects that they might partake in to diversify the local economy.

The red-haired elder swivels at her approach and swings his cane at her face. She doesn't notice her finger squeeze the trigger of her rifle as her whole body recoils from the blow. The knock of the rifle against her chest surprises her as does the sudden pop of bullets.

When the elder falls back onto his behind she assumes that he has lost his balance trying to strike her, until points of blood spring up over his shirt, turning the white cloth a red that darkens before her eyes. Then the two other elders decide to drop to the ground too, their open eyes still watching her; movements at the periphery of her vision are blurred so she does not recognize the grey shadows as her comrades advancing on the prostrate men.

'Hold fire!' shouts Lieutenant Afrah.

Filsan looks down at her feet and sees bronzed beetles scuttling over them. She presses one boot on the other, and the beetles are stilled, transformed into empty bullet shells.

The elders are slumped over each other like drunks; a howl sweeps over the plain as first one woman and then another and then another rushes to the dead and dying bodies.

Filsan tries to step forward but her boots feel cemented down.

Lieutenant Afrah aims his Kalashnikov at the young men in the crowd. 'Get back! Back! Back!'

A group of soldiers corner the youths and force them back to the cleared space at the centre of the threadbare settlement. Filsan notices for the first time how thin their calves are, just shafts of bone below their frayed sarongs. They are hustled away, hands on the back of their afros, to squat in the sun until the soldiers depart.

An old woman pulls the wives off the corpses and shrouds the men's faces under a shawl. She says nothing but turns to Filsan and points a finger; whether it is to lay blame, mark her out for retribution or curse her, Filsan cannot decipher.

'Get in the truck, *jaalle*, we will secure the area,' Lieutenant Afrah orders.

Filsan peers down at her distant boots. 'But I can't move.'

Afrah clicks his fingers and a conscript no older than fifteen comes to his side. 'Escort her back to the truck.'

The conscript takes her elbow gently, like he would with his grandmother, and leads her forward as she stumbles over the broken ground.

'You did well, *jaalle*,' he keeps repeating in her ear, as they trek the half-mile back to the vehicles.

'But what happened? Who killed them?' she whispers.

3

Filsan smoothes her palms over her wooden desk, enjoying its solidity; she closes her eyes and sees the elders looking back at her. Captain Yasin makes an aeroplane from a card and throws it at her desk; it glides just short and lands beside her feet. It is her request for leave stamped with 'APPROVED'. Filsan will soon be back in her yellow room with the cherry-print curtains. She craves Intisaar's cooking, her crispy lamb *sambuusi*, the grilled fish served with spiced and sweetened vermicelli, and hot oily *bajiye* dipped in green chilli sauce. Intisaar the maid, paid a thousand shillings a week, has been everything a mother should be to her; while her own children were raised by their grandmother she laboured in the malign atmosphere of their silent house. Filsan writes down a list of things to buy Intisaar from Hargeisa, items that show she knows her and has been thinking about her – a silver necklace or even a gold one if she can afford it, imported Taarab records, support bandages for her swollen knees. The last item might be the most appreciated now that Intisaar has crossed the border from middle age into old age; at fifty-seven the marrow starts to dry up, she said in her musical Bajuni accent, from then on you are just waiting for your bones to turn to dust.

Filsan opens a window to clear the room of the Captain's cigarette smoke and stands idly for a moment watching the wind shake desiccated leaves into the yard. 'You want to come to Saba'ad with me?' Captain Yasin's voice startles her. 'I'm going to check on the militia there for the paramilitary report.'

The report *I* will end up writing, thinks Filsan as she sinks into her chair.

'Come on, it will be good for you to see them.'

'What about these files?'

'They're not going to walk away, are they?' He pulls her up from her chair. 'Come on. It is an order.'

Filsan scribbles a note on her desk with her whereabouts and follows him to the jeep.

Saba'ad is twenty miles north-east of Hargeisa. The largest of five refugee camps in the north-western region, it has grown and established itself as a kind of satellite town and stretches as far as the eye can see. Twenty thousand Ethiopian Somali refugees scratch out a living here, having first fled the fighting between '77 and '78 and then the subsequent famines in eastern Ethiopia.

The camp's residents live in a mishmash of dwellings scrabbled together from donated tarpaulin, acacia twigs, old cloth and scavenged metal. Dust blows up in large gusts from the denuded landscape. Filsan covers her nose and eyes against the sand and keeps close behind Captain Yasin. At different points of the camp, various charities maintain schools, clinics, community centres; German, Irish and American aid workers mark out their own fiefdoms with flags and acronym-heavy placards. Looking down on the camp brings home just how great Somalia's humiliation was in the war; these people have land, homes and farms just a few miles away but subsist here on gruel.

Captain Yasin had told the militia leader to meet him by the burial ground to the west of the camp and the men are waiting, around fifty or so, squatting between the rocks placed to mark graves. The fighters are ragged teenagers in sarongs and vests; they are armed with long sticks and wear sandals made of tyre rubber. They rise as Captain Yasin and Filsan climb towards them.

'Is this all of you?' Captain Yasin asks.

The militia leader is tall and skeletal; a green cap obscures his eyes. 'No, we have more but they are tending what animals they still have.' His voice is grainy, dry.

'This is Corporal Adan Ali, she will be working with you too.'

They squint in Filsan's direction.

'We need to know how many of you there are before we can arrange proper arms.'

'When we have our weapons then we will come out into the open. Not before.'

The leader scrapes pictures into the grit as he speaks; straight lines, suns, hills, curved horns. 'We are waiting for the signal.'

The teenagers watch her with benign interest, their arms draped over each other's shoulders; they have the lean limbs of marathon runners but are penned into this prison of sand and rock.

'It won't be long now. You must gather as many men as possible. Organize them. Discipline them,' Captain Yasin exhorts.

'It will happen.' The leader hawks and spits into his drawing. 'What will you give us for the time being?'

The teenagers lean forward to hear the response.

'We will set aside more rations for you but there is little we can do until we are able to take control of the city.'

Filsan looks up quizzically.

The leader nods, defeated. 'We will just wait, then.'

'Don't despair. Soon your fortunes will change for the better. Within the month you will have rifles, RPGs, transport. This girl will make sure of that.' He gestures to Filsan.

She doesn't understand what he is referring to. Why would they give RPGs to these refugees when Somalia already has one of the largest armies in Africa? She wonders if he has drawn her into weapon smuggling. She imagines what her father would say if she were court-martialled over something so squalid. Turning on her heels she abandons the gathering and traces the route back to the jeep. Captain Yasin is soon beside her but she speeds on, ignoring him.

'What's wrong?' He pulls her arm back.

'Let me go!' She wrenches it free, not caring that he is her superior.

'Wait, Filsan! What's the problem?'

'I will report you, Captain, you can commit as many crimes as you want, but you won't drag me down with you.'

'What crimes?'

GRANTA

THE MAGAZINE OF NEW WRITING

SUBSCRIPTION FORM FOR UK, EUROPE AND REST OF THE WORLD

Yes, I would like to take out a subscription to *Granta*.

GUARANTEE: If I am ever dissatisfied with my *Granta* subscription, I will simply notify you, and you will send me a complete refund or credit my credit card, as applicable, for all un-mailed issues.

YOUR DETAILS

MR / MISS / MRS / DR ....

NAME ....

ADDRESS ....

....

POSTCODE ....

EMAIL ....

☐ Please tick this box if you do not wish to receive special offers from *Granta*
☐ Please tick this box if you do not wish to receive offers from organizations selected by *Granta*

YOUR PAYMENT DETAILS

1) ☐ Pay £32.00 (saving £20) by Direct Debit
   To pay by Direct Debit please complete the mandate and return to the address shown below.

2) Pay by cheque or credit/debit card. Please complete below:

   1 year subscription: ☐ UK: £36.00   ☐ Europe: £42.00   ☐ Rest of World: £46.00

   3 year subscription: ☐ UK: £99.00   ☐ Europe: £108.00   ☐ Rest of World: £126.00

   I wish to pay by ☐ CHEQUE ☐ CREDIT/DEBIT CARD
   Cheque enclosed for £_____ made payable to *Granta*.

   Please charge £ _____ to my: ☐ Visa ☐ MasterCard ☐ Amex ☐ Switch/Maestro

   Card No. ☐☐☐☐☐☐☐☐☐☐☐☐☐☐☐☐

   Valid from *(if applicable)* ☐☐☐☐   Expiry Date ☐☐☐☐   Issue No. ☐☐

   Security No. ☐☐☐

SIGNATURE .... DATE ....

Instructions to your Bank or Building Society to pay by Direct Debit

BANK NAME ....

BANK ADDRESS ....

POSTCODE ....

ACCOUNT IN THE NAMES(S) OF: ....

SIGNED ....

DATE ....

DIRECT Debit

Instructions to your Bank or Building Society: Please pay Granta Publications direct debits from the account detailed on this instruction subject to the safeguards assured by the direct debit guarantee. I understand that this instruction may remain with Granta and, if so, details will be passed electronically to my bank/building society. Banks and building societies may not accept direct debit instructions from some types of account.

Bank/building society account number
☐☐☐☐☐☐☐☐

Sort Code
☐☐ ☐☐ ☐☐

Originator's Identification
9 1 3 1 3 3

Please mail this order form with payment instructions to:

Granta Publications
12 Addison Avenue
London, W11 4QR
Or call +44 (0)208 955 7011
Or visit GRANTA.COM

'Don't think I'm stupid. I may be a woman but I can't be fooled so easily.'

'What are you talking about?'

Filsan stops abruptly and lowers her voice. 'You are selling arms.'

He bends back with laughter. 'You're crazy! Selling arms? To them? And what would they pay me in?'

'So why tell them they will receive rocket-propelled grenades?'

He pulls her close. 'Because that is what the government wants. We can't talk about this here.' He takes her arm again and marches her to the car.

'Get in the jeep,' he orders. 'I can't tell you everything but I will tell you what I know.'

They drive away from Saba'ad in silence and only when they have reached the long, empty road to Hargeisa does Captain Yasin feel comfortable talking. 'The government has decided that the situation as it stands is untenable. If the NFM continue to attack a village here, a battalion there, other clan militias will become emboldened and soon we will be fighting on twenty fronts.'

Filsan has never seen him so serious before. She watches his sharp profile and feels that old desire for him creeping up on her.

'They, all of the leadership in Mogadishu and Hargeisa too, have decided that there has to be a change.'

'What kind of change?'

'An end to it all. The whole population must be resettled to prevent the terrorists taking over.'

'Empty Hargeisa?'

'All the towns, Hargeisa, Burao, Berbera, anywhere the rebels might gather.' He wipes sweat from his upper lip with his wrist.

'When will this happen?'

'Not confirmed.'

It seems sensible, final, an improvement on this constant, draining game.

'How do you know about it?'

Captain Yasin smiles. 'Ahh, don't you know that I am in the inner circle?'

'When will the rest of us be told?'

'When it is absolutely necessary and, Filsan, please, you cannot tell anyone about this, or we will both end up in jail.' He holds her gaze in the rear-view mirror.

'Don't insult me. I am not some market gossip. I take my work more seriously than anyone else.'

'I know that.' He nods. 'That's why I told you.'

4

The next day, Captain Yasin leaves for lunch alone but as evening approaches, when her fingers sting from the impact of the typewriter keys, he mooches over to her desk and asks what she plans to do with her evening.

'Read, Captain.'

'Poor girl, is that the extent of your existence?'

Filsan sits rigidly. 'I am not here for fun. I want to make something of myself.'

'Life is to be enjoyed.'

'For layabouts and street boys, maybe.'

'No, for you and for me too. Let me take you out to dinner.'

Filsan's eyes sweep down to her hands. 'I don't know.'

'I don't know? Are your books really more interesting than me?'

'I have work to do.'

'As do I. Let's discuss it over a meal.'

Captain Yasin waits under an electricity pole a hundred yards from the barracks. He appears thin and angular in a white shirt that glows fluorescent in the dim light. She has changed into a pair of flared jeans and a loose red tunic with a shawl over her shoulders. They meet awkwardly and shake hands under the light of a nearby tea stall, her hand tiny in his.

'Roble, pleased to meet you.' He hides his grin.

'Filsan, likewise.'

Walking beside him, Filsan feels a static charge as if the cables above are lightly electrifying them; it surprises her how good it feels to stand beside a man and know that he has picked her from all of the other women he could have.

Roble leads the way with his hands in his pockets and makes small talk about the restaurants he likes, the hotels that serve alcohol, the best places to meet senior officials.

He draws her away from the road as a truck passes perilously close; the curfew is imminent and civilian vehicles rush to their destinations despite the derelict condition of the road.

They turn right at a checkpoint, he raising a hand in greeting to the group of soldiers behind the barrier, and enter the Safari, an open-air restaurant with tame wildlife roaming the grounds.

It is packed with men in uniform, seated on white plastic chairs around tables set unevenly into the gravel beneath. Red light bulbs hang in a chain from one corner to the next and the drone of a generator masks the music from two large speakers.

The men glance up from their card games and meals to judge the woman in their midst.

'Is this OK?' Roble asks, pointing to a dark table under a bougainvillea bush.

Filsan knows what the stares mean. That she is a whore to be seen in public with a man she isn't married to. Their eyes are still on her as she slips into the chair. A waiter in a black bow tie and shoes with the soles slapping free appears quickly beside Roble.

He orders two colas and a lamb platter.

Slowly attention drifts away from Filsan back to the red nucleus of the restaurant.

'*Bedus*.' Roble smiles. 'You would think they have never seen a woman before.'

'Uneducated, that is all.'

'Or jealous.' Roble strokes her little finger with his knuckle.

'Don't do that.' Filsan snatches her hands from his reach.

He raises his palms in acquiescence.

'Why are you not married already?'

'No one has wanted me.'

'Do you know the reason why?'

'No, why?' Filsan smiles with surprise. She decides to be candid tonight, to not hold back for once.

'Because you act like you don't need anybody.'

'I *don't* need anyone but that doesn't mean that I don't want certain things.'

'And those certain things are?'

'Someone by my side, on my side, who I can share my thoughts with.'

Roble lights a cigarette, adding another pinprick of light to the dark. 'Thoughts about the organizational budget of our office, or other thoughts?'

'All kinds. You wouldn't guess how far and deep my thoughts reach.'

'*Ahh*, so you are philosophizing up there in your little room.'

The waiter returns with a tray piled high with rice and a lamb shoulder and two cola bottles rough with reuse.

'Sometimes, and other times I am just wishing something good would happen in my life.'

'Something like me?'

Filsan raises an eyebrow. 'That is very arrogant.'

'Accepted, but is it wrong?'

'I don't know yet. Why have you suddenly become so attentive?'

'Time. We have much less time than we realize, especially as soldiers, and I don't want to wait for anything.'

Filsan lifts the bottle to her mouth to hide her smile. 'That is very dramatic. But our office is pretty safe, isn't it?'

'For now. But don't worry, you have me to protect you.'

'I think *I* would be better at protecting you.'

'You would type them into submission, I'm sure.'

Roble walks Filsan back to the barracks. The curfew has shut up the civilians inside their homes, with only the faint smells of charcoal and spice and paraffin lights hinting at their existence. The street is dark and deserted, apart from the squeak and rustle of stray cats chasing mice and the soldiers at the checkpoint talking softly over the hiss of a radio. Filsan looks up; the sky stretched over them like a dome is alive with stars; thin black clouds with haloes of white and silver pass over the half-moon. It is a city up there, teeming with life.

'You know that on clear nights you can spot satellites?'

'I've heard that. In Mogadishu there are too many lights to see anything like this.' Filsan carries on staring at the heavens and stumbles over a stone.

Roble catches her by the waist and rights her; for a moment her hands rest on his and then she pushes them away.

They stroll slowly to the barracks, unafraid. Filsan remembers reading once that the night was made for lovers, each pair invisible to the rest. It had been in a romance novel she had found under her bed, left behind by her American cousin Rahma.

'You should stop here in case anyone sees you,' Filsan says, turning to him and holding out her hand. 'See you tomorrow.'

Roble chuckles at her formality but shakes her hand.

He waits for her to pass the sentry gate and enter the compound. Out of sight in the stairwell, Filsan watches him turn and walk away. She feels a pang in her chest as he strides, head bowed, into the dark. He seems so vulnerable, prey to whatever ghosts or beasts might assail him. Filsan begins to blow a kiss at his back but feels ridiculous and just follows his white shirt as it disappears into the night like a ship's sail surrounded by high waves and low clouds. ∎

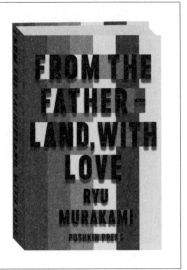

EUROPA

David Szalay

DAVID
SZALAY

1974

David Szalay was born in Canada. His
family moved to the UK soon after, and he
has lived here ever since. He has published
three novels: *London and the South-East*,
The Innocent and *Spring*. He is currently
working on a number of new projects –
'Europa' is an excerpt from one of these.

It was ten o'clock in the morning and the kitchen was full of standing smoke and the smell of the stuffed cabbages. 'So you're off to London?' Emma's mother said. Though she was not an old woman, probably not even fifty, she had the sour demeanour of someone disappointedly older. She looked much older too as she moved ponderously around the kitchen in an old blue tracksuit, or leaned heavily on the grim, antiquated gas cooker.

Gábor said, 'We'll bring you something back. What do you want?'

'You don't need to bring me anything,' she said. Her hair was dyed a maximal black. White roots showed. Outside the window, its sill crammed with dusty cacti, an arterial road growled. She lit a cigarette. 'I don't need anything,' she said.

'It's not about needing,' Gábor told her. 'What do you *want?*'

She shrugged and lifted the cigarette to her seamed mouth, to rudimentary dentures. 'What have they got in London?'

Gábor guffawed. 'What *haven't* they got?'

She put a plate with a single pickle on it, halved lengthways, on the small, square table next to Balázs's Michelangeloesque elbow. (His mouth working, he acknowledged the plate with a nod of his head.)

Gábor said, 'We'll find you something. Whatever.'

'You've got business there, have you?' the woman said.

'That's right.'

'And your friend?' (Balázs went on eating.) 'Has he got business there too?'

'He's helping me.'

'Is he?' She was staring straight at him, at 'Gábor's friend' – a sun-toughened lump of muscle in a tight T-shirt, skin tattooed, face lightly pockmarked.

'Security,' Gábor specified.

'How's the cabbage?' she asked, still staring at Balázs. 'OK?'

He looked up. 'Yeah,' he said. 'Thanks.'

She turned back to Gábor. 'And what's Emma going to do while you two take care of your business?'

'What do you think?' Gábor said. 'Shopping.'

They weren't actually friends. They knew each other from the gym. Balázs was Gábor's personal trainer, though Gábor's attendance was sporadic – he might turn up four or five times one week, then not for a whole month, thus undoing all the work they had put in together on the machines and treadmills. He also ate and drank too much of too many of the wrong things. When he did show up, Emma was sometimes with him, and sometimes she was there on her own. These days she was there more often than he was – Monday, Wednesday, Friday, every week. All the guys who worked at the gym wanted to fuck her, Balázs wasn't alone in that. He wanted it more than the others though. It was getting to be an unhealthy, obsessive thing.

She didn't even acknowledge him when she came into the kitchen. Without seeming to (he was lighting a Park Lane) he noticed that she was wearing the cork-soled platform shoes that made him think of pornography. In fact, he had an idea that Gábor – like not a few of the members of the gym, with their BMWs parked outside – was somehow involved in the production of pornography. One of the BMW drivers had even offered him a part in a film, had offered him a month's wages for one day's 'work' – Balázs had the well-muscled, tattoo-festooned look the producer favoured. His lightly pockmarked face was apparently not a problem, though the man had intimated that his size might be. Balázs had turned him down; partly to leave no hint that he was worried he might be too small, he had told him, or implied, that his girlfriend wouldn't let him do it. That wasn't true. He had no girlfriend.

Nor was it that he didn't need the money. He did. He needed whatever bits and pieces of extra work he could find. He had been employed by Gábor as a minder several times already – usually when he visited people at their offices, often in smart villas in the leafier parts of the city – though what Gábor did exactly, and what his business was in London, Balázs did not know.

The easyJet flight to Luton was four hours delayed due to the late arrival of the aircraft. Gábor took this quite hard. He seemed especially concerned about Zoli, whom he was unable to reach on the phone. Zoli was evidently some contact or associate of his in London, who would be meeting them at the airport, and Gábor was frantic at the idea that this Zoli was already on his way to Luton and would have to wait there for hours.

When Gábor finally got through to him, Zoli already knew about the delay. They were by then installed at a table in the sun-dappled interior of the small terminal. Gábor finished apologizing to Zoli and put down his phone. 'It's all right,' he said.

Balázs nodded and took a mouthful of lager. The two men each had a half-litre of Heineken. He wondered how it would be in London. He imagined meetings in soporific offices, himself standing near the door, or waiting outside. For Emma, though, this was a sort of holiday so she and Gábor would probably want to have some time to themselves. Well, that was fine. He just had to know when to leave them alone, when not to hang around.

It was extremely stressful, he found, to be in her presence outside the safely purposeful space of the gym. It was the same in the car, in Gábor's Audi Q3, when she was there. Sometimes Gábor would go in somewhere and leave them in the car together – she in the front, Balázs in the back – and he would be so intensely aware of her presence, of the minuscule squeaks when she moved on the leather seat, or flipped down the sun visor to tweak an eyebrow in the vanity mirror, that, just to hold himself together, he had to fix his eyes on some object outside the darkened window and keep them there, unable to think about anything except how he had masturbated to her, twice, the previous night, which did not seem a promising starting point for conversation. They never spoke. Sometimes they would be alone in the car for twenty minutes – Gábor was always away for at least twice as long as he said he would be – and they never spoke.

What she was like 'as a person' he had no idea. There was something princessy about her. She seemed to look down on the staff in the gym – she wasn't friendly with them anyway. The women who worked there hated her, and it was assumed that she was with Gábor, who was slightly shorter than her, for his money. She always listened to music while she worked out, possibly to stop people trying to talk to her. Sometimes she would have a tea – usually organic peppermint or something – in the little cafe. Balázs had never seen her smile.

He had been surprised to see what her mother was like, where she lived. He had expected something smarter, something in Buda maybe, a house with roses in front and a well-preserved fifty-year-old offering them coffee, not that wreck of a woman living in that hole of a flat. The time-browned tower block, the odours and voices on the stairwell, the neglected pot plants by the yellow window where the stairs turned – these things were all familiar to him. Most of the people he knew emanated from places like that, himself included. That she did, however, was a surprise.

He finished the Heineken and said something about stepping outside for a cigarette. Gábor, waggling his fingers at the screen of his phone, said, 'Yeah. We'll just be here.' She did not even look up from her magazine.

He smoked on the observation terrace, from where, through a barrier of hardened glass, you could watch the planes taxiing to the end of the runway and taking off at intervals of a few minutes. Standing there and watching them through the feeble heat haze, the sound of the engines coming to him across several hundred metres of warm air made him think of the days he had spent at Balad Air Base, with the rest of the Hungarian unit, waiting for the flight home. He now looked back on that year with something like nostalgia. He should have stayed in the army – it was safe there, and there were things to do. Now he was just treading water, softening, waiting for something to happen . . . What was going to happen, though?

Gábor was standing there.

He lit a cigarette, a more expensive one than the Park Lanes Balázs smoked. 'Sorry about the delay,' he said.

Gábor seemed nervous. It was as if he had something to say but wasn't sure how to say it.

Balázs had started to think that maybe Gábor didn't have anything to say after all, so long had he just stood there smoking furtively, when he said, 'I should tell you what we'll be doing in London.'

There followed a few seconds during which they stared together at the scene in front of them – the smooth-skinned planes waiting in the sunshine near the terminal, and the other, smaller vehicles zipping around with a sense of urgent purpose on the quilted tarmac.

'Emma,' Gábor said, as if she was there and he was addressing her.

Balázs half turned his sun-reddened head.

She wasn't there.

Gábor said, 'Emma's going to be doing some work in London.'

They watched as a narrow-bodied Lufthansa turboprop started its take-off. After a few hundred metres it leapt into the air with a steepness of ascent that was quite startling, as if it were being jerked into the sky on a string. They watched it dwindle to a point in the sky's hazy dazzle, and then, at some indefinite moment, disappear. Then Gábor said, 'And your job . . .' He found a more satisfactory pronoun. '*Our* job is to look after her. OK?'

Balázs simply nodded.

'OK,' Gábor said, with finality, having performed what was obviously an embarrassing task. 'Just thought I'd tell you.' He dropped his cigarette and extinguished it under the toe of his trainer. 'See you inside.'

Mimicking his employer, Balázs toed out his own cigarette. (His shoe was a hard, square-ended, faux-leather thing, manufactured somewhere in South-East Asia.) Then he lit another, and squinted out at the shimmer standing on the tarmac.

2

Zoli met them at Luton Airport in a silver Mercedes.

The flight had been uneventful. The plane was full, but Gábor had paid for priority boarding and they had seats together – Balázs squashed into the window seat, Gábor stretching his legs in the aisle, and Emma between them, listening to her iPod and staring at the rigid plastic seat back a few inches from the tip of her nose. When the plane's ascent flattened out and the drinks trolley approached, Gábor bought himself and Balázs little cans of beer – two each – and Emma a Diet Coke.

With barely enough space to lift the beer to his lips, Balázs concentrated on the window. There was nothing to see, except a section of wing and fierce light on the endless expanse of white fluffiness far below. You would fall straight through it, he thought, solid as it looks. He wasn't sure, now, that he had understood what Gábor had meant when he said that Emma would be 'doing some work' in London. Had he even heard him properly? The light hurt his eyes and he half lowered the plastic shutter. He folded his swollen hands in his lap and sat there, his mind snagged on those questions and on the serrated whisper of her headphones, only just perceptible over the massive white noise of the labouring engines.

Zoli was tall and not unhandsome, and managed a moustache without looking silly. He also had an air of slightly savage intelligence about him – he was in fact a fully qualified doctor, though not currently practising. It was true that there was an unhealthy puffiness to his face, a swollenness, his eyes protruding more than was ideal, but Balázs did not notice these things until he saw them, intermittently, in the rear-view mirror – he was sitting in the back of the Mercedes with Emma, the lowered leather armrest emphatically separating them – as they made their way towards London.

They did so with single-minded speed, Zoli pushing the powerful car through holes in the traffic on the motorway. Holding on to the spring-hinged handle over the window, Balázs saw fleeting past a landscape somehow more thoroughly filled than any in his own country. It seemed more orderly. It was very obviously more moneyed. Even now, in the middle of summer, everything looked fairly plump and fresh.

Gábor lit a cigarette. He was sitting in the front with Zoli, who immediately told him to put it out.

Gábor apologized and pressed it into the ashtray.

Still forcing the car forward, Zoli pulled the ashtray out of its hole, lowered his window and shook it out into the loud wind. When the window was up again, he explained that he had borrowed the car from a friend of his who had a luxury limousine hire service. He had promised he wouldn't smoke in it.

'Sorry,' Gábor said again. Then he said, 'This is the new S-Class, yeah? Nice car. Very nice car.'

Zoli agreed vaguely. He looked in the rear-view mirror and for a moment Balázs saw his swollen eyes.

Zoli was in his mid-thirties probably, only a few years older than the others. Even so, Gábor was having trouble relating to him as an equal, something he normally managed quite easily with older and more important-seeming men, a quality that was probably the source of much of whatever professional success he had enjoyed. They *had* made some small talk as they drove out of the airport – though even that was abruptly ended (Gábor was in the middle of saying something) when Zoli had to pay for the parking – and, as they headed into London, Gábor's usual effortless friendliness seemed to have faltered. Whether that was because he was simply intimidated by Zoli or for some other reason, Balázs did not know. Seeing them shake hands with some formality in the arrivals lounge the situation had seemed to him to be this: they had met before but did not know each other well. Zoli and Emma, on the other hand, seemed never to have met. Gábor introduced them, again with a strange sort of formality, and Zoli was very friendly to her – a wide smile, a pair of kisses. To Balázs – obviously the minder, with his shit clothes and his muscles – he had offered only a peremptory handshake. Then he had hurried them to the short-term parking lot. They were in a hurry because, as Zoli said, 'there's one tonight' – whatever that meant – and what with the delay they were pressed for time, as they had first to go to the flat. Zoli, it seemed, had sorted out a flat for them to stay in while they were in London.

They spent some time stuck in traffic, the flow of the motorway silting up as it entered the metropolis. They were slowed by traffic lights. (The air conditioning was on – outside the tinted windows London, what they were able to see of it, sweltered.) Then there were smaller thoroughfares, a more local look to things. There were neighbourhoods, parks, high streets, overflowing pubs. Smudged impressions of urban life on an electric summer evening. It went on for over an hour. Then they arrived at the flat.

It was on a quiet street with a few trees on it. Small two-storey houses, all exactly the same. They waited with their luggage and duty-free while Zoli opened the front door, swearing to himself as he struggled with the unfamiliar keys. The flat was on the upper floor of a house, up some narrow stairs, at the top of which there was another struggle with the keys, and then they went in. One bedroom, white and sparsely furnished. Balázs would take the sofa in the living room, which overlooked the quiet road. On the other side of the landing, lurking mustily, was a windowless bathroom, into which Emma disappeared with her washbag as soon as they arrived.

The men waited in the living room, Gábor on the sofa, Zoli pacing slowly and taking in the view from the uncurtained window and then pacing again, and Balázs just standing there staring at the old lion-coloured carpet and its mass of cigarette burns and other blemishes. From his sprawl on the sofa, Gábor wondered out loud whether there was somewhere to get something to eat. Zoli offered only an uninterested shrug. He said he didn't know the area well – like the Mercedes, he said, he had borrowed the flat from a friend. He himself lived in another part of London. Turning back to the window, he said the high street was nearby – there would be something there.

'D'you mind popping out,' Gábor said to Balázs, 'and getting some kebabs or something?'

Balázs looked up from the carpet. 'OK.'

'Do you want something?' Gábor said.

The question was addressed to Zoli, but he was still staring out the window and didn't answer.

'Zoli?' Gábor said, slightly tentatively. 'D'you want something?'

'No,' he said, without turning.

'OK. So, yeah, just get some kebabs,' Gábor said.

Balázs nodded. Then he said, 'How many should I get?'

'I don't know. I'll have one. Do you want one?'

'Uh . . . Yeah.'

'And Emma might want one. Four?' Gábor suggested.

The stairs were almost too narrow for his shoulders, he almost had to make his way down sideways. The downstairs hall was dark, despite the frosted square pane in the front door, which opened as he neared the foot of the stairs and admitted a youngish woman in a charcoal trouser suit.

It was very warm and light out in the street, a nice soft evening light that flattered the parked Merc. He lit a Park Lane, and then set off through the little mazy streets of pinched, identikit houses in the direction Zoli had indicated. It took him twenty minutes to find the high street, and when he did there seemed to be nowhere selling specifically kebabs. He walked up and down, sweating now in the summer evening, his orange T-shirt stuck to his skin. He noticed a Polish supermarket, and the number of non-white people in the street. Then he phoned Gábor. 'Is chicken OK?' he said.

Gábor didn't seem to understand the question. 'What?'

'Chicken,' Balázs said emphatically. 'Is it OK?'

'Chicken?'

'Yeah.' He was standing outside a fried chicken place. The street lights had just flickered on, greenish. There was a faint smell of putrefaction. 'There's this fried chicken place . . .' he said.

'Yeah, that's fine,' Gábor told him. Then, 'I mean – does it look OK?'

Balázs looked at the place. 'Yeah, it looks OK.'

'Yeah, fine,' Gábor said. 'And don't be too long. We've got to leave at half eight.'

Balázs slipped his phone into the hip pocket of his jeans and stepped into the pitiless light. There was a small queue. While he waited he studied the menu – some backlit plastic panels – and when it was his turn, ordered without mishap. (His English was quite fluent; he had learned it in Iraq – it was the only way they could communicate with the Polish soldiers they were stationed with, and of course with whatever Americans they happened to meet.) He had trouble finding his way back to the flat and had to phone Gábor again for help. Then they sat in the living room, he and Gábor, on the low sofa, eating with their hands from the flimsy grease-stained boxes. The overhead light was on in its torn paper shade and the stagnant air was full of loitering smoke and the smell of their meal, and in the hurried eating of which Balázs was so involved he did not notice Emma's presence until Zoli spoke.

Then he lifted his head. His mouth was full and his fingers were shiny with the grease of the chicken pieces. She was standing in the doorway.

'Wow,' Zoli said, as if speaking Balázs's thoughts. '*Wow.*'

Sitting in the pearly Merc, Balázs found an after-image of how she had looked, standing in the doorway, still singed into his vision as he stared out the window at other things. The London night was as glossy as the page of a magazine. Nobody spoke now as the smoothly moving Merc took them into the heart of the city, where the money was.

3

It was awkward, especially that first night. In the driver's seat, Gábor seemed morose – he spent a lot of time with his head lolling on the leather headrest, staring out through the windscreen at the plutocratic side street in which they were parked. Unusually for him, he hardly said a word for hours at a time. The hotel was a few minutes' walk away, on the avenue known as Park Lane – after which Balázs's inexpensive cigarettes, he now learned, were named.

When they had arrived, Zoli made a phone call and they had been joined shortly afterwards by a young woman, also Hungarian, whose name was Juli and who, it seemed, worked at the hotel in question. Zoli introduced her to Gábor and Emma, and then she, Zoli and Emma – lofty and precarious on inordinate heels – had set off, and Gábor had told Balázs that the two of them would be waiting there, in the car, until Emma came back.

It was a pretty miserable night they spent there, mostly in silence exacerbated by the tepid stillness of the weather. There were instances of listless conversation, such as when Gábor asked Balázs whether this was his first time in London. Balázs said it was, and Gábor suggested that he might like to do some sightseeing. When Balázs, showing polite interest, asked what he should see, Gábor seemed at a loss for a few moments, then mentioned Madame Tussauds. 'They have waxworks of famous people,' he said. 'You know. David Beckham. Whatever. Emma wants to see it. Anyway, it's something for you to do, if you want.'

They lapsed then into a long silence, except for Gábor's index finger tapping the upholstered steering wheel, a sound like slow dripping – drip drip drip – slowly filling a dark sink of preoccupation from which Balázs's question, asked some time later, seemed mysteriously to flow.

He asked Gábor how he knew Zoli.

'Zoli?' Gábor seemed surprised that it was something Balázs would have any interest in. 'Uh,' he said, as if he had actually forgotten. 'Friend of a friend. You know.' There was another longish pause and then, perhaps finding that it was something he wanted to talk about after all, Gábor went on. 'I met him last time I was here, in London. He suggested we set something up.' In the shape of light that fell into his lap from a street lamp, Gábor studied the Tibetan inscription tattooed on the inside of his left forearm.

She tapped on the misted window just after five in the morning. It was light and quite cold. Not much was said as Gábor, waking, unlocked the door and she got in. Nor while he fiddled with the satnav. Then he switched on the engine, set the demister noisily to work on the windows, and they pulled out into the empty street.

She looked tired, more than anything, still in her skimpy dress and heels – though now she had shed the shoes and drawn her legs up under her on the seat. The two men had managed a few hours' sleep while they waited; it was hard to say whether she had. Her brown-ringed eyes suggested not. Her residual alertness seemed chemically assisted.

'Everything was OK?' Gábor said eventually, while they waited at a traffic light.

'Mhm.'

'Are you hungry?' was his next question, a minute or so later.

'I don't know,' she said. 'Maybe.'

'You should eat something,' he advised.

'OK.'

They stopped at a McDonald's and Balázs was sent in, sensible, in her presence, of his own obvious stink – he had been wearing the same T-shirt for twenty-four hours. She wanted a Big Mac and large fries, and a Diet Coke.

'Thanks,' she said when he got back to the car and, turning in the passenger seat, passed her the brown bag.

Was it the first word she had ever spoken to him?

He said, 'No problem,' though she might not have heard, as at that moment Gábor started the engine.

She pushed the plastic straw into the cup's lid and started to drink.

Zoli showed up in the middle of the afternoon, while they were all still asleep. From his position on the odorous sofa, Balázs was woken by his music, or perhaps by its sudden stop, as he parked in the street outside.

His main purpose was to pick up his share of the money and Gábor emerged vague and tousled in a singlet and boxer shorts to hand it over, which he did in the recessed corner of the living room that had been turned into a derisory pine kitchenette. Zoli then handed out strongly chilled lagers and, as they opened them, asked after Emma. She had not been seen – not by Balázs anyway – since the morning, when she had disappeared into the bedroom as soon as they got back to the flat. Gábor had joined her soon after, leaving Balázs to press his face into the strange-smelling sofa back in an attempt to escape the light that flooded the room as he tried to ignore the sounds from the street, intermittent but easily audible from the first floor. At about ten o'clock, still unable to sleep, he had masturbated under a weak shower to a torrent of fragmentary pornographic set-ups, involving Emma in a vaguely delineated hotel room, of the sort that had filled his head all night. A shocking quantity of seed turned down the plughole. Some time after that, with a T-shirt tied over his eyes, he fell asleep.

A few hours later Zoli turned up.

'So everything went OK?' he said, and swigged.

'Yeah, I think so,' Gábor said, with a sort of sleepy snuffle. They were standing at the pine breakfast bar.

'I know him, that guy,' Zoli said. 'He's OK. He's a nice guy. I put him in first because I knew he wouldn't cause any hassle.'

Gábor just nodded. He was wearing his glasses, not his contacts, which gave him a look of bookish vulnerability.

'Some of the others I don't know,' Zoli went on. 'I'm not expecting any hassle.'

'No,' Gábor said.

'These aren't people who want to talk to the police, to journalists, you know what I mean. They've got too much to lose. Some of them are famous, I think.'

'Yeah?' Gábor said. He didn't seem interested.

'I think so,' Zoli said, with a nod and a swig. 'She still asleep?' he asked.

'Yeah,' Gábor said.

Zoli didn't stay long, and after he left Gábor went back to bed. If he had had a bed, Balázs might have done the same. Instead he went out into the blinding day and got another box of chicken pieces from the same place as the night before. Then he lay on the sofa with the window open, smoking and trying to read a book, *Harry Potter és a Titkok Kamrája*; he was working his way slowly through the series. He found it difficult to focus on the story. Then he found it difficult to focus on the words.

When he woke up she was standing in the doorway, in a dressing gown. He had no idea what time it was. It was still daylight.

'Hi,' she said in a neutral voice.

'Hi.' He sat up quickly. 'What, what time is it?'

'I don't know. Gábor wants to go shopping.' She tilted her head as if looking at something upside down. 'Is that any good?' she asked.

'Uh.' He picked up the book and looked at the front, as if the answer might be there. 'It's all right,' he said. He tried to think of something else to say about it.

She stayed there a few moments more, in the mote-filled afternoon light, as if she was waiting for something. Then she yawned, and left.

Later, when they were sitting in the parked Merc, Gábor told him about the shopping trip – two and a half hours in the scrum of Oxford Street, followed by a meal in the red velvet interior of an Angus Steakhouse. They had been talking more than they had the first night, the two men. It was drizzling. Maybe that helped, the way the surrounding hubbub softened the silence. The fact was, they did not know each other well. Even in the context of the gym they were not particularly friendly. Gábor's friendliness shone without favouritism on everyone, but he spent more time talking and joking with other members of the staff – with András, with Attila – than with Balázs, in spite of the fact that Balázs was his personal trainer.

At about midnight, Balázs left the Merc and went through the drizzle to the nearby KFC, which was open till two, to get their 'lunch' – two 'Fully Loaded' meals.

Taking his seat again, he found Gábor in a pensive mood.

'Sometimes I worry about my attitude to women,' Gábor said. Water trickled down the window against which his head was silhouetted. 'D'you worry about that?'

Balázs had just bitten into his chicken fillet burger and could not immediately answer. When he could, he said, 'What d'you mean?'

'Just my attitude to women,' Gábor said miserably. 'Maybe it isn't healthy.' He turned to Balázs, 'What would you do in my position?'

'What would *I* do?'

'Yeah, if you were in my position.'

'What d'you mean?'

'If you and Emma were . . . whatever,' Gábor said. 'Would you let her do this?' he asked.

Balázs said, 'Would I *let* her?'

'Yeah.'

'Uh,' he said. He was having trouble imagining, with any emotional specificity, the situation Gábor wanted him to. 'Don' know,' he said. 'Maybe.'

'You would?' Gábor sounded pleased.

'Well . . . I don' know.' Balázs tried to think about it honestly. 'Maybe not,' he said. 'It depends.'

'On what?' Gábor asked.

'On what . . . You know . . . I don' know . . . What sort of relationship . . .'

'*That's* it,' Gábor said, finally turning his attention to the food in his lap. 'What sort of relationship you want. That's my point. That's what I'm talking about.'

'You're worried it won't be, uh . . . *positive* for your relationship?' Balázs said, encouraged by having seemingly hit the nail on the head and wanting, as well, to talk about Emma some more.

'Yeah,' Gábor said simply, and pushed a sheaf of French fries into his mouth.

'Well . . . D'you talk to her about it?'

Gábor shook his head, and spoke with his mouth full. 'Not really, to be honest. I mean, I try sometimes. She doesn't want to.'

They ate.

'It's her birthday next week.' Gábor sounded slightly wistful now.

'Yeah?'

'Yeah. The nineteenth. I'm taking her to a kind of wellness spa place.'

'Yeah?' Balázs said again.

'In Slovakia. They've got this luxury hotel up in the mountains there. We've been there before. Kempinsky Hotel. You know those hotels?'

Balázs frowned slightly, as if trying to remember, then shook his head.

'Fucking nice,' Gábor told him. 'There's this kind of lake, surrounded by mountain peaks – she loves that shit. They've got every kind of treatment,' he said. 'Literally. You know. Mudbaths, whatever.'

4

The days passed, and every day was the same, from Zoli's visit in the mid-afternoon, through the long night, to the stop at McDonald's in the smeary sun and the spasm in the mildewed shower, which smoothed the way to sleep.

Still, his sleep was poor. He felt stretched thin with fatigue, felt as insubstantial sometimes as the sails of smoke that sagged in the windless air of the warm living room. Sometimes he felt transparent, at other times insufferably solid, but all the time there was the small furtive thrill of inhabiting the same space as she did. Of using, for instance, the same bathroom. The small, water-stained bathroom was full of her stuff. He examined it with intense interest. If her proximity thrilled him, however, it tortured him also in the long pallid hours of each afternoon, as he lay on the sofa knowing that she was there, on the other side of the flimsy wall, at which he stared as if trying to see through it, while the fantasies unspooled in his smooth, pitted head.

As for her, he marvelled at how fresh she seemed. If on Monday, which was the fourth day, she looked a little haggard and hungover when she appeared at four o'clock in the afternoon in her towelling dressing gown, it was nothing she was not able to magic away, more or less, with twenty minutes in front of the bathroom mirror.

Monday was the night they had the problem, the night of the incident. It was still early, not even eleven, when Gábor got the text message.

'Shit,' he said.

'What is it?'

'It's from Emma.'

'What's it say?' Balázs asked.

'Nothing.'

'Isn't that the signal?'

'Maybe it's a mistake,' Gábor said.

'Isn't it the signal?' Balázs asked again.

'Yeah,' Gábor sighed. 'OK,' he said heavily, 'let's go.'

He was scared, Balázs thought. That's why he was taking the hammer – he had a hammer with him, he kept it under the driver's seat. Now it was up his sleeve.

They started to walk towards the hotel. Shaking his head, his face full of sorrowful intensity, Gábor said, 'I was really hoping this wouldn't happen.' Once he had lit a cigarette, he phoned Juli, who was working nights all week. She said she would meet them at the staff entrance – a little low door in the side of the building, set in a deep doorway, up a sticky step.

She was waiting there, smoking nervously, when they arrived. 'What is it?' she said. 'Is everything OK?'

'Don't know,' Gábor said.

'What happened?'

'Don't know,' Gábor said again.

They followed her to the service stairs. 'It's the fourth floor,' she told them, handing Gábor the key card. '404.' Gábor nodded, and he and Balázs started solemnly up the stairs.

Scuffed walls, a neon tube over each landing.

'You ready?' Gábor said.

Balázs shrugged.

Gábor said, 'This is where you earn your money.'

'OK.'

'I'll make sure she's OK, you deal with him. I mean, if there's any trouble.'

'OK.'

'And the minimum of necessary force, yeah? I know I don't need to tell you that. We don't want . . . You know what I mean.'

He was worrying about the police, obviously. It was something that was on Balázs's mind too. 'Why don't you leave the hammer here?' he said, stopping.

'What?'

'Leave the hammer here. You can get it later.'

'Why?'

Balázs wondered how to put it. 'Look,' he said, 'if . . .' He started again. 'Let's say the police get involved, and you've got a hammer . . . A *weapon*. D'you see what I'm saying? We won't need it anyway.'

'Well . . .' Gábor was doubtful. 'We won't need it?'

'No.'

'OK.' He shrugged. He put it down quietly and they passed through a fire door into the moneyed hush of the hallway on the other side, where they searched in the smart light for 404. When they found it, they listened at the door, heard nothing. Then Gábor swiped the sensor, the lock whirred and disengaged, and they went in.

'What's this?' Gábor said. He sounded surprised, almost disappointed.

There were three people in the room, which was large and well lit – Emma and two Indians, all sitting down, and all seemingly waiting patiently in polite silence.

'OK, listen,' one of the Indians said immediately, standing. 'We want to talk to you.' He was much the older of the two of them and had been sitting on an upholstered chair between the tall, draped windows.

Gábor ignored him and said to Emma, in Hungarian, 'What's going on?'

She shrugged. 'There are two of them.'

'I can see that. What's been happening?'

'Nothing.'

Gábor turned to the older man – who was wearing a tweed jacket and seemed to be waiting for him to finish speaking to Emma – and said, in his faintly American-accented English, 'Only one of you can be here.'

'Yes, this is what we want to talk to you about,' the man said.

'Only one of you can be here,' Gábor told him again.

'I understand, I understand . . .'

'OK, you understand. So one of you go. Please.'

The Indians – the older with his nice jacket and manners, his elegant cologne, the younger scrawny in a Lacoste polo shirt, and still in his seat – were profoundly unintimidating. There was a fairly obvious sense that Balázs, standing with his massive arms folded near the door in a turquoise short-sleeved shirt with meaningless numbers inexplicably printed on the fabric, would be able to deal with them simultaneously if necessary. The older man's exaggerated politeness, with its subtle edge of suppressed hysteria, may just have been down to that.

'I understand,' he was saying yet again. 'The young lady told us that only one of us could, uh . . . you know,' he said. 'I understand. That's OK. That's OK. My, uh, my young friend . . . will be . . . doing that.'

Moving only his eyes, Balázs looked at the younger man. He was about twenty perhaps, or even younger, and, slumped slightly in his seat, staring at his loafers, seemed not even to be following what was happening.

Gábor said to Emma, again in Hungarian, 'Do you have the money?'

She nodded.

'Who paid you?'

She pointed to the older Indian, who said, 'I just want to watch.'

Gábor turned to him. 'What?'

The man said again, 'I just want to watch.'

'You want to watch?'

'Yes.'

Gábor said, succinctly, 'Fuck off.'

'Is it a problem?'

'Yes, a problem,' Gábor said in a louder voice.

'Why?' The man seemed sincerely puzzled.

'Why? *Why?*' In what seemed to be a sudden loss of temper, Gábor seized the Indian by the scruff of his jacket and first swung and then started shoving him towards the door, until Balázs, packed into his lurid turquoise shirt, intervened and separated them. There was a moment of tense quiet while Gábor, evidently struggling to maintain a professional demeanour, focused on his shoes. Then he looked up and said tautly, 'It's a problem, OK. A problem. Please?' With stiff politeness, an extended hand, he showed the man the door.

The Indian was starting to sweat. Nevertheless, he seemed determined to negotiate. Panting slightly, he said, 'No, just a minute. Please. I also say please. Just a minute.'

'Let's go,' Gábor said.

'Please,' the man went on. 'Let's just talk for a minute. Let's just talk. Your friend said the money was for a whole night with the, the young lady. Your friend said that.'

'Yes,' Gábor said, with strained patience.

'Now, listen,' the Indian said, his pate starting to shine, 'what I want to suggest is, uh, that we only take, uh, an hour or two of her time – *but* that I'm allowed to watch. Just watch! Is that fair? Doesn't that seem fair?'

'Look, this is a nice Hungarian girl,' Gábor said. 'She don't do stuff like that, OK?'

'Oh, she's a nice girl – of course she's a nice girl.'

'Yes, she's a nice girl. Let's go.'

'OK, you want more money,' the Indian said, as if surrendering, as Gábor took hold of his arm. 'How much? How much? A thousand pounds,' he offered.

Gábor, transparently surprised by the size of the offer, did not say anything. He swallowed cautiously and looked at Emma.

'OK? A thousand pounds?'

'Uh,' Gábor said, frowning as if trying to work something out. He seemed unable to do so, however, and finally said, 'It's up to her.'

'Of course!' The man turned smartly to Emma. She was sitting, with some dignity, in a tub chair, wrapped in a towel, her long thighs, which the towel did not hide, scrupulously parallel. The man said, 'A thousand pounds, madam, simply to sit in the corner. I'll be as quiet as a mouse. What say you?'

Even the young Indian lifted his overlarge head, with its cockatoo-ish plume of blow-dried hair, and looked at her now as they all waited to hear what she would answer.

'Just say no,' Gábor said to her, in their own language. 'Just say no, and we'll get rid of him.'

'Why?' she said finally. 'What difference does it make?'

Gábor's face underwent a very slight distortion.

'What difference does it make?' she said again.

'You'll do it then?'

She shrugged, and Gábor turned to the waiting Indian, who had not understood the exchange, and said, 'OK. Where's the money?'

'I, uh, I have it here.' He took from the inside pocket of his jacket a tan leather wallet.

As he counted out the money, Gábor said, 'You just watch.'

'Of course, of course,' the man said distractedly.

'You don't touch.'

A shake of the shining head. 'No.'

'Any trouble, we'll be here.'

The man held out the money. 'I promise you, there won't be any trouble.'

'Give the money to her,' Gábor said.

'Oh, excuse me. *Madam*?'

Emma stood up – even without her shoes she was taller than the dapper man – and took the money and put it in the small handbag that was on one of the tables next to the brocaded expanse of the bed.

'OK,' Gábor said to Balázs. 'Let's go.'

Gábor hardly spoke for the rest of the night, his face swallowed by shadow in the parked Merc. He had speculated bitterly, as they walked back, on the nature of the Indian's perversion, but once they had taken their seats on the anthracite leather, he seemed to have nothing more to say.

The previous night had also challenged his composure, though not nearly to the same extent. Zoli had told them, when he came as usual to collect his money, that the client for that night did not want to go to the hotel, so they should go instead to his house. It turned out to be in a grand square of stucco terraces. The two men had watched through the windscreen as Emma, in the familiar little flesh-coloured sheath of a dress, went up the steps to the porticoed entrance, with its big hanging lantern, and pushed the doorbell. A minute later the house swallowed her.

'Whatever,' Gábor said.

The house spat her out at four in the morning, just as the birds started to sing in the railinged gardens.

She was drunk. As they drove through the empty streets, she apologized for hiccuping, and then, when she couldn't stop, seemed to get the giggles.

'You're in a good mood,' Gábor said, fixing her momentarily in the rear-view mirror. 'D'you have fun then?'

'Don't be stupid,' she said softly.

'You're drunk.'

'Yes, I'm drunk. I've had about two bottles of champagne.'

'Champagne?' Gábor said. 'Nice.'

She ignored the sarcasm. 'Not really.'

'No? Did he make you drink it?'

She turned to the window, to the blue streets, dawn seeping into them. Monday morning. 'It helps,' she said.

Later they had to stop so she could be sick on the steps of a shuttered shop. ■

AFTER THE HEDLAND

Evie Wyld

EVIE
WYLD

1980

Evie Wyld runs Review, a small independent
bookshop in Peckham, south-east London.
Her first novel, *After the Fire, a Still Small
Voice*, won the John Llewellyn Rhys Prize
and a Betty Trask Award. In 2011 she was
listed as one of the *Culture Show*'s Best New
British Novelists. She was also shortlisted
for the Orange Prize for New Writers, the
Commonwealth Writers' Prize and the
International IMPAC Dublin Literary
Award. 'After the Hedland' is an excerpt
from her second novel, *All the Birds, Singing*,
forthcoming in June 2013 from Jonathan
Cape in the UK and in 2014 from Pantheon
in the US.

We are a week from the end of the job in Boondarie. I'm in the shower at the side of the tractor shed watching the thumb-sized redback that's always sat at the top of the shower head. She hasn't moved at all except to raise a leg when I turn on the tap, like the water's too cold for her.

The day has been a long and hot one – the tip of March, and under the crust of the galvo roof the air in the shearing shed has been thick like soup, flies bloating about in it. I'm low on shampoo, but I use a good slug of it, and feel the suds run down my dips and crevices, the water cooling off my lower back where the scars get hot and throb with the sweat. Above me is a fast-blackening sky – the night comes quickly here, not like in the city where you could spend all night at work and not notice its difference to the day, other than the slowing off of customers. The first stars are bright needles, and in the old Morton Bay fig that hangs over the tractor shed and drops nuts on the roof while I sleep, a currawong and a white galah are having it out, I can hear the blood-thick bleat of them. A flying fox goes overhead and just like that the smell of the place changes and night has settled in the air. Someone moves outside the pallet board screen of the shower and I still my hands in my hair.

'Greg?' I call, but no answer. I turn the tap off to listen. The redback sets down her leg. 'Greg?' The suds are still thick in my hair and they keep up a crackle in my earholes. I think of being found alone and taken away, back there, tied up and left to rot in the long dry grasses. There is a smell of fat and eggs frying. Someone steps quietly around the shower. It could be any of the team, could be Alan, who is getting deaf these days, looking for electrical tape or kerosene or batteries or rags. But it is not, that much is clear from the change in the air. 'Greg?' I am less than 150 km from Otto's, the closest I've been since I left Gaymont, but still, in seven months, I've travelled up and down the country and even if he has a nose like a bloodhound, I've covered my tracks. *I've covered my tracks.* I mouth the words.

The pallet to my right darkens, and through a punched-out knot in the grain of the wood, an eye appears, and I back away from it, my voice gone.

'I know about you,' says the eye. 'You don't fool me, I know about you and what you've done.' The voice is thick and sticky and there's that smell of rotten eggs and lanolin together and whisky and unwashed places. *I've covered my tracks, it's been seven months and I covered my tracks*, but my heart is beating fast, and I have to put up my hand to the wall to steady myself. The spider reacts, turns in a small circle, settles again. The eye twitches, and I think of driving my thumbnail right into it, but I can't bring myself to touch it, and there is nothing else sharp to poke with. The eye slides up and down, the iris is a milky blue. 'I know what you're about,' says the eye. It disappears and the shadow moves away. My heart drums. I look through the knot in the wood and see Clare staggering off in the direction of the shearing shed. He's been away the week, and he has found something out.

I bolt from the shower without washing off the suds, round the side of the shed to my sleeping quarters. I pull on pants, shorts and a singlet and then I begin stuffing everything else into my backpack. *If you were so sure he'd never find you* says my head *why are you so prepared to leave, why do all your belongings fit in a backpack?* Everything is in there, except my shears, which I left on the bench next to the wool table to sharpen in the morning. And the carapace of a cicada that Greg gave me last month when he asked if I'd go to the Gold Coast with him once the job was done. I hold it in my palm and it vibrates with my pulse.

'Just spend a month at the water. Fishing, swimming, drinking beer,' he'd said. 'Get the dust off us before the next job.'

I put the skin back down on the ledge and go to find Greg in the dinner hall.

Almost everyone has gathered for tea, and I scan the bench for Clare, but he's not there. I sit down next to Greg who is talking to Connor about boat engines, and I try to make it clear I want to talk to him by putting my hand on his shoulder. He squeezes my thigh under the table but doesn't turn around, too involved with his conversation.

'. . . corroded so far, it broke through and dropped down into the bilge,' he says.

Connor is drinking from his can and he says, 'Yep. That's just the way she'll go – people forget.' His voice becomes high-pitched and incredulous. 'As far as an engine is concerned – water's your enemy.'

'Yep,' says Greg and I shift about next to him. I don't want anyone else to know there's a problem.

'You right?' asks Greg, distracted by my fidgeting.

'I need to talk to you,' I say quietly.

Greg looks at me a moment, takes a swig of his drink and snakes his arm around my back.

'Can we go somewhere?'

'Tea's coming out.'

'Yes, but.'

'Whisper it.'

I lean closer to him. People assume we are having some sort of moment, I suppose, and no one could be less interested. A grey steak arrives in front of me and trays of boiled potatoes get passed down the line.

My mouth goes dry. 'Have you seen Clare yet?'

'His truck's back, he'll be around somewhere. Why – what's he owe you?'

'Nothing. I just. Look, can we go to the Gold Coast?'

He gives me a hopeless look, like he doesn't know what on earth is the matter with the woman. 'Yeah. I suggested it. What, are you having a stroke or something?' He puts six large potatoes on his plate, passes the tray, which I pass on to Stuart on the other side of me.

'I mean now. Can we just hop in the truck and go now?'

'Why? What's happened?'

'Nothing's happened. I just want to go now.'

Greg looks confused. 'Well, so do I, but we've got to finish the job.'

'Why?'

Greg is chewing on a lump of steak. 'Why? Because these are me mates, I'm not leaving them a man down. Besides, we go early, we don't get the bonus – it's just a week we've got left. Not long.' He swallows.

'Can you just trust me that we need to leave now?'

He puts his fork down. 'Why do we *need* to leave now? What is the difference? You rob a bank?'

I open my mouth to speak, but there is nothing I can tell him.

'See,' he says, picking up his fork again, 'there's no problem. Everything is simple. It's just hot is all, we'll be at the coast in no time.'

Another tray starts to come down, with sausages on it. When I pass this to Stuart he looks at me strangely.

'No snag for you?' he says.

'What?'

'On Jenny Craig or something?'

I ignore him, but Greg notices too, and waves the sausages back. 'Wait wait wait, if she's not eating I'll have hers,' and he spears two extra.

'Why do you get the extra?' asks Stuart.

'Because she's my woman.'

'What? That's not right.'

'Fair dinkum,' Denis says from down the end. 'She's his woman, means the snags pass on to him.'

I wish I had taken the sausages.

I have until the end of tea to convince him.

Greg has eaten my steak, and two large bowls of tinned fruit cocktail with the shining red cherries and the pale cubes of melon are distributed along the table.

Someone barks, 'What, no ice cream?' and Sid tosses a couple of bricks of it, the kind you cut with a pallet knife and which are bright yellow like cheese, and Connor hacks off a two-inch slice and dumps a ladle of fruit salad on top.

'Love it when the ice cream mixes with the syrup,' he says loudly to anyone who wants to know, and then he picks out the red cherries one by one with his fingers, his pinkie held up high. He lines them up at the side of his dish. 'But those little fuckers can get bent.'

Clare appears in the doorway with the night behind him. The strip lighting in the shed makes him look like he glows. He holds on to the door frame and scans the long table. I wait for his eyes to settle on me, and when they do I see a look of pleasure on his face that I recognize. I am trapped. Greg's thigh pumps blood next to mine. Connor scrapes the bottom of his dish with his spoon and Steve, next to him, flicks one of the red cherries so it darts onto Stuart's lap. Stuart gives Steve the finger without looking up from his bowl. Alan at the top of the table is reading the paper and is not interested. He drinks his beer. Through all of it, Clare looks at me and I know I'm done, I know the end has come. He enters the room and walks slowly past me. I try not to crane to follow him, I try not to anticipate his next move. He puts a hand on Greg's shoulder and bends down to him, and I tense myself for the end. Greg looks up and Clare hands him a Violet Crumble and Greg's face opens out into a smile.

'Good man,' says Greg, 'now I don't have to get involved with this horse shit,' he says, nodding at the fruit salad and pinching open the purple wrapper as he does it. Clare ambles on by, just giving me a sidelong glance. Greg breaks the end off his bar and hands it to me. While Greg is turned away from me, I crumble it to dust under the table.

I pick up my shears from the wool shed, and do not think about what will happen next. The shed smells of sweat and dung, lanolin and turps. I can't imagine being away from it. A possum scratches on the tin roof. I walk slowly back to my quarters, stand for a moment in the dark where I can see the warm slice of light in the dinner shed. Where I have a side view of Greg, who is laughing, who brings a beer to his lips, who drinks, who puts it down and wipes his mouth with the back of his hand. I bite the tip of my tongue and I try to think of some last-minute plan that can stop this. Nothing comes and I turn away and follow my feet back to my quarters.

Clare is lying on my bed with his boots on, smoking a roll-up. I stop in the doorway, but he's heard me coming and he's ready with a toothy smile for me. I stay in the doorway, wondering if I can turn around, walk back to the wool shed, hide under a fleece.

'Know where I was all week?' he asks, swinging his legs off my bed and leaning forwards. 'Come in out of the doorway, love,' he says. 'You look like a prostitute.' He grins wider, if that is possible. He blows smoke out and it fogs the air between us.

'Planning a trip?' he says, in the voice of someone off the TV. He kicks my backpack gently. There is so much excitement in his voice.

'Ben tipped me off about the posters – pictures of you plastered all around the place down there. Did you know that? I had to go and see for myself – but they're you all right.' He pulls from his back pocket a scored and folded piece of paper. He unfolds it slowly, chuckling to himself, and holds it up to show me. There I am in black and white sitting on my pink pony doona cover, smiling for the camera. There's a Care Bear on my lap and my hands are digging into it, not that you can see my hands, not that you can see the bear or the doona cover or the old man taking the photograph or the dog guarding me outside. You can only see my face, the smile for the camera. In capital letters it says MISSING at the top and I catch the words 'Granddaughter. Danger to Herself', at the bottom, but I can't read it all because things have gone dark.

'I rang the number, Jake, and you know what I found out?'

'I don't know what you're talking about. He's not my grandfather.'

'Oh, I know all that. That poor old bloke, "Otto". We had a good long chat. I went to see him on his farm, just a pen of dead sheep, and all he can talk about is how you killed his dog and how you took his money and he was only trying to take you off the street. Said you took everything that was dear to him, took his truck even, poor old cracker couldn't get into town, had to rely on the salvos to come once a week with groceries until he got his old banger working. Saw what you did to that too, smashed it up pretty bad.'

'I didn't, I just –'

'I saw it. The old bugger cried when he talked about his dog, Kelly.'

'I just –'

'Shhh,' Clare says, but loudly. He gets up off the bed in one fluid movement and walks towards me slowly, takes my forearms where they hang limply by my sides. He moves me over to stand in front of the workbench and he leans into me, crotch heavy. My mouth waters. I look over at the doorway. What would happen if Greg appeared there now?

'What you've got is, you've got two options here. Maybe I'd be persuaded to keep my mouth shut.' Clare's breath is hot fudge on the side of my face. He whispers in a way that sounds like soon he'll be shouting. 'You can show me some of what you've shown everyone else at the Hedland.' My heart tumbles around my body. A stupid part of me thinks, *he might not say anything*, and is quieted by the part of me that knows it will not end, and I cannot stay here and that I have been stupid to grow comfortable. 'Little bit of affection – I'm not asking for much – I wouldn't fuck a mate's lay – maybe just the mouth,' and I can see exactly how it will all be, the back of the throat, the hair grasped in a ponytail, and the words he will say while he does it, and then afterwards how it will only be worse, how he will be rid of me either way, and with a flourish. 'Or,' he says, trailing his finger along the outer curve of my breast, 'or I can let old Otto know where to find you. Or the police.' He starts to unbutton my shorts, and he tugs my singlet out from them, and puts a hand down, scrabbling with his fingers to get beneath my underwear. 'I won't even have to tell Greg, they'll do it for me.' He scrapes a finger over my crotch, and like a mechanical game at the fairground, something is triggered and I punch him in the jaw with my right and he goes down, out cold and bleeding on the floor.

I cannot do up my shorts because my hand crunched badly against Clare's face, and it has turned into a meat fist, throbbing and swollen.

I leave the room without looking back at him, but I can hear him beginning to shift about in the dust and a wet groan comes from him. I am fairly sure that I have broken his jaw.

2

There is a moment that I see things change with Greg. Waking up with him in my bed becomes something that happens, and the small time we have before work is as important as the rest of it. We do not watch each other sleep like they do in the movies. If one of us wakes first, we wake the other with a rough shake. 'Hey, wake up'.

We talk like magpies, gabbling out the words like we're in competition with each other. I do push-ups while he talks, and move his feet up and down as he rests them on my shoulders. He tells me about his father, who is dead, but who could eat a whole watermelon with just a spoon and the top cut off like a boiled egg. 'Heh, he was the fattest fucker. And proud of it – some doctor tried to tell him to lose weight, and he said, "What would I be then? I would just be Joe, I wouldn't be Fat Joe any more, and who would care when I died?" Heh. Fat fucker.'

And when it's my turn, I do sit-ups, which are easier to talk around, and Greg plants his feet on mine to spot me. He never mentions that it's strange, he never says *careful, you'll get too manly*. I tell him the in-between bits of my life, the bits that are available. Learning to shear, my friend Karen, and further back, the sharks, the bush.

In the morning, Sid finds out weevils have made it into the flour.

'I don't particularly mind,' he says. 'I'm just saying in case anyone has an aversion to having the buggers in the bread.' There is silence while the table takes this in, and it is broken by Alan shouting from behind the wool shed.

Something has taken a bite out the side of one of the rams. He's not dead, just looks like someone tore past him and took a chunk out. Flies swarm the wound. Connor shoots the ram while we all stand around. The animal twitches.

'Just nerves firing,' Denis says to me, like I am a hysterical woman who needs comforting. But I'm thinking how quick it was and what a mercy. One second horribly wounded, feeling flies lay their eggs in your flesh and watching the currawong circle, and the next, in a flash, all is safe. I will learn to fire a gun, I think.

Alan stands next to me. 'Come on,' he says. 'We'll have a drive around, see if we can find a feral dog or something.' Connor and Clare move the ram's body out of the pen while the rest of the sheep look on. There is no way of telling what they think.

In the truck I'm alone with Alan. This has not happened before, and he's got something he wants to say. He keeps coughing into his fist and then looking over at me as I drive. There is nothing for miles, nothing but that desert heat wobble, and now and then a rabbit, which Alan picks off and we scoop up as we drive past until we have a brace. It's not silent, but all we say are things like, 'Over there,' and 'Bloody got him,' and 'A little bit bloody closer.'

After an hour, when I'm thinking about how much time is wasting and how far ahead of me the rest of the team will be, Alan tips the bullets out of the rifle and sighs.

'There's nothing bloody else out here,' he says and then he turns to me. 'I don't normally bloody interfere in anyone's business,' he says, and I grip the wheel. 'But I've been meaning to say, I think it's not a bad thing, you and Greg.' I wait for *but* . . . and it doesn't come. 'You're both good bloody blokes, and the thing is that I've known Greg a while and he's a good bloke.' The air in the truck is heating up and I wonder if I should start to drive home or if starting the engine now would be rude. 'And you're a good bloke, and I reckon together, two good blokes is a good thing.' Alan is red in the face and I wonder why he is putting us through this. 'Thing is, what I'm bloody getting at, is that you gotta ignore the bloody loonies in life, and listen, there are one or two of them in the team. Not bad blokes all in all, but . . . lonely blokes maybe.'

'I'm not sure –'

'Listen, just. Don't be bothered by Clare is what I'm bloody getting at. He's a lunatic, a good bloke, but a lunatic, and he's messed himself up with the business with the kid . . .' Alan shakes his head. 'Arthur's mum sent a letter – he's trying to learn to write with the other hand – lot of good that'll do him, kid can barely read. Anyhow.'

'Has he said something?'

'Look, it's not even about that.'

'What did he say?' I keep my voice steady and my eyes on the heat wobble in the distance.

'I'm not interested,' says Alan. 'Look, I'm not interested in what my team have done before. Hell, I've bloody got a past, we've all got pasts – you want to find one of us who chooses to be out here without a past, I'd bloody pay to see that. Denis, he's been doing this his whole bloody life – fifty years of this. You think there isn't something he's getting away from?' He looks at me and I can tell he wants me to know something, and for a second I think *what did you do, Alan?* 'What I'm saying is,' he carries on, 'Clare can be a whingeing bitch. He's a good bloke, but a whingeing bitch. And I don't take any notice of him or of the past. Let's not forget Clare and Greg are best mates. He's just acting like a prick because he's jealous, but he can't admit to that because, well – he's a prick. But what I'm saying is maybe talk to Greg about it – get him to go out for a night with Clare, just the two of them. Might quieten him down a bit.'

'I'm not forcing Greg to hang out with me,' I say. My face is hot and there's an anger I wasn't expecting.

'I'm not saying that – I'm just saying if we're all living together like we are – might be the . . . political thing to do.' He sniffs loudly. This has gone further than he wanted it to.

In the silence he holds the rabbits up by the ears, out of the open window of the truck. Each of them is cleanly done behind the shoulder. He holds them high in the air, breathing through his mouth and watching beads of thick blood drop from them onto the orange dirt.

'Was thinking to take 'em back for Sid, thinking he might make a bloody casserole or something.' A fly settles on the wound of one of the rabbits. He leans back and throws the dead rabbits in a high arc away from the truck. 'He'd only make 'em taste of bloody arseholes anyway,' he says and we drive back to the station. I itch to get back to work.

'Catch a shark?' Greg asks and I smile at him. I don't feel like speaking. Clare keeps his back to me.

At smoko, Sid comes in, bright red and snarling. 'Right, which one of you useless fucktards did it?' he says, standing at the top of the table. I look down the line of men, trying to work out what has been done and who has done it. Clare is smirking behind his moustache.

'What's the bloody drama now?' asks Alan, just coming in as Sid drags his glare away from the table.

'Come and see for yourself,' he says, and when he moves to the back where the kitchen is set up, we all stand up and follow. Everyone crowds around the flour barrel, and when Sid takes the lid off, there's a bum print there.

'It's not fucking funny,' shouts Sid above everyone's honking laughter. Greg doubles over like he's in pain.

'Well, we can rule one person out,' says Alan, wiping his eyes. He points to the edge of the bum print, where you can make out another print. 'Culprit's got balls at least.'

'Up to Boondarie next week,' Alan announces at tea. 'Hot as a bloody dog's gut up there.' It's as far north as I've been since leaving, but the people of Hedland won't mix with the people of Boondarie. Still, my mouth goes dry and I scull a beer to dampen myself down.

Sid makes bread out of the weevily bum flour, and it sits, turning to rock, in the centre of the table. No one will touch it, not even Stuart, not even with a fork.

The light is out and Greg has his large thumbs in the dips of my pelvis, and the shed is hot and dry. I feel out of myself tonight, like my bones have become too heavy for my flesh. The heat gets itself in under the metal roof during the day and it stays there at night, making the spiders sleepy. I loop my fingers in Greg's hair, to let him know I'm still paying attention and to try and remind myself to keep focused. A frog is creaking outside, and so maybe soon there'll be rain hammering the roof. Sometimes when it rains, which is not often, it feels like the drumming will knock the spiders off and onto my bed.

The frog stops, and there is a cool breeze that swims into the shed, like the kind of wind rain makes when it's on its way down. Greg sighs, I remember where I am, and grasp harder at his hair. Something large and black darts through the doorway, skitters along the far wall and under the workbench, and I bounce up in bed, knocking Greg in the face with my groin and taking a clump of his hair with me.

'The fuck?' he says, holding his face with both hands.

'There's something in here,' I whisper, though whispering is pointless against Greg's noise.

'What something?' He examines his palm for blood from his nose and then feels for the spot I ripped his hair from. 'Fuckin' needed that,' he says.

'Under the workbench, something big.'

He looks up at me, his expression changes. 'How big?'

I'm feeling under the bed for the hammer but I can't find it. Greg lifts himself off the bed and gives his head a small shake to clear it. He goes lightly over to the switch and turns it on. The strobing strip light does nothing but throw shadows.

'Like a big dog.'

The strobe settles, but there are still shadows and places to hide. The workbench is covered by a blue oilcloth that hangs down and hides the space under it. Greg picks up the metal pipe that leans against the wall. I'm glad that he kept his underwear on – I think *this would be so much worse if he was naked.* I have made his nose bleed, but he ignores it, lets it flow down onto his lip, while he holds the pole with both hands like a cricket bat. He treads carefully and slowly towards the workbench, and his eyes dart around finding new shadows. The hair on the back of my neck prickles. I try not to think of Kelly, or picture Otto outside holding a gun, watching. Holding his cut-throat too. He will kill Greg then he will do me slowly. Kelly will snap at the air by my face as she watches me die. He will cut off my hand and give it to her as a prize. *Kelly is dead,* I think, but the thought is not a comfort.

I take the corner of the oilskin in my fingers, look to Greg who raises the pipe, ready to strike if something runs out. He tells me with a nod of three to lift it, and I make my own countdown and jerk the cover up. Under the workbench, there is nothing. Greg lets his arms fall at his sides and the metal pipe clangs on the floor.

'Jesus,' he says. 'If you weren't in the mood you just had to say.' I look at him to see if this is a joke, but I can't tell.

Later, when he sleeps next to me, I get up out of bed and, careful not to wake him, I pull on a shirt and some shorts, and leave the shed. It is cooler out. I concentrate on breathing, sucking the cool air in, blowing the hot air out. The night sky is crisp with stars and I sit on the fence, listening to the cicadas and the night birds, the bandicoots and rats and all the live things that are out there, breathing with me. Not far away, the sheep are a dense and silent cluster. I feel the pull of being alone, of answering to no one, the safety of being unknown and far away. I sense a small movement behind me and turn just in time to see a shadow in the doorway of the shed. But it's Greg, I know his shape, and he doesn't want me to have seen him, and I don't want him to have seen me, and when I get back to bed an hour later, he feigns sleep and I feign sleep too and soon we are both asleep. In the morning he looks closely at my face.

'Strewth,' he says. 'You look like you've been plugged in both eyes.'

3

Outside Kambalda is a shearers' pub, which isn't much more than a galvanized shed with a bar and tables made out of railway sleepers. They serve whisky in mugs and everything else is canned. You're supposed to bring your own cooler, and I make a mental note to pick one up next time we see a shop, which could be weeks from now. I'm at the bar, warming a mug of whisky in my hands and taking longer than I should as I turn over how I ended up at this bar in the middle of a desert with the smell of a barbecue coming in through the open wall of the shed, and with all these men, not another woman in running distance, and how is it that this is a strange comfort, and how long will it last before something finds me again and I have to go somewhere else.

Clare is beasting Bean, calling him nicknames that don't mean anything much but which make the kid go red in his pale cheeks, as if his real name wasn't bad enough. *Nippy Balls, Sour Tit, Pussy Willow.* He won't leave the kid alone, but it is pretty funny.

'G'wan, Ball Ache,' says Clare, 'show us where your dick's hidden.' Clare pulls a stool up opposite me and gestures for Bean to sit. 'Let's see who wins a wrestle between you and Alice the Goon here.' Mostly the men laugh, but not all of them. There's a quiet moment when Bean and I look at each other. I would like for this not to happen, and when Bean sits opposite me with a look of drunken determination coming over him, it breezes through me that if I let him win, then maybe he'll get less of a hard time. But I won't do that, I know it as I settle my elbow on the table. Bean will have to fend for himself, he might be small and awkward, but I am a woman on a sheep station. We grip hands over the sleepers, position our elbows to everyone's satisfaction, and money starts getting laid down. I catch Greg's eye and he smiles at me, holds up twenty dollars. I see Bean's white bicep bulge like a new potato, and there's a countdown shouted by everyone. The kid's face goes red and fierce, his lips pull back from his teeth, and it's not a total pushover. There's some strength in him, but mainly it's the strength of fear, like those times you hear about kids lifting lorries off their parents. Our fists wobble in the centre, but soon Bean has used up his burst of self-belief, and his face sweats and he is tired and done. I start to push his arm down, and I see in his face the huge disappointment; he had thought this was his time to be hoicked onto the shoulders of the men but once we are three-quarters of the way down, he has no way back up and I flatten him and everyone cheers and whoops, and Bean lays his head on his spent arm.

Later, when I am drunk, and Bean has been relegated back at the end of the table, where Denis now and again asks him a question and then doesn't listen to the answer, Greg sits himself in front of me and puts up his massive arm. I laugh and he laughs and I put my arm up too, like we're about to wrestle, but all we do is grip hands like that.

'Strong lady,' he says.

In the morning, I wake up in between Greg's bear arms and I hold my breath and count to fifty. OK, I say to myself, OK, and I check through my body from the feet up. All is warm and nothing hurts except the crick in my neck from lying on his arm. The smell of him, lanolin and whisky that has been sweated out in the night.

The sun is rising and there won't be long before the gong goes and work starts, and with the hangover worming in my guts I try to roll softly from the bed. In a sitting position, I'm about to make it, when Greg springs from where he is lying and makes a noise like a lion, grabs me by the waist and wrestles me back into the bed growling and grunting into my neck and squeezing me hard. It takes me a few seconds to understand that this is a joke and I laugh.

Just like the other times it has happened, the rest of the day we will catch little looks at each other and I will worry and feel good and feel sick and trip up over my feet. At smoko he will sit opposite me on the bench and touch my knee under the table, and when I look up at him he will wink. It's getting so when he touches me, I don't even think about pushing his hand away and I will even give myself a shock by walking past him while he's bent over a bucket washing his hands, and thwacking him on the behind before I can stop myself. He will jump up and crack a smile that cuts his face up into segments – it's a face I like, it's wide and has a tendency to smile.

Clare is missing from tea and I see him over at the phone stand behind the shed. He's nodding and he's looking at me in a way that I don't like. He turns his back, and finishes up the call. I drink deeply and feel better. It's just the paranoia, and maybe I could lighten up on the drinking.

'Who's that?' asks Greg, when Clare comes back to the table. He doesn't often use the phone, none of us do, other than poor Bean who misses his sixteen-year-old girlfriend in Rockhampton.

Clare looks up brightly. 'Just Ben – letting us know what a dickhead he is. Reckons he likes the uni course, reckons next time we see him he'll be air-conditioned and rich.'

'Ha!' says Greg.

'Prick,' says Connor.

Clare looks at me and smiles. I shift in my seat.

Bean sits apart from everyone else. Greg strides past and clunks a beer down in front of him without speaking, and the boy's face opens and he looks happy as he sits there chewing his meat and drinking his beer.

Later, Clare is in a bad mood with the drink, and even Denis seems to enjoy winding him up.

'Getting a bit soft around the middle,' Denis says, prodding Clare's gut with a bony finger. 'Finding it slows you down in the shed?'

'Get fucked, you old cunt,' says Clare, but it only makes Denis chuckle and his eyes shine. Denis is too old to say much to, and so Clare rounds on me. 'Y'know,' he says, 'they won't have a woman at sea – reckon it's bad luck. They reckon a clothed woman on board is bad luck, angers the seas.' I square myself up and look directly at Clare, but he doesn't want to meet my eyes. I know I look hench, but I can feel a nasty beat to my heart.

He knocks back the rest of his drink. 'It's just not right, it's just not,' he belts out. 'In me old man's day, there's no way they would have tolerated it.'

'I dunno,' says Greg. 'Your old man gave you a girl's name. Reckon he might have been quite progressive.' Everyone laughs a bit.

Clare is red in the face and Greg smiles behind his drink. Clare stands up abruptly and sways over the bench.

'You'se are all fuckin' poofs,' he says and flounces away into the night.

With Greg breathing like a tanker next to me, I draw up a contract in my head with Dad. This will not go on for long, I will keep moving. In return he will sink beneath these new memories, just for a while. I can keep it all at arm's length because there is nothing here yet to connect me to that time, with those people, other than the marks on my back, which are pinked over enough to look like they happened in a past that can be left alone.

In the morning Greg traces the scars with his fingers.

'Those are hell good,' he says with real admiration in his voice. 'How'd you get 'em?'

I turn and look at him and feel that countdown, how it could go either way. 'Bad relationship.' Greg shifts up the bed and puts his hand on the back of my neck, like there's something I deserve comfort for. I can let myself believe it just for now that I am some kind of victim. He lifts my hair up and I can feel him looking. He kisses the top bone of my spine and says, 'I'll kill him.' And there it is, the lie, and it becomes real, another contract signed, stamped and dated.

There's a yell, which turns into a scream. Greg shoots out of bed in his undies and runs towards the noise. By the time I make it over to the shed, everyone's standing in a circle around the grinder. Blood is misted up the wall and Bean is on the floor sobbing and holding what is left of his hand. Greg is trying to get him to hold it up above his heart, but the kid won't have it, can't stop looking at it.

Someone's gone to call the flying doctors and Alan comes running out of the house, his face white and red at the same time. He pushes men out of the way and squats down on the other side of Bean, inspects the hand and holds out his palm to Connor. 'Gimme yer bloody singlet,' he says quietly, and Connor strips it off.

'OK, Arthur,' says Alan to Bean, 'bloody doctors are on their way.' He tears the singlet in two down the middle and ties it with a firmness that makes me wince, around the kid's wrist. 'There's nothing here can't be sorted out,' he says and Bean carries on sobbing. There's no getting to him.

'What the fuck was he doing on the bloody grinder?' Alan hisses at us. Clare is standing at the back with a hand over his face. He raises his arm.

'He was sharpening my teeth for me.' There's a silence, deeper than before, and everyone turns to look at Clare. Alan's mouth drops open, but he doesn't say anything. Clare walks a little way away from us.

'We'll get yer mum on the bloody phone,' says Alan to Bean. 'She'll be there by the time they've got you sorted out.'

When the plane lands, they're worried about the blood loss, and

Alan goes with them to the hospital. Bean is blue in the lips as he's carried, between Alan and the medic, into the plane. Clare kicks over and over again at a stump of wood stuck in the earth.

We get on with work, I go back to roustabout without being asked, just seems the right thing. Clare is slow and hardly makes his quota. No one talks. The next morning, Alan is back and you can hear him going off at Clare round the back of the sleeping shed.

'What the fuck were you thinking? The bloody hand's gone, mate. Kid can't read. Certainly can't fucking write now. What the bloody fuck do you think he's going to do for a job? That's it, you've fucking fucked it. I had to tell his mother – fuck, I told her I'd bloody look after him.' It goes on, and every question Alan asks is left unanswered by Clare. Everyone pretends not to have heard any of it, and Clare comes limping pale into the shed to start work. Most of the men make an effort to turn their backs to him, Denis mutters something under his breath. But Greg slaps him on the shoulder and says 'You right?' Clare nods and takes up his position. I get a sheep over to him and it's all go but we work in silence.

Just after midday Alan comes in and when he sees me flinging a fleece onto the table he goes apeshit. 'Why in filthy bloody fuck are you doing that?' I stiffen and feel my eyes stretching wide. But the shouting's not for me. He turns to Clare and points at him, 'You, you useless fuck, until further notice. You're bloody roustabout, not Jake.' Clare's mouth is open. 'I'm not losing a prime shearer just because you can't look after your own shit.' I don't know where to look or what to do. No one moves. 'Jake, where's your bloody kit?'

'Back in my room.'

'Go and get it. You're on.' I take a second to respond. 'G'wan, get!' he barks, and I scuttle off across the yard to my room. It's awful, it's humiliating for Clare, poor Bean's life is wrecked, Alan is all kinds of fucked up, but I can't stop smiling. ■

DRIVER

Taiye Selasi

TAIYE
SELASI

1979

Taiye Selasi was born in London to
Nigerian and Ghanaian parents. She holds
a BA from Yale and an MPhil from Oxford.
Selasi made her fiction debut in *Granta* in
2011 with 'The Sex Lives of African Girls',
which was selected for *Best American Short
Stories* in 2012. Her first novel, *Ghana Must
Go*, was published in March 2013. An avid
traveller and documentary photographer,
Selasi lives in Rome. 'Driver' is a new story.

I am the full-time driver here. I am not going to kill my employers. I have read that drivers do that now. I will make just a few observations.

First, to state the obvious. My employer is a generous man. He buys many gifts, for many women, none of whom is Madam. I judge not, lest I be judged. This is between him and his God. *My* God would smite him right there in the garden. Madam would weep for her flowers.

Madam says her flowers are the toast of all of Ghana. I would note that all of us do not, alas, have bread. But the flowers are spectacular. They line the drive in pots. They burst into flames of yellow petals. They pretty the concrete walls. I had never seen such beautiful flowers until I came to work here – or I had, but only wild ones, free. Not fed, as at the zoo. Every morning Madam walks among these gorgeous flowers in an Angelina *buba* with a glazed look on her face. She runs her fingers lightly through the petals as one fingers strands of wispy hair of women for whom one buys gold-plate trinkets. I'd also note that once before I passed her bathroom window – which is oddly low, and stranger still, undressed – while she was bathing, and I had the thought that Madam might receive more gifts more often were she not to hide her body in that dark green swamp of cloth.

Madam has the contours of a girl I knew in Dansoman and sculptures sold at Arts Centre and Bitter Lemon bottles. Slender top and round the rest. A perfect holy roundness that is proof of God's existence and His goodness furthermore. Her skin is ageless, creaseless, *paint*. Her lower back a hiding place. The colour brooks no simile. If you have been to Ghana, you know. If you have never been to Ghana then you might not understand the way the darkest skin can glow as with the purest of all lights.

I slipped across the alley to the quarters that we servants share, a single room with piled-up latex foam instead of beds. Mamadou, the watchman, says that we should ask for proper beds and Sundays off and cooking gas, but no one ever does. We huddle in our single room like very sunburned Boy Scouts with the faded shirts we've washed to death, dead, hanging from the ceiling, and we listen to the crickets or the new cook's ancient iPod, with things that we should ask for piled up, soft, like folded clothes. There used to be some women here, apparently, a laundress and a multi-purpose housegirl; where they slept I do not know. When my employer married Madam and she moved here with her half-caste teenage daughter, called Bianca, all the women were let go.

I slipped into this Boy Scout room and stood against the concrete wall, my heart attempting break-out from its skin-and-muscle jail. I was frightened that she'd seen me and would think that I had meant to look, that I had not been idly walking by but lurking. *Peeping.* On the wall of our room is a sign with the rules written out on a torn piece of cardboard. There is a similar sign in the hallway that houses Accra Mall's public toilet. It reads:

1. No washing of kitchen items.
2. No changing of clothes.
3. No buying & selling.
4. No standing on the toilet bowl.
5. No brushing of teeth.
6. No sex.
7. No smoking.

In smaller font, 'all offenders will be prosecuted', signed in cheerful colours, 'Accra Mall'. Our sign is much shorter. ATTENTION is written in red. In black:

1. No stealing.
2. No peeping.
3. No urinating on flowers.

There is no handwritten consequence, but I could guess my fate. I am the only servant with a real education, which is to contextualize my reasoning skills and not to judge my colleagues. I've been offered a place at the University of Ghana – incidentally, our president's alma mater – and would have enrolled this summer had my dad not fallen ill. It should have been my sister's job to move back home to care for him, but Merriam has children and her husband Nii said no. I didn't mind. My dad had worked a thankless job for all my life, the thanklessness of which he realized only when he left. For fifteen years he drove the head of Mensah Mines, 'Boss' Mensah, from his home in Trasacco Valley to his mine in Obuasi and back again. Boss adored my father – and who doesn't adore a smiley man? a dimpled, deferential, diminutive man? – but more importantly trusted him. In all those years, no missing cash, no leaks of information, no convenient turns down darkened alleys lined by armed Liberians. Boss's children Barbara (Babs) and Basil (Bossy Jr) call my father 'Eja' (father), having known him all their lives. Boss's second wife still sends us music-playing Christmas cards with yellow packs of Berger Nut as if we're kids, and starving.

Seven hours' driving in a single day for fifteen years, the windows up, the A/C on, Boss chain-smoking in back, and still, when Boss's smiley driver broke the news that he had lung cancer the only thing Boss had to say was, 'Send your boy to me.' My father smiled, and bowed, and coughed, and came back home elated that his good and kind employer would attend to my school fees. My mother ironed my only suit – the shirt of which now hangs here, dead – and told me to 'speak proper', although she knew she didn't have to. For my thirteenth birthday my father gave a deeply touching gift to me: his most cherished possession, for which we are named, his *Merriam-Webster* dictionary. 'Knowledge is power,' he said to me, and kissed me on my forehead, perhaps the first time that my father ever kissed me, and the last. To indicate her knowledge of my consequent vocabulary, my mother tugged my tie-knot tight and winked. 'My clever Web Star.' She said my name the way I love, as if it were two separate names, as if I were a superhero, an attaché to Spider-Man. She also cooked her groundnut soup, which Babs and Bossy Jr loved and always asked my father for, although their cook could make it. My father's nephew Kojo drives a taxi. When he came for me, my father made me sit in back, which Kojo understood.

We drove out to Trasacco Valley daydreaming of eating soup, then gazing at the houses with an equal aching appetite.

'This one's mine,' said Kojo, slowing. He pointed to a pillared house.

'Then you'll be pleased to know that I have bought the house next door.' We laughed. We rolled across a sleeping policeman. I steadied the pot of groundnut soup. I noticed that my hands were trembling, breathed, re-tightened my tie. When we reached the Mensahs' massive palace we stopped and sat in silence, with the growling of the engine and our stomachs growing loud.

'I will wait for you, Webster,' Kojo said. His voice was soft and serious. I hadn't imagined he'd leave me there, but nodded, and said, 'Do.'

He didn't wait long. Needless to say, my school fees weren't on offer. Neither were my dad's astounding medical expenses. 'I've asked my sister to take you on,' said Boss, lips glossed by orange oil. Though he'd told me to come at one o'clock, I'd found him eating lunch. 'She has come to her senses, finally, and has left the heart of whiteness to get married to a proper man, a Ghanaian, friend from PreSec. So. We'll see how it goes.' He took a bite. 'At least the bastard has some cash. That last one, the *obroni*, died a pauper. No excuse for it. Here I am a black man in a racist world and look at me.' I looked at him. 'While that one, born a white man, dies in debt.' A bite. 'I told my sister plainly. Look. Nice bastard. Wants to marry you. Say yes. Come home. Enough of all this mopey-dopey shit.' A bite. 'A woman of a certain age must be a bit strategic. With a daughter, too. A pretty girl.' He drained his wine. 'But stupid. You can guess who paid her school fees, eh?' He pointed to his meaty chest. 'For all those years. No longer. Now they're on the bastard's dime.' He laughed. 'The girl came, too. Same age as you.' He wiped his mouth. 'How old are you?'

'I'm eighteen, sa.'

He looked at me as if I'd just walked in. 'Why does Noor keep sending you those stupid bloody children's cards?'

'I couldn't say, sa.'

'How old is your sister?'

'Twenty-four, sa.'

'Bloody hell.' Boss decried the flagrant waste of blinking singing Christmas cards, the trouble with a Muslim wife with no regard for money. Then he shared his thoughts about the helping out of household help, i.e. better not to get involved and set a bad example. Aid one, all ask. No end in sight. A hundred dying grandmas, beating husbands, pregnant mistresses. Of course I understood? I did. He rang a bell. He smiled at me. A *kontomire* leaf between his teeth. A houseboy came to fetch me. 'Oh! I almost forgot to ask.'

I turned to him, prepared to field the question of my father's health. 'He's brave,' I breathed, a reverent murmur.

Boss didn't hear. 'Can you drive?'

I am the full-time driver here, and this is how we pay for it: my mother working round the clock, we children sending wages. I could have taken another job, a slightly more ennobled job, but nothing that would leave the time that this does for my studies. Driving means waiting and waiting means reading. The money is good and my colleagues are sweet. If I were caught peeping I'd lose my job driving. So I stood there and prayed, back to wall, *please make sure she didn't see me please make sure she didn't see me in Jesus's name I pray amen,* then opened my eyes to the cook.

Bulu has been cooking here for seven years, an important fact, as Jean-Louis the junior cook arrived just after I did. I have no idea where Bulu comes from. Bulu is not a local name. But he looks to be ocean-fed, stocky and muscular: central casting Ga. Jean-Louis is younger, maybe twenty, tall, a Beninois. His shirts remain an undefeated white despite the heat. He also wears a jacket with his name in navy cursive that his last employers gave him when their Lagos gig was up. Jean-Louis insists that though these last employers were truly kind – a Norwegian with a childless wife and braying guilty conscience who, decrying the size of the servants' quarters in relation to their mansion, had insisted that each servant have a bedroom in their house – the downside to their kindness was the constant chipper chit-chat. It wasn't enough to feed them well. He had to know them well, too. Better a boss, says Jean-Louis, who couldn't care less about your life than questions from a boss who couldn't hope to understand it. When curious Jørg was recalled to Stavanger, he gave all his servants the option to come. Jean-Louis considered, but he doesn't like the cold. A Beninois friend suggested he 'Go west, young man!' and so it is that Jean-Louis now sleeps on piles of latex foam, unquestioned.

Madam sought this second cook to make her meals less fatty; my employer likes his meat with lard and stew submerged in oil. Since moving back to Ghana, she has started drinking heavily and never walks for longer than it takes to reach the car. While my employer keeps himself in shape by riding at the Polo Club and getting up at dawn to golf and jogging through the neighbourhood, Madam seems to move as if through fog from house to garden to house with very little action taking place beyond these walls. I have mentioned how I feel about the consequential shape of things. But Madam is less grateful for the graciousness of God. She insisted on a second cook, a francophone and *skinny* cook, to make her figure less like an inverted question mark. Bulu takes offence at this, although he never says it; he has simply set his umbrage on our pile of folded clothes. He doesn't speak to Jean-Louis, but took an instant shine to me, perhaps because I never draw attention to his thieving.

That first time, he strolled in with green-yellow pawpaws and tossed one to me where I lay on my foam. 'We're not meant to take any food from the house,' I said. I pointed to the cardboard.

'I took these from the tree,' he said.

'But isn't that stealing?'

'Stealing from what? The earth?' Bulu laughed, slicing open his pawpaw. The juice dribbled down both his chins.

The second time, I'd driven him to grocery shop, our weekly task. I was reading *Maths: the Basic Skills* while Bulu did his shopping. Madam demands that Bulu shop, and only shop, at Bekaa-Mart, where expats spend my monthly pay on plastic bags of apples.

Madam claims she can't digest untreated local produce after decades out of Ghana; my employer isn't sold. He points to the use of pesticides, the cost of goods at Bekaa-Mart, the fact that Boss's wife and her two piggish brothers own it. But Madam is insistent. She wants Folgers coffee, Red Delicious, soya milk, spaghetti sauce, genetic engineering.

Bulu appeared with shopping bags. We loaded them into the boot of the car. He lumbered into the passenger seat. 'Where to?' I said. He pointed. Across the street from Bekaa-Mart a group of local women sell fresh produce out of makeshift stalls in the lot of the filling station. I frowned. 'For what?'

'*Chalé*. For vegetables.'

'You're meant to shop at Bekaa-Mart.'

'It's too expensive,' Bulu said.

'It's not your money. It's not your choice.'

'Eh! Madam never notices. The stickman never notices. I have a list of things to buy. I buy what's on the list. Job done.' I glanced at *Maths: the Basic Skills*, now lying on the dashboard. 'What's the difference?' Bulu shrugged. 'You understand?' I understood. The difference between what he spent and what she *thought* he spent on groceries would be roughly thirty, forty Ghana cedis every week.

Now Bulu was standing there looking quite sweet with a frown of concern on his Buddha-fat face. 'Why are you crying?'

'I'm not,' I objected, but found that I was when I swiped at my cheek. I dried off my face with my navy-blue shirtsleeve and hurried back out into nine o'clock sun. Her bathroom was empty, the window gone foggy. I went to go soap off the car.

Second, several weeks ago I dropped off my employer at the Oak Hotel on Spintex Road, on Sunday afternoon. I didn't think too much of it. We've passed this place a thousand times while driving to and from the house in gated Airport Hills. It looks more like an office park or conference hall, this Oak Hotel, with tiny windows, perfect squares, a dull, generic lobby. My employer doesn't go to church, though Madam does and had that day; I dropped her off at ten and would return for her at four. The daughter, Bianca, used to go when I first came but promptly stopped and now most often lounges at the beach with friends on Sundays. 'Wait here, please,' he said to me, got out, and strode across the lot, a rather dashing figure in his Zegna-replica suit.

My employer is a handsome man, in stellar form at fifty years; he wears his silver beard trimmed short, shoes pointy, collars starched. I would guess by the size of his five-bedroom house that he isn't as rich as his brother-in-law, perhaps on account of his overstretched domestic empire (a classic problem). He runs a waste-recycling plant, the first of its kind in the country I'm told; was married two times when he lived in the States and left behind some children. On occasion he'll raise his voice on his phone in the back of the car but it never lasts long, and ends with his chuckling, adjusting his cufflinks and cooing to me, 'Please excuse that.' A man of careful manners. Wears a mask, is what I'm getting at. But clement as employers go, no hauling over coals. He's been in Accra now for seven years but still doesn't know how to get around town, how to bob and weave through the narrowest streets of Osu or evade Spintex traffic. 'Webster! You're a *wiz*ard!' he'll say, as I bring him more swiftly to this or that meeting, or pick up a box from a jeweller to drop off for this or that East Legon housewife. But I suppose his years as a divorcee – which would seem to outnumber his years as a husband – have left him with habits that effort, affection and honest intention can't break.

I think he cares for Madam, whom he met one night some years ago at Boss's yearly Christmas bash before she lost her husband. I've heard him say on his mobile phone that Madam is the 'best of both worlds', a wife with Western etiquette and West African expectations. 'A Ghanaian woman raised in Ghana wouldn't speak French, for example,' he said. 'But these worldly women who don't know *Ghana* just don't work for me. You need a wife who can charm the guests *and* mind the staff, do you know what I mean?' The person on the phone must have known what he meant. My employer chuckled. 'Of course you do.' These days I so rarely drive the two of them together that I barely hear them speaking Twi or English, much less French. But they must have had a good night once. The engagement ring could be a world, a sparkling globe of diamonds on a band of Mensah gold. There's a photo on his key chain of the two of them in bathing suits at White Sands; he is holding her as one holds brides and babies. Her slender shins are dangling off his elbow, head of braids tossed back; his chest is taut with effort, to a flattering effect. Bianca sits behind them on a beach chair, either scowling at her mother's handsome lover or else squinting at the sun.

A note here on Bianca.

'Bia.'

Boss was wrong in both regards. Bia isn't pretty. At least, she isn't pretty to me. I know that here in Ghana we're obsessed with skinny half-caste girls, ascribing as we do some magic power to their paleness – but I'm not that way inclined: as said, I take my berries plump and dark, and Bia looks to my eyes like a beggar from Mauritius. Monochromatic, with wispy legs, and wispy threads of squiggly hair, her magic-skin the colour beige of satin sheets and crème brûlée. Her eyes are pretty, I'll give her that, the same as Madam's, wide and sad, slow-blinking as a baby doll's, two perfect Os of silence. The colour is different, light instead of Madam's melt-and-pour dark brown, the glassy gold of tiger's eye. The problem is the smile. When Bia smiles her pink gums show above her tiny pearls of teeth, which are half the size of normal teeth and still look cannibalistic – but the eyes don't smile. The brows don't move. The cheeks don't lift. The jaw goes stiff. Only the lips move, parted and stretched, as if pulled by two strings to her ears. This is why I'd found her so unnerving when I first arrived and why I still can't meet her eye when picking her from school.

'My uncle says that you're my age,' she'd chirped the day I started work (that day I never went to sleep, still hopped up on caffeine). Bia goes to Lincoln School, where all the foreign students go, despite her plea to stay abroad for senior year of high school. My employer says that boarding schools in England and New England peddle hash, hegemony and homosexuality. Further, they cost a fortune. Madam imagines that 'experiencing Ghana' will encourage her 'overly Americanized' daughter to embrace her African identity. Further, it will make for a good college essay. Needless to say, I have yet to see anything particularly Ghanaian about Bia's 'experience', which mostly involves swimming pools, blow-dryers, smartphones and chauffeured sport utility vehicles. Still, I suppose she was trying to be nice that day. She jumped in front, where Bulu sits, and smiled the small-toothed, flat-eyed smile. 'Do you want to go grab some coffee?'

Not knowing how else to respond to this, I said, 'Yes, ma'am,' and started the car. I wanted to ask her to move to the back but lacked, perhaps, the courage.

'You can call me Bia. Everyone does.'

'Yes, ma'am,' I said, hearing 'can', thinking choice.

'Webster! Noooooo! Just Bia!'

'Yes, Bia.'

'Dude, I'm not like . . . *them*.' She touched my hand. I shifted gears. Her four slender fingers fell, startled, away. She laughed a short and throaty laugh, and fiddled with her hair. 'I don't believe in all this twisted slave-becomes-king hierarchical shit.' She flicked her abandoned fingers at me, as if I had conceived of said shit. 'It's a hold-over from colonization, Webster. That's all it is. Repressed self-hate. *They* had to call their masters "sir" so now they make you call them sir. The British treated *them* like shit, so now they treat their staff like shit. My mom, whatever, it's what she knows, but, dude, no. I'm not like that. My dad was American. I guess he still is. I mean, I guess you don't lose your nationality when you die. Or maybe you do. That would make war a joke. But that's my point, you know? *I* am a liberal! *I* am a pacifist! I went to school in Massa*chu*setts! I don't believe in war. Or sir. I'm normal. I'm like *you*!' She laughed. I tried, but coughed instead. She was waiting for me to say something.

I said, 'Under three things the earth trembles, under four it cannot bear up: a servant who becomes king, a godless fool who gets plenty to eat, a contemptible woman who gets married, and a servant who displaces her mistress.'

Bia laughed her throaty laugh, a sound of light, bemused contempt. 'Shit! Webster knows Shakespeare?'

'Yes, Bia,' I said. 'But that was from the Bible.' I pulled into the parking lot of Bekaa-Mart and stopped the car. I looked at her. She looked confused. 'Shall I go buy the coffee?'

'The –? Webster, noooooo,' she cried again, then hugged, or somehow tried to hug me. With our seat belts on, the best she could do was a cheek pressed against my right shoulder. 'It's, like, a thing you *say*, "get coffee".' She lifted her cheek. 'Is there Starbucks in Ghana?' I drove her to Deli France Cafe in Airport Residential. 'You have to come inside,' she said. I went inside. She ordered in French. The Lebanese man who took her money looked at me in judgement. We sat at the counter with our double espressos. 'I know how you feel,' she said. I swallowed. I don't drink coffee. My heart was racing. I wanted to leave. I nodded. She smiled. 'About your father. My uncle told me. My dad and I weren't super close. He left us, like, ten years ago, but still, it sucks, you know? You know how he met my mother? At Harvard. He's Jewish, so his mother freaked. They had to run away together. How romantic, right? Then I was born and things were cool except for he's an alky so my mom has to ask Uncle Boss to pay, like, mortgage and tuition. Then my dad decides to leave her for this Tex-Mex yoga artist chick he met in fucking *rehab*. Like, cliché much? No, I know. I used to go and stay with them in Santa Fe for Hanukkah, and things were cool except for she's a bat-shit fucking hippie. The man gets *liver cancer* but is all "no pharmaceuticals", so then of course he wastes away and – God, I don't stop talking, right?' She continued talking. 'It's just, the chicks at school are *lame*, like nice, but fucking sheltered, and my mom – well, shit. You see her. DNR-depressed. Like, dude. *You* chose this guy, not me.' Her mobile rang. 'Shit, this is her.' She answered. 'I'm at coffee, Mom.' The smile. 'A friend.' She winked at me. 'He's no one. You don't know him.' She smiled again and touched my hand. Again, I pulled my hand away. But I thought to myself, and still think now, that Bia isn't stupid.

On the Sunday in question, some weeks ago, while Madam sang and fanned herself and emptied her purse in support of her prayers for lost souls and lost kilos, my employer entered the Oak Hotel. The sliding doors slid smoothly shut. I found a spot with decent shade and opened *Open City*. I didn't even notice when my cousin parked beside me in his newly tricked-out taxi; Kojo had to honk three times. His car was now a neon green, with Rasta-themed interior decoration, seat covers of wooden beads, JAH RASTAFARI decal. 'Webster!' he mouthed. We rolled down our windows. The cold air from mine kissed the warm air from his. 'No Woman No Cry' drowned the sound of his question. He turned down the music. 'You like it?' he called.

'*Too* much! But how?'

'Jah bless me good!' He held up a small battered baggie of weed. 'Webster, we'll eat like kings one day!'

'The food in prison, you grinning fool. Put that away!'

'Who's grinning? Me? *You* driving Mister Daisy!'

'Ha!'

'I missed you, oh! Too long, *chalé.*'

'Too long, indeed, mein cousin.'

He laughed his bright, infectious laugh, as if I'd told a funny joke, and I laughed even harder, making Kojo laugh the more. It seemed years since I had seen him, since I'd sat in back pretending that my cousin was my driver and my father would recover. I'd heard from my mom (who had heard from *his* dad) that Kojo had found a second job: selling drugs to white tourists at Labadi Beach, on Wednesdays at Kokrobite. I hadn't believed it. His taxi confirmed it. On the clock, both, we did not leave our cars. We leaned towards each other through our windows, as through cages, and we laughed until our jawbones hurt then sat there, smiling, hurting.

'How is Uncle?' Kojo asked.

'Alive, thanks be to God. In pain.'

'*Chalé*, why? You should have called your cousin Doctor Kojo! My boy there at Labadi, Yaw, his auntie, too, was suffering. Bad. He gave her ganja. Poof! No pain. I have some for Uncle. Free gift. Respeck.'

I thanked him. 'What are you doing here?'

'You sleep? Bianca dropped just now. Aren't you here to pick her? Eh! Fine girl, oh. Sweet, sweet, sweet. I brought her from Labadi Beach. I don't think she knew that I knew who she was. Girls, they love my taxi, oh!'

I forced a smile. 'I sleep for true.'

'You working hard. Bless up! *Mi ko.*' He started his taxi.

'*Ye beshia bio.*'

With three cheerful honks, he reversed and drove off, 'No Woman, No Cry' blasting, crackly.

In the hour that followed I stared at the faded blue-greys of the Oak Hotel lobby. In retrospect, I see that this was not a part of their plan. Typically, my employer will ring on the mobile he gave me whenever he's ready. I'll drive to the door of wherever he is, to minimize his time in the heat. I never sit and watch for him. I read until the mobile rings. It was purely by chance, as I stared through the glass, that I saw them appear in the lobby. Peculiarly, the first thing I felt was faint pride that he knew – that they both knew – my habits. They'd been watching me, passively, as I had watched them, without attention, observing my patterns. They took it for granted that I would be reading. They didn't glance out at the lot just to check. They walked into view just as calm as could be, my employer a half-step behind her. She was doing the thing that she does with her hair, pulling it all to one side, twisting it up, letting go. This time, however, she stopped with the twist. My employer kissed Bia on the back of the neck. She smiled that strange smile then she let her hair go. She stepped to one side, out of sight.

My employer found his mobile in a pocket and dialled. The sound of the ring in my lap made me start. The clamshell dropped to the floor by my feet. I fumbled to find it. 'I'm here, sa,' I said.

'When I call please answer on the first ring, Webster.'

'Yes, sa. I'm sor–' But he'd already hung up.

My heartbeat was a talking drum. I started the car. I pulled to the front. I glanced at the lobby as I held his door open, but didn't see

Bia, and got in the car. I turned on the radio, to BBC World, which he usually likes, but he said, 'Turn that off. I can't hear my thoughts.' I turned off the radio. 'What are you waiting for?'

'Nothing, sa.'

'Home.'

A third and final observation re: what happened here this morning. I do not mean to say that I did the right thing. But every now and then I'll think of Boss there at his table and his 'woman of a certain age' and then of my dad, and the way he still smiles when he first sees my mom in the morning and laughs (though it hurts) at her jokes, and the way she will kiss him, asleep, breathing laboured, a ghost of a man with the weight he has lost, before kneeling to pray for him, clutching her cross through her dress, and I'll think that we're lucky. Though the roof in our house has a hole, the couch too, though our toilet is a glorified latrine out of doors, though with all of us working we still come up short, I will think that we're loved, that we're lucky. I was thinking of love when I woke up this morning. I dressed and was going to go soap off the car when again, as had happened, I passed Madam's window and found her just stepping, pure light, from her shower.

A note here on the matter of what happened to the driver who was working here before me, i.e. when Madam moved in. I once found his groundnuts while cleaning the Rover, which only my employer and the driver may use. These are the groundnuts you get wrapped in plastic with grilled sweet plantain on the side of the road. It is an exquisite combination, the sweet-soft plantain and the groundnuts with skins on, so salty and dry. As my employer is allergic to nuts, I grew curious: who had been driving when Madam arrived? Boss had referred me a month or so after. I enquired with Bulu, who snorted and laughed. 'Poor fellow,' he said. 'Had a weakness for women.' I didn't see how my employer could judge him for that. 'Read that your Bible, eh? Thou shall not covet.' Jean-Louis entered and Bulu stopped laughing.

It was only today that I thought of Poor Fellow, the skins of his groundnuts there under the brakes. I passed by the window and looked up and saw her, but this time she saw me and looked at me, too. Our gazes, like magnets, got stuck to each other; we stared through the glass and we didn't look down. Her eyes, wide and sad, seemed to ask me a question. My eyes, wide and sad, gave an answer. She smiled. She turned from the window, her bottom uncovered, and entered the bedroom and kicked shut the door.

Fifteen minutes later she came floating through the garden with her fingers trailing, lazy, through her flowers' bowing heads. The massive green *buba* swished-swayed all around her. I froze in a crouch by the Rover's back tyres. My hands were still wet when she drifted towards me. I stood up to greet her but couldn't quite speak. I stood with the suds dripping down to the concrete. She walked through the puddle and stopped, at my face. 'I know what you saw there,' she whispered, not angry. I nodded, not breathing. She held both my cheeks. 'You're good at keeping secrets. I know that.' I nodded. 'You think I am beautiful. I know that, as well.' There were tears in her eyes, little fragments of diamond. Her skin smelled like lotion and soap and reprieve. 'Will you keep it a secret? If I help with your father?' There were tears in my eyes as her hands took my waist. Bianca was starting her school day at Lincoln. Bulu was scowling at Jean-Louis, mute. Mamadou was sleeping. My employer was teeing. My God would have held her back, too. ∎

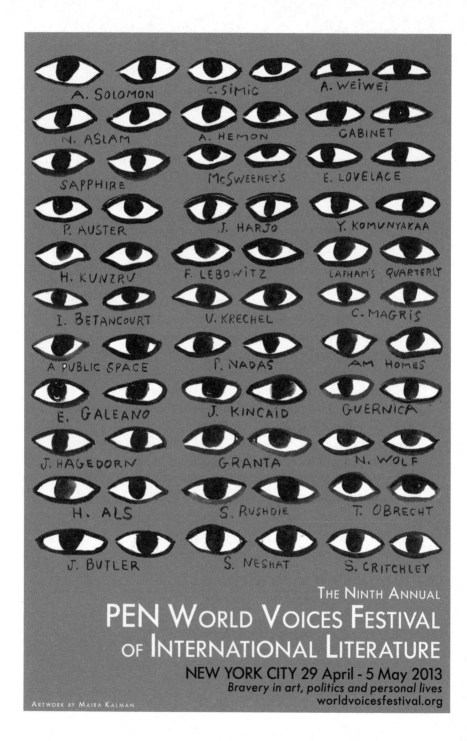

A. SOLOMON
C. SIMIC
A. WEIWEI
N. ASLAM
A. HEMON
CABINET
SAPPHIRE
McSWEENEY'S
E. LOVELACE
P. AUSTER
J. HARJO
Y. KOMUNYAKAA
H. KUNZRU
F. LEBOWITZ
LAPHAM'S QUARTERLY
I. BETANCOURT
V. KRECHEL
C. MAGRIS
A PUBLIC SPACE
P. NADAS
AM HOMES
E. GALEANO
J. KINCAID
GUERNICA
J. HAGEDORN
GRANTA
N. WOLF
H. ALS
S. RUSHDIE
T. OBRECHT
J. BUTLER
S. NESHAT
S. CRITCHLEY

THE NINTH ANNUAL
PEN WORLD VOICES FESTIVAL
OF INTERNATIONAL LITERATURE
NEW YORK CITY 29 April - 5 May 2013
Bravery in art, politics and personal lives
worldvoicesfestival.org

ARTWORK BY MAIRA KALMAN

SLOW MOTION

Adam Thirlwell

ADAM THIRLWELL

1978

Adam Thirlwell was born in London. He is the author of two novels, *Politics* and *The Escape*; a novella, *Kapow!*; and a project with international novels that includes an essay-book, *Miss Herbert*, which won a Somerset Maugham Award, and a compendium of translations edited for *McSweeney's*. He was selected as one of *Granta*'s Best of Young British Novelists in 2003. His work has been translated into thirty languages. 'Slow Motion' is from a novel in progress.

[Edison Lo wakes up]

When I woke I was looking upside down at a line of velvet paintings on the wall above the bed. Jesus was standing on his halo beside a very bright Madonna – I mean the religious kind, not the disco version. In between the two of them was a tropicana beach – it was a palm tree, a palm tree, a palm tree, some blue sand. I thought perhaps I liked them, these velvet paintings. I liked the very bright vibe. But also I knew that although I liked the vibe it was not the vibe of my usual bedroom, just as the girl who was sleeping beside me in what seemed to be a motel room was not my happy wife. I felt like my head was somewhere else and I also felt very sick. My head was sick. I knew my phone was there beside me somewhere and I knew that I should look at it but I really also didn't. If at this point you put me on a chat-show sofa and asked me how I was feeling, I'd have to tell you that I basically was feeling very sad.

[to discover that he might be doomed]

Because I really am no big shot, or hoodlum. I am no *player*. Girls make me shy. In this role of high-speed macho I was about as authentic as the white chicks doing gang signs for photos. It really wasn't normal for me to wake up and not know how I got there. A normal pastime for me was to be intent on mathematical problems, or models of voting patterns in different democratic states. Nevertheless, this new thing went on happening and I was powerless to stop it. My head was definitely very bad. High outside the walls, planes were presumably drifting as usual like goldfish in the empty air, and down here on the terrible earth a girl who was not my wife was lying there beside me. I knew her name, at least. Her name was Karly. She was blonde and when you saw her in a bar her hair was this gorgeous listless mass to one side of her neck but on reflection she wasn't a natural blonde. She almost had no hair between her legs but the hair that was there, a tuft, was definitely dark. The light began to fry the nylon curtains and Karly continued to sleep.

[so over breakfast he tries to think about it]

But, however, even if you're bewildered or sad you have to carry on. I remember one bodhisattva phrase – *keep cool but care* – and that phrase is never wrong. It's almost certainly a rule to live by and such rules should always be treasured. So I got up and dressed and considered how I was going to return home, I mean in what state and with what explanations. But it was also very early. It was both way too late and also very early so I thought for now I would start with getting myself some breakfast, because sometimes the only way to be is to just take care of the ordinary things. You have to think things through in stages. I walked out into the car park and along to the motel restaurant. From the booth in which I sat I had a very bright view. It was nothing special. Beside my car there was what looked like a Caddy Hearse but I ignored it. And maybe this was a mistake – to ignore what other people might consider a definite sign. If you're used to the unfranked letters arriving at your house, or phone calls where a man asks if he's got through to the chapel of rest, I mean if you're alive to the mafia ways of telling a man he's marked or savaged or doomed then maybe it could be said that I made a mistake. But I always missed the obvious. I don't know why. Other people got into the ordinary things like petrol-station car parks and Coca-Cola parasols, or whatever – the coffee-machine coffee. But me, no. I was much better at my own ruminations.

EDISON LO'S CHILDHOOD DINERS

Mr & Mrs Lo drove him out to the motorway junctions where there were replica drive-in restaurants with American memorabilia on the ceilings, like a Quaker spinning wheel, or electric guitar. And these restaurants served him up his favourite meal: a pale virgin pina colada, beside a bacon cheeseburger, settled in its wicker nest, beside its softer nest of fries.

It was very bright and very sad inside this diner. The radio was talking to itself but I had nobody to talk to, so I sat down in my booth with a view of the empty signscape, and read through the laminate menu. I waited. I looked out the window. I kept looking at my watch and then the landscape for ten minutes: my watch and then the landscape, my watch and then the landscape. I really don't like waiting. Finally, a waitress emerged from the kitchen. Her name was on her breast pocket. This name was Quincy. In another font, another badge was wishing me a nice day. And it was a nice day, no question. It was cartoon nice, if you had not woken up in an adulterous and guilty state.

    – I was waiting ten minutes, I said.
    – You said what? said Quincy.
    – I'm not making a formal complaint, I said. I just think you should know that I came in, I think, ten minutes ago. It's really nothing.
    – Uh-huh, said Quincy.

I don't think she really cared but at least I'd tried to help. I ordered my vegetarian breakfast. My style of eggs was sunny side up. My choice of juice was orange. I did want the hash browns. I ate my fries with gusto. I added the ketchup and mustard. And when I finished, having dragged some toast across the red-and-yellow plate, I rubbed my glasses clean with a wipe that Quincy had provided for my fingers. It was kind of her because people's hands are often covered in germs. It's always good to be cautious. The wipe made my glasses smell pure but they now also stung my eyes. I looked out over the horizontal electric lines, then the horizontal lines painted on the tarmac. Then I looked out over the vertical STOP signs. The world was as empty as that. I felt very trapped and very sad.

[and develops a temporary solution]

Although of course *in retrospect* I was nowhere near as sad as I should have been because in retrospect Fate was about to juice me even more than it already had. Fate was all around me, like the crimping on a beer-bottle top. But already I thought it had and this was enough to make me feel just very frazzled. I was thinking about the home life of Edison Lo and considering if some kind of confession would be really and truly required. Because I do not like to do things that are wrong. I am totally against it. And one thing that does seem wrong is to wake up in a bed beside a woman who is not your wife. Although also I was counter-thinking that so far I had no proof or evidence that anything other than sleep had occurred in this motel room, which was at least hopeful, if you're thinking morally. Must a man be judged for sleeping beside a woman who is not his wife? Are we so very totally medieval? But I wasn't thinking about this problem as methodically as I would have liked because I had a heaviness in my bowels and it was kind of preoccupying me too. As I walked back to my motel room where Karly was presumably waiting in some sleepy spaced-out manner, with eyeliner smudged in a way that would no question be appealing, I was suddenly regretting not using the bathrooms in the restaurant. Because while on the one hand I didn't like going back inside just to use the bathroom, on the other hand the thought of returning to my room and sitting down and exploding in the small hutch next to where Karly was sleeping . . . This didn't please me at all. But then I thought of a solution that made me proud. And now I wonder if I hadn't had this thought if things would have been different, and I wouldn't have been too late. It's never obvious at what point you can use this language of in retrospect or too late. They seem like normal phrases but they conceal much more than is useful. But this is anyway what happened. Before going back to the room, I decided, I would do the necessary checking out, and then silently take my backpack – because I travel with my backpack every day, it goes with me everywhere I go, partly because there's no end to the possessions I need to keep on my person for luck or voodoo or habit but also it's just the most useful method overall, I think – and steal away. And afterwards I would go and get a coffee in a diner somewhere else and use whatever bathroom they could offer me and that was where I would plan how I would return to Candy in such a way that she didn't entirely hate me. This wasn't obviously usual for me – to leave a girl in bed without saying a proper goodbye. I would definitely admit that it seemed perhaps impolite. But in the end you have to choose among politenesses. Also though I was in a very dark panic there was in me a sense that this did have a macho charm. It's not so great to admit it but as I stood there at reception, while reading a calendar for the wrong month and the wrong year, I allowed myself this grizzled moment of glory. You, kid, I was thinking, are paying for a girl to sleep. It also occurred to me that if this kind of thing was happening then I really did need more sustained medical attention. I needed more consideration applied to my pills. But that was only a parenthesis. And I would like to also assert at this high point of pause and idyll that while, sure, it had some kind of machismo, this way of thinking, it also showed concern, and this was always something that Mr and Mrs Lo liked me to show. They liked it when I thought about other people. So I did it more. I tried very hard. The man who was at reception this early in the morning seemed kind of sad so I thought about him as well. He had a difficult job, I was thinking, an arduous job, which presumably necessitated answering phones to the people supplying the kitchens, as well as kids calling for a practical joke, and a woman arriving at four in the afternoon needing a room right now, and so on, as well as the preparation of check-in and check-out forms, and the monitoring of the pool maintenance team, and also the use of the credit-card machine. It was not easy at all. It was exhausting. His name was Osman, and Osman, I was definitely thinking, seemed sad. He turned round to find a stapler or other office accessory and there was a scar on his neck, behind the ear. Maybe in the heyday of Osman he'd been some Caucasian warlord, but events had so conspired that Osman was now here: in a chain motel, taking calls. While at home he kept his videos where he surveyed his troops and I hoped that he did, because it's important to keep some kind of link to your past.

    – Have a nice day and come back soon! said Osman.
    –You too, man, I said.

I did mean it. A woman wearing headphones who was possibly Filipina was swabbing down the wooden decking outside the rooms. I wanted to give her a gentle smile but she didn't see me.

THEN EDISON IS VISITED BY AN APPARITION

Then he thought he saw his dead grandmother walking towards him, at least it looked like she looked in photographs. She seemed relaxed. But when he was closer she was no longer his grandmother. She was nobody at all.

I could see the exit route back to something that I could call my ordinary life. It was very close. Inside the room, the light was now brightly bleaching the curtains. I tried to turn off the ceiling fan because it was making this blurry kind of noise but instead I only turned on the bedside light. Karly didn't notice. I walked across to the desk, where my bag was propped. And although I was anxious to make what the pulp fictions must have once called *the perfect getaway*, I also wanted to kiss her goodbye. I don't know if that's the pulp style too, I think it isn't, but still isn't that right – to kiss a girl goodbye while she's sleeping? Isn't that what romantics do? So I walked to the bed, and bent over her. Karly was sleeping on her front, and beside her nose on the pillow there was a thin dark slick of blood.

[but his plans change]

Everyone thinks they will not be there when someone dies, I mean when someone dies who is not their endless and married love.

Everyone thinks that things happen in certain orders but of course they don't or not always. Terrible combinations are always possible and in fact I'm not sure they're combinations, so much as aspects of the same thing. This was the knowledge that was being forced on me while I stood there. I was fading in and out. I was like a hologram or optical illusion. Or like a neon sign. I mean, I was switching on and off and I was sinister. I looked down. What kind of big shot are you? I was saying to myself. A fucking small one. I looked up. The ceiling fan was still going round and round. That was basically a version of me too. I looked back down at Karly. Yes, everyone thinks they know the order in which things will happen but in fact this is not true at all. And also whether something has happened or not is not always obvious. I think we tend to over-exaggerate the idea that things are real. Or at least I was trying to think how real something was when it was so far entirely private. I mean, do your own mini quiz. When a gorgeous girl tries to kiss you in the back of a taxi when you're both high on ketamine, do you go home and tell your wife? I do not think so. You keep the gorgeous blonde to yourself as a stereoscope slide for winter evenings and therefore basically she does not exist at all. Or when your husband knows you do not smoke but you do in fact smoke a cigarette, why do you upset his peace of mind? And so you do not. In which case, has anything really happened? That's what I mean by nothing happening, or one of the things I mean. It was only known to me and so it was maybe not known at all. Although it's not so easy to really think this.

HIGH-SPEED DESCRIPTION OF KARLY'S BLOOD

The blood looked red to him but in close-up the blood seemed black. It was a red liquid that was turning black, or a black liquid turning red.

I tried to say Karly's name, but it wouldn't – my voice. I tried to breathe and that was difficult too. It was like my heart was somewhere on the surface of my body. I could still taste the stale-egg taste from breakfast in my gullet. In other words I felt very much under-prepared, like the nightmare where you are giving a PowerPoint presentation but leave behind your laptop in some stranger's coupé. I felt definitely ill at ease.

[so Ed tries to reconsider]

If you imagine me at a speed-date session being asked to define myself I'd easily say I was a model citizen. I don't think that's exaggerated. My grades in English were good, my grades in mathematics were spectacular. I read the classical texts. I had a talent for exams. I am aware that not everyone has this talent nor the opportunity for such talent and I am very grateful. I am grateful for the privilege of these things. Do good, said Mr and Mrs Lo, and you will prosper. Take exams, be cool. But I really wasn't sure now if this was, after all, enough. It turns out that you can have all the ancestors you want, they can hover in the air around you like candyfloss, but still, they cannot help you. Inside the room, my thinking was slow like dub music. I tried to consider the options that this body presented, of which one was that I was looking at a suicide. I was remembering an article about a kid who went to sleep and woke up to find a girl jumping out the window. I didn't really want to think that now that boy was me, but then the only other possibility was that somehow she had had a seizure or attack. And naturally the whole narcotics business was the main culprit or cause for this in my head. But also I wasn't right now so interested in causes, I was more interested in *what happens next*. I'd never thought of a life like a structure or building but it was exactly like that, my thinking, because I was picturing those videos where buildings get blown up, where they just curtsy or dissolve from within. And I didn't think I could be expected in this situation to know what to do. I looked out the window. The view outside the window was very still. Perhaps I shouldn't have been so surprised, because life had definitely been a recent narcotic cloud, but there it is,

I was total shit and terror. The bathroom contained two hand towels, two bath towels, a bathrobe and a bath mat. In the toilet bowl some paper from the night before had inflated like a parachute or squid. On the wall there was another velvet painting: the naked torso of a black woman, with shiny breasts and sunglasses, against a turquoise background. While outside, my car was parked, oh outside where there was also sunlight and the sky and everything was ordinary. Clouds gathered. Clouds dissolved. If I'd turned on the radio I would have heard a voice explaining the effects of the weather system in our city, but I didn't, because I was running the hot tap, washing my hands. And I was thinking about Karly. I mean, one thing I am good at is rationalizing. I was doing the logical arithmetic. I had checked out without mentioning that there was a woman in my bed; I had sat in the restaurant unnoticed for over ten minutes. And although of course it was possible to do the ordinary thing, the legal thing, to go back to a man called Osman and explain, in abject supplication, that I'd found a body comatose or lifeless but not quite, in my bed, but that I had nothing to do with this situation, or only in the most minor way: yes, I suppose I could have returned to Osman to discuss the problem of hospitals and police, but the voices in my head were strange. The voices in my head, they did their own thing. They tended to prefer the idea that help should be anonymous. And in this they were probably right.

[and he begins to clear up]

Her left arm was behind her back and her left cheek was squashed softly against the pillow. It was like a Kodachrome of a kid sleeping or a cherub but it also wasn't. I just needed to mop up the blood on the pillow beside her, because it seemed the tender thing to do, and I always try to do the tender things. I don't think at this point I had finally decided on my project. I took a bath towel and laid it on the blood. The white terry cloth became maroon. And I was thinking that maybe this was the first time I had ever seen another person's blood, I mean in such lavish quantities. I didn't want to touch it but I knew I had to. I had this fear of someone else's blood, like I had this fear of coming inside a girl without a condom. I don't think these are unusual. I think these are the fears that everyone's been taught. I took the towel up and tried to rinse it in the bathtub – which meant that I was leaving a tiny trail of blood on the bathroom floor which was tiny but basically gross. Then, kneeling on the side of the bed, I gathered Karly in my arms, from behind, and gently lifted her chest; and it felt wrong, touching her breasts like this, but I didn't think like that for long because this was when a cry of horror overtook me. I couldn't help it. It came out of my mouth much quicker than I knew. I was trembling. I held her there, as if I were performing some kind of slow-motion Heimlich manoeuvre: first gazing at the pillow, which was a mess of polyester and vomit and possibly more blood, a total horror show, then gazing sideways at what once was Karly's entire expression, but all the expression was gone. I held her there. I bent to her face and her mouth smelled like vomit but also it was warm. And well, I think if you want to know what Fate feels like, it feels like this. You are holding a body in your arms. No, in fact I could make this more precise. This is what Fate feels like. You are holding a body in your arms, and then you hear a knock at the door, and then you hear a key card being slotted into place. That's how it feels. I would possibly argue that maybe it would be nice if just one time Fate used a more original ringtone. So I dropped Karly, gently, to the pillow again, and ran to the door. The Filipina woman was facing me. She was carrying a mop and brushes. I didn't have time to check if I was bloodstained. I probably was. Maybe people don't care any more. Maybe in the modern world blood is no surprise. But me, I was always old-fashioned.

FILIPINA
Housekeeping.

EDISON
But I'm still here.

FILIPINA
This room is not occupied.

– But I'm here, I said: hopeful, esperanto. She looked in and I suppose she maybe saw a pair of naked legs. She looked at me. It was just about plausible that I was a mini donjuanish type, or at least I hoped it was.

FILIPINA
They said you gone.

EDISON
We're leaving.

FILIPINA
Ten minutes. Ten minutes, mister.

It was probably then that my plan became obvious to me, which was possibly a movie plan but I think also a plan of carefulness. I was thinking that there were maybe two or three things that were true. That I needed to get Karly some medical help, that I needed to do this in some kind of secrecy, and that speed was very necessary. It was a difficult trio but maybe not impossible. I wanted Karly to be OK and I wanted to return to my ordinary life, or at least the possibility that I still had an ordinary life. It was like I had crossed over or been transformed. And I suppose other people have their ways of thinking this through. Mr Lo would do it by calling this the devil. He has the devil ranged against him. I think this is in fact one of my earliest memories: standing in my water wings on a Sunday morning, waiting for my father to return from church so that he could take me to the swimming pool. My father believes in devils. Me, I do not. But I do believe in monsters. I remember the Egyptian monsters in the museum and they make me very fearful still, those pictures of the green god and his dog-god of judgement, the devouring god with his crocodile head. Although at least the dog-god stays down below.

Whereas this felt more like what happens when the gods above decide to lope down here, and when they do they kill you. Have you ever met a god? It's like this. They just can't help themselves. They're very sorry, the gods, but they are going to fuck you up. Like the child-eating goddess who would very much like to but just cannot, cannot stop herself from guzzling your little daughter. Or like the gods who once demanded that three temples should be built for them in one night. And dawn, so goes the record, came too soon – and so these aforementioned deities descended and smashed the scaffolding up, like gang-rape footballers.

[then leaves the room]

So I began the crazy project of delivering Karly's body to the care of trained professionals. It was kind of the time desperation of being on a PlayStation with the power run down to zero and you're almost at the completion of a personal best. But obviously also worse. It was like time was gone, but also stretched. As gently as I could I dragged Karly, under the armpits, so that her legs flopped onto the floor beside the bed, then lowered her torso to the ground. It wasn't totally easy but still it was easier than dressing her in her dress again. That was like dressing a difficult toddler, like maybe a toddler who's overtired and isn't wanting to leave the dance class. Her arms were difficult and her legs were suddenly longer than seemed possible. Still, I dressed her in a way. But before we could leave I realized that first I also needed to make the room look neat. So I slipped off the bloodied pillow, and also the sheet with its vomit and saliva. I think if I could have spoken, my voice would have been much lower, a proper bass, like when they put voices in slow motion in the horror flicks, or when the batteries in a tape player ran down, in the era when they still put songs on tapes. I didn't know what to do with this sheet and pillow and the previously mentioned sodden towel. I had a shopping bag but it, I now discovered, was punctured with two holes. Who does this? Who is in charge of making holes in plastic bags? What kind of sadistic factory? I had my backpack but my backpack if I could avoid it would not get bloodied and smeared because then I would have to abandon it, which did not worry me for the backpack but for its possible future existence as evidence against me. I looked to the bin in the bedroom. The bin in the bedroom was a bucket of stainless steel. But in the bathroom the pedal bin contained an unused plastic liner, neatly folded. With my hand inside, I made it unfurl, like those bags for picking up dog shit. Then gently – maintaining the bag unfurled – I squashed the pillowcase and sheet inside it. Then the bloodied towel, but the bag was now gaping open and the blood was very much visible. So I took the shoelaces from my sneakers. In my worry and terror I couldn't tug the laces out: the laces stuck, the laces were dirty and so I scrabbled at the interlacing and was going to cry. Finally two laces hung from my hands. My feet sort of wallowed slackly in my hipster shoes. I strangled the bag with my laces, then gently placed it on the floor. I know that in some way the theft of a sheet and towel was definitely a crime, and a crime that no doubt would be discovered, but it seemed a miniature kind of crime, the kind that just leads to something extra on your credit card – and this was definitely a better crime than the discovery of blood and then the consequential thinking on the part of the authorities. But with the sheet removed I now also noticed that the mattress had this formless stain, a sort of horrible discoloration. It was like nothing I'd ever seen. I can't compare it. It's like trying to compare kapok, or tundra. And in these situations I think Mrs Lo would always say that you should just do the minimum possible and so I decided that this would be what I'd do. I would turn the mattress upside down. But a mattress is bulky. And I am only small. I sweated and heaved. I manipulated the dense sprung mattress so that it moved through a nondescript circle. I curled it up over itself where the mattress stalled, for a moment, on the crest of its sodden wave. Then it collapsed from under itself and flopped to horizontal. I re-dressed it with the duvet. Which meant that the problem remaining in the four minutes I had left before the housekeeper returned was to try to manoeuvre Karly's body out of the door and into my car in a way that looked as normal as I could manage. First I went to the basin in the bathroom and tried to scrub my fingernails, but it didn't have much effect so very quick I stopped. I still needed the toilet very much but this was no longer an option, so I returned to Karly, and we left.

[and gets back into his car]

I wonder if because this is the era of mass calculations is maybe why I managed the situation. There are so many calorie counts and fitness reps and email checks in the average day that in fact it's much less strange, this manoeuvring of bodies, than you might think. It's just a different way of thinking tasks through in detail. I dragged Karly to the threshold. I tried to do this gently but in the end, of course, I didn't really. Then I was having to make sure that I could hold her up to about the level of my shoulders and I was regretting suddenly the unspent time in the gym, the many hours of newspaper reading and YouTube videos. The entire history of my wasted time seemed sad to me, like it turned out to be a menace where no menace had previously been visible, and I berated myself that, vigilant as I always was for signs of menace, I had not noticed that the true menace was right there, when I had been doing nothing more than just existing. At the door I did another filmic thing, that filmic thing of looking left and right. It was daylight and this isn't an easy condition for introducing a comatose body upright into a car. I was also thinking that in my attraction to the taller woman I had possibly overreached myself. But still, the Filipina maid was gone somewhere, to call her son or just stand and look at the cars on the motorway. No one else was there. For one moment, Fate was off buying itself a burger or an apricot juice. I was trying to open the passenger door of my car, and I could see the entire future sequence of events unfold and then it was like those moments in the stories of the saints when the sage who has lived all his life in the desert or maybe forest receives a lunatic bath of light, a deep revelation. I would like to call this vision love, or something like it. Also it was maybe nostalgia. It was just as if very sleepily I could feel Candy breathe beside me and I thought I was going to cry but I gradually didn't. There were a few dead trees around, possibly palms, and they were making dry clickings; the palmettos were a sequence of old clocks. I pushed Karly inside, with my hand over her head, very gentle, like a halo. Then a shoelace loosened on the bag that I was holding and the towel became visible: a slack red smear. I thought that the whole thing was going to fall open and it made me panic but it didn't. I sort of slung the passenger belt over Karly and fixed it and shut the door. And I was walking round the car and was just sort of paused at the boot when I started to shake. I couldn't easily match my hands to what I wanted them to be doing. I suppose, I told myself, this happens. Then I realized that Quincy was regarding me from a cigarette break. Because there's no reason why a life should not come complete with a laugh track, none at all. I say cigarette break but of course I have no idea. She was just standing there, at the restaurant door, and she was starting up this middle distance conversation.

QUINCY
Want a cigarette?

EDISON
Sorry?

QUINCY
Want a cigarette?

EDISON
I don't know.

QUINCY
You don't know?

EDISON
I mean no.

We paused on this obviously not satisfactory conversation. I was
hoping it would mean she'd stop but she didn't.

QUINCY
What's your name?

EDISON
My name?

It's sometimes useful to look like me, I mean the way I look to certain
people, and this was one of those occasions. So I just stared at her.

QUINCY
You from round here?

EDISON
Uh, no.

QUINCY
From where?

EDISON
From China?

QUINCY
China? Really? I worked once at the what was it – the Garden, in
Hong Kong? You know it? They did these char sui buns –

EDISON
I've only been there once.

QUINCY
The Lei Garden?

EDISON
Hong Kong.

QUINCY
Well. No harm done.

[where he contemplates his terrible fate]

And she wandered away in this weird dazed souvenir condition that left me in a state of envy or melancholy that was also still totally panic. By which I mean: Was it right for me to be so punished? All I'd done was wake up beside a woman who was not my wife. Is this so untoward? I might not have even kissed her. I really didn't think the grand things were real – like murders and death and destruction – it never occurred to me that such things could really happen in a life, and now that something like this was happening it was making me amazed and also confused. Yes, I think it was about then that the first inkling began to occur to me – like the way you see a cat drift through some amateur porn footage and just sit there, it occurred to me as backgroundly as that – that I might be doomed. It was like the moment you look up in the air at some distant passing plane and just think for a sad moment that its engines might possibly be failing. I really did feel that this was unfair. I wanted another me! – at liberty, like a squiggle . . . When I play Dungeons & Dragons I am an elf, and my weapon is a longbow. I am taking kazoo lessons from a sweet woman on the Internet who lives somewhere near Kansas City. My favourite piece of music is called 'With 100 Kazoos'. My favourite food is this vegetarian goose thing I once had in San Francisco which I liked for its ingenuity. Reading want ads makes me sad. I have no meanness in me. Whereas just make sure, Fate was telling itself, as it contemplated the picture, like a connoisseur, that no level spot of ground isn't trampled over with blood. I don't think this is an exaggeration. It fits the facts as I see them. I would have preferred it if Fate had concentrated more on the future of, I don't know, Aldebaran but it seemed that no, it preferred me. And in response I would like to say that this was in no way fair. Or I mean, no, this is what I was thinking. Elsewhere they are in their black ship somewhere, your enemies, the pirates are out in the port, and drinking champagne. They are in the dark tanker. That is everyone else. But you are here and on your own. And you are no longer into the poetry of the Buddhist sages, or movies filmed on hand-held cameras or whatever. The whole culture is not the point. It is no longer yours – the culture. I was feeling suddenly empty, like I was the Windsor Plantation that with just one careless cigarette gets suddenly converted and becomes the Windsor Ruins. I was pulling out of the car park in a car whose steering, I was now thinking, was shonky, and needed to be seen to, but if this was a problem it was not as much of a problem as the possession of an unconscious girl. I think that's obvious. And I was saying to myself: Kid, you are currently the least talented gangster in the world. Or, in other words, you were always way-out innocent. Your mother always said it was your sweetest characteristic. And now look at you. ■

THE END OF ENDINGS

Steven Hall

STEVEN HALL

1975

Steven Hall was born in Derbyshire. His first novel, *The Raw Shark Texts*, won the Borders Original Voices Award and the Somerset Maugham Award, and has been translated into twenty-nine languages. 'Spring' and 'Autumn' are excerpts from his upcoming second novel, *The End of Endings*.

Autumn
September–November 2014

I

This is what I know for sure. Andrew Black, author of the popular Harvey Cleaver detective stories and my friend of almost ten years, died two days ago, on 28 November 2014.

That much is fact. It means that every day for the last thirty-eight years, a human being named Andrew Black was alive in the world, he grew from being a baby, to a child, to a man. He learned, he acted on the world and reacted to it acting on him. His life grew out of those actions and reactions, with each new hour always built upon the last. For every day of the last thirty-eight years, Andrew Black woke up where he'd gone to sleep and carried on pretty much where he left off. Every day, that is, except for the last two, because for those two days, Andrew Black has been dead.

We can add further facts – the facts of our respective histories, the circumstance of our meeting and so on, but I'll deal with those things later. Then there's the fact that Andrew and I exchanged a series of letters over the last three months of his life, and the fact that the letters I received from him during that time reported, not only a theory that seemed to trouble him very much, but also a string of unusual events in which he claimed to have become involved.

There's also the matter of the postmark on his final letter. By which I mean only to say the letter had a postmark, and that the postmark still exists as a physical thing made of paper and ink (the envelope sits beside me as I write this) and inarguably displays certain information in a series of letters and numbers. I don't mean to suggest that the information itself is beyond question, or that it is cast-iron proof of anything.

But that's it for the facts. Everything else I have to say remains wide open to challenge and interpretation.

I'm writing this not to prove anything or argue any sort of case, but simply as an attempt to make some sort of sense of it. I have this particular ship should be a-headed. And though all this heroic straining at the rudder until backs break and eyes pop is a noble enough pursuit, I am sure, I have long believed that the wiser man, when finding himself thus assailed, might initially ascertain from whence and to whither these currents flow, and secondarily, if there might not be some way to ride them a spell and thereby steer and manoeuvre their worst excesses unscathed, just as the skilled Indian brave pilots his canoe through the wild Colorado rapids.

Now accepting all that, reasoned I with myself, cutting up my supper, *let us first take sight of our predicament. You're not for turning away the work as you need the money so, and you've maybe got this business under your skin some too. But – you can't settle happy with the job neither, for if this Spear is, as it seems, some poor delusional, then you'd be a mighty cruel fellow to do him down so in the New York Tribune. Well then* (and here is where all that picking and piloting just mentioned comes about), *perhaps what you should rightly do is find out more about John Maxwell Spear, the better to make your decision. Yes, that's it. That's the way, all right. You learn for yourself if he's showman, dupe or madman, and then this question of whether to write for Lockwood will quick be all a-solved, won't it? For if he's truly sick or foolish, then that's your time to give it up, is it not? But if he's after all a fraud, well then, take the work with clear conscience. Aye, and with duty even. Good, good. Yes, and that's the matter settled.*

The great problem with giving the current its head, of course, is that a fellow may think himself cleverly steering, dodging, picking and choosing his way all the while, when in truth, he is doing no such thing at all. ■

idea that if all the disparate elements that made up those three months could be pinned to the page – like butterflies on a card in a museum – then maybe some larger pattern might reveal itself. What this pattern might be, what it might mean, I don't know. Truthfully, I don't hold out much hope. The more I've turned it all over in my mind, the more the vague logic I'd perceived as being there becomes impossible to grasp, in the way that saying the same word over and over makes it seem strange and, ultimately, meaningless.

Black himself was a fan of that trick, I remember. The repetition of a single word until it came to feel empty, nothing but a collection of sounds. I suppose that's why I'm thinking of it now.

It won't be enough to look at the last three months in isolation. It's not always necessary to understand how a person lived in order to understand how he died, of course, because it's not always true that a life leads to a death in any direct, meaningful way. But with Black, the two feel intimately, unavoidably, connected.

M y name is Philip Quinn. I'm going to try to tell Black's story, all of it, in the best way I can – without resorting to half-grasped explanations of my own making, or unjustifiable connections between the different parts. That said, there's nothing I can do about the principle rule of writing – one thing comes after another – letters make words, words make sentences, sentences make paragraphs, paragraphs make pages. Some kind of imposed structure is unavoidable, though I'm sure Black himself would call it a fundamental requirement – 'finding the line'. But Black is dead, and I don't know that I can believe in his techniques any more. Maybe I haven't believed in them for a long time. What I'm trying to say is that I *can't* know how the story of Andrew Black fits together, or if it fits together at all. I can't even know that all the things I'm going to write about here are relevant. In fact, I'm fairly sure some of them won't be. But my only option is to cast the net as wide as possible and include everything and anything that might conceivably matter.

We'll just pin down the butterflies, then see what we can see.

accept his commission. For, despite my general disdain of what ha[d]
n recent times come to be known as 'the spiritualist movement', and
despite the ever-lightening load of my purse, which, truth be told, was
now close as could be to having no weight at all; despite these things
had precious little interest in making cruel sport of a man who'd so
clearly lost his reason.

And yet.

And yet, as afternoon became evening, and as evening became
right, this noble letter of mine did resolutely remain unwritten.

I would say it was the turning away of such a valuable commission
that stayed my hand and kept me from throwing in the work, and in
ruth that was the greater part of it, but also, I'll confess now, I found
myself unable to entirely rid my thoughts of John Maxwell Spear and
his nonsensical contraption.

Quietly, yet persistently, the matter played upon my mind.

This note, this letter, I should correctly have written to put an end
to all involvement with the strange spiritualist and his engine, did
most stubbornly and consistently refuse to come into being throughou
the morning and afternoon of the following day. I had told myself tha
should at last compose the letter when my work was done, but ere
long that hour was come too — and there, look, is your narrator, packing
away his papers and ink and not writing any letter at all but instead
picking up his lamp and leaving his study altogether, thinking only to
find himself a bit of supper before bedtime.

'Well,' said I to myself, as I sat at table with a plate of bread and
cheese. 'Well now.'

For it is a very true thing, I think, though not one so widely professed
as might be, that though a man may always — and with all clear thinking
and good intent in the world — seek to steer the ship of his life along
the wiser, more advisable latitudes, there exist certain currents that car
occasionally make the turning of his rudder in one way or another a
much harder task than might generally be supposed, for they, thes
urrents, often have other undisclosed ideas of precisely where tha

2

A little before midday on Monday 1 September 2014, and I am one of 927 people watching my wife sleep.

If that seems like a very specific number to be quoting, three months later and after everything else that's happened, it's because the website had a viewer counter under each camera window, so I could always see just how many people had clicked through. If the number was a big one – and 900 plus was pretty big – I'd make a note of it for later.

The Post-it is still here now, one of many stuck around my note board:

Mon 1 Sept = 927

By then I'd been watching Imogen sleep for most of the morning, through the fuzzy green night vision of Dorm Cam Two. All that time, she'd been lying on her side, facing out, with the duvet pulled up under her chin. That's how she always slept, although when she slept like that at home, she'd usually do it turned away from me, facing the wall. This meant that for all of my watching Imogen on a computer screen, and from 8,383 miles away, I'd learned more about how my wife looked sleeping than I ever did from lying next to her in bed. It reminded me of the trouble scientists have studying very small things in laboratories.

I drained my 'I ♥ Coffee' mug and set it back on the desk.

On-screen, the duvet rising and falling with my wife's breathing and a slight digital fuzzing were the only things to give the image away as a live feed, and not a flat, dead picture. And, as none of the webcams had sound, the scene was utterly silent too.

In every traditional sense, nothing at all happened.

The counter clicked up to 945 viewers. I made another note.

I stared at the brown loop in the bottom of the coffee mug, then tipped the last lukewarm drops into my mouth.

There's something fascinating about watching a person living in real time. The long pauses. The stillness. Sleeping, staring, thinking, reading – all played out in their true, vast and blank entireties. Putting

ny man amongst his spiritualist congregation had even the slightes
scientific education as might conceivably assist in the implementation
of their task. Instead, ongoing instruction and guidance in the
development of the mechanism was to be provided by a host of spirits –
and these calling themselves 'The Electricizers' – a ghostly troop which
did, according to Spear, count among their number none other than
he late Benjamin Franklin!

Setting the letter aside at last, I sunk my hands deep into my pockets
then gave over to a good long spell of pacing about to prompt the
wheels of my mind into some sympathetic action.

Whilst striding about my parlour like this, I happened to notice
now the portrait of my wife had grown a little dusty, so I stopped my
marching and lifted it down from the mantle.

'A prayer engine,' said I, polishing the frame with my sleeve
Prayers for power. What do you make of it, Emma? And – though
t's said he had a very fine brain in his head while his heart was stil
a-beating – what would you make of being told what's what by . . . the
ghost of Benjamin Franklin?

But my wife only stared from her glass casing, lips pressed tight
replaced the portrait and took up Lockwood's note a second time
reading the whole thing again at the windowpane.

It seemed clear to me that this John Maxwell Spear might only
resolve himself in one of three ways: he was an out-and-out charlatan
an honest dupe seduced by this new and unfortunate fad for ghost-
knocking and table-tipping; or else he was a poor and pitiable soul in
he grip of some lunacy or other.

Given the clear impossibility of his undertaking and the ease with
which any mechanism might be tested against its stated purpose (and
his to say nothing of a chief adviser some sixty years in his grave), i
struck me that the third of these was by far the most probable state o
ffairs.

Yes, this Spear was likely naught but a cracked delusional.

I decided then that I would write a letter to Lockwood that very
fternoon and express therein my deep regret at being unable t

those familiar little islands of talking, arguing and laughing that we always thought were *what people are* into wide empty oceans of context. And then, at the other end of the scale, the opposite of those stillnesses – the rare, powerful, private things – the truthful, the revelatory, the sexual. Those one-in-a-million moments that probably won't happen while you're watching, but just might, just might, just might . . .

The phone rang, loud in the quiet house.

I jumped, grabbing the handset before it could ring again.

'Hello?'

'Hello, Euston,' said Imogen. 'This is Eagle One.'

On the screen, her fuzzy green body slept soundly under her fuzzy green duvet.

'Hello, stranger.' The hardness in my voice surprised me.

'Don't be like that, I haven't got long.'

'No, I wasn't. I didn't mean it like that.'

'I did say I didn't know if I'd be able to call.'

'I know, that's fine. I'm not. I wasn't meaning anything.'

'Promise?'

'Yeah. It's just the first time I've said anything all day. I'm . . . strange.'

'Ah, that'd do it,' said Imogen-on-the-phone. 'I did want to call when I got back, but we ended up being on site longer than I thought and it would've been like 3 a.m. or something over there.'

Imogen-on-the-screen showed no signs of waking up. She just carried on taking her slow, deep breaths – in . . . out . . . in . . . out . . .

'It's fine, I'm just feeling a bit weird, a bit . . .' The word I wanted to use was *flat,* but I didn't. '. . . abstract. Hello?'

'Hello. I'm here. Hello?'

'Hello. I can hear you.'

'What did you say? Abstract?'

'Yeah, like, as in, not all here.' I thought. 'It's not seeing people. I should probably go out later, walk around and normal out.'

'That sounds like a good plan. You should definitely do that. Get some sun and have some fruit.'

'I think I will.'

In reading such as these, the city man might justifiably suppose that New England has been restocked of late with peasants, squires and knights from the Dark Ages of Europe!

However, it was in the collective testimony of a second bracket of letters that our Mr Lockwood placed rather more faith. It seemed a good portion of the more level-headed correspondence regarding the spiritualist's machine had been generated by result of a meeting between Spear and a small group of engineers out of Boston some weeks previously. A number of those engineers, knowing full well of the *Tribune*'s interest in, and regular reporting on, all things mechanical, had subsequent mind to convey the absurdity of Spear's undertaking to that publication, for doubtless they could hardly believe what was being proposed themselves.

Mr John Maxwell Spear, Lockwood then explained, did by these several, reliable sources believe himself to be constructing some manner of engine, but an engine the like of which had surely never been suggested or even fleetingly fancied by any sane practitioner of that most logical and mathematically informed discipline of engineering. For the fuel intended to galvanize Spear's engine was not coal, nor oil, nor wood, nor wind, nor water – but prayer. Prayer! Yes, when sufficiently stimulated by honest religious devotion, it was claimed, Spear's engine – once complete – should reliably and consistently bring forth a plenitude of actual motive power!

But let's have all this praying business straight between us, afore we go any further. If you should've come to me around this time asking questions on this business of faith, I'd likely have told you I was at least a passable Christian soul. I was all for church of a Sunday morning and saying my prayers on bended knee like all the rest, but, come now – all things where they are meant!

But Lockwood's letter was not yet entirely read nor finished with, and still more of the curious and improbable was to be described therein afore the report was done.

Again at the word of these certain Boston engineers, the newspaperman did now additionally relay that neither Spear nor

'Sun and fruit stop a person from being abstract, that's a well-known fact.'

'I didn't know that.'

'Oh yeah, there's nothing better for it. So. What're you doing now?'

The whole time, I hadn't taken my eyes off the screen. 'I'm watching you sleep.'

'Oh God, you're not, are you? Am I thrashing around? I've been having the weirdest dreams.'

'No, you're just lying there. All still and serene.'

'That's something, then.'

'No, you're really very calm. And you had a 945 a minute ago.'

'Jesus. How many?'

'Nine hundred and forty-five.'

'Hang on, I'll write that one down. Nine, four, five. And I'm not doing anything?'

'No. Nothing. You're breathing. But, no.'

Imogen-on-the-phone thought a moment.

'It's funny,' she said. 'It only bothers me when you tell me the numbers, the rest of the time it's like the camera thing isn't, well, I don't mean it bothers me really, but you know.'

'Yeah.'

'Actually, it is bothering me now I'm thinking about it. I'm waving at them.'

'You should.'

'I'm doing it right now.'

Imogen-on-the-screen lay fast asleep. In . . . out . . . in . . . out . . .

'I'll wave back when it comes up,' I said.

'You're lovely.'

'Thanks.'

'I do miss you, you know.'

'I miss you too. How's it going?'

'God. Slowly.'

On 1 September 2014, Imogen is on the other side of the world, doing research. She is looking for one small spot on a very remote

Later, deep into the night, when at last I capped my ink, put out my lamp and drew the cold and lonely blankets up around me, my thoughts turned once more to Lockwood and his curious note. By now my eager reply would be bagged, bound and far distant, thundering to old Manhattan under the great steam plume of an overnight locomotive.

The following days were governed outwardly by the quiet industry of the writing desk, though there reigned too a vague inconstituted anticipation, evidenced by nothing more than a slight brightening of my mood as I went about my large and empty farmhouse which was then, in the month of March, still a colder and onelier place than in years past. Welcome as the green shoots of spring, then, the arrival of a second letter from the *New York Tribune*.

Yes, our good Mr Lockwood replied most expeditiously, supplying such information on the strange apparatus as was at his disposal and, upon reading barely the first few lines of his letter at the post-office doorstep, found myself in complete agreement with the newsman and his initial summation – a most peculiar undertaking indeed!

With boots still upon my feet and door barely closed behind me, I roused the fire some, then eagerly installed myself by the drawing-room window, the better to read this latest in full.

'Of the dozen reports concerning Spear and his mystical mechanism, fully one half,' Lockwood noted, 'were to be considered hyperbolic in the extreme', and these most generally dealing in wild and fervent accusations of blasphemy, crimes against the Lord God and his Creation and, in one instance, even a-joining Mr Spear and his spiritualists with that seven-headed monster most terribly set forth in the Book of Revelation. 'Though if we are to be warned that Mr Spear s the Beast itself, one of its heads or merely a lesser, diabolic accomplice, is difficult to ascertain, for correspondence of this type is typically rather lacking in the more practical specificities.' Lockwood also made mention of several other letters in this wild bracket – including a text founded almost entirely upon a single phrase, 'The Electric Messiah' – copied to the fill line of a full sheet of foolscap – before concluding that island, where she believes the single most important act in the entire history of humanity may have taken place.

'But you're still getting a good general movement, right?'

'In patches,' she said. 'But it's not like they just went from east to west or something.'

'I suppose that would've been – Oh, hang on.'

'What?'

Imogen-on-the-screen flicked her sleeping green head as if to shake something away.

'You're dreaming.'

'Told you. Very weird dreams.'

'I think you're going to wake up in a minute.'

'I am. Listen, I've got to go. I'll try to call tomorrow, but if not, I'll call Wednesday morning.'

'OK.'

'My time.'

'OK. And get them to sort out your laptop.'

'I will. But Johnny says it's killed itself.'

'Nice.'

'I know. Shit, right. I really need to –'

'OK. Love you.'

'I love you too. And go out.'

'I will.'

'All right, bye.'

'Bye.'

'Bye bye bye –'

The line cut to a flat buzz.

I kept the handset to my ear for a moment then clicked it back into the dock.

Imogen-on-the-screen frowned in her sleep and tugged at the duvet. The viewer counter had been falling steadily, but once she'd started to dream it stabilized. Now it climbed back up in ones and twos towards the 900 mark.

I waited, watching, arms folded.

You'll have noticed, I dare say, how crafty Lockwood made no mention of the *purpose* of this 'curious and improbable' machine in his note, thereby compelling me – a man of the inquisitive sort, for good or ill – toward writing him after the specifics.

Now I was, at that time, hard at work on a story in several parts for *Putnam's Monthly Magazine*, though I confess I took very little pleasure or satisfaction from the work, the plot of the thing being (by strict instruction of the editor) an all too familiar flags-and-gunpowdery sort of a brew, with a sugary flip-flop of lost love amid the cannonballs to help down with the swallow. Truly, this dreary job suited me not one bit, and I found myself increasingly reluctant to take to my writing desk each morning, yes, and even when firmly entrenched there, would oftentimes be given over to staring at my unused paper and thinking: *Oh, would that I might give these waiting sheets, if not some very grand story in exchange for their quitting the green glades and the peaceful leafy life, then at least something not so bashed and chopped and regurgitated that it should feel read and written some three times already.*

But such idle, rebellious thoughts made no very big difference to my being about the work regardless, for against this displeasure of mine, against the desire to get well away from Potter (the hero of my *Putnam's* tale) and from the dull hours of inky scratching in his honour, there stood two colossal and immutable facts. One: my recent books had sold very poorly, with my latest failing to find print at all. Two: as everyone knows, a man can do little very well without money, save starve to death or join the fishery. So take to my desk I did each morning and there I wrote that *Putnam's* adventure whether it pleased me to or no.

But to receive this letter from the *Tribune* – well now.

I have never much fancied myself a journalist but I can scarce deny that adding my name to a newspaper's pay sheet had considerable appeal, my situation being as it was. Further, as I have said, Lockwood's letter intrigued me greatly, and in any case, drafting a reply supplied ample justification to set aside that grey stew of a manuscript for a few moments, and to think imaginatively upon other matters.

Almost before I knew it, I'd a fresh letter paper in hand and promptly set to in finding just what this 'curious and improbable' machine was all about . . .

Imogen jolted awake, eyes flashing about in a panic before realizing where she was. She relaxed as she got her bearings, rubbing her face with her palms, propping herself up on an elbow and then looking around the dorm. Seeing she was alone, she leaned out of bed and flicked on the lights.

The green instantly flared to a white blank. Then the dorm re-emerged in full colour.

My wife climbed out of bed and walked out of shot in her pyjamas. I waited.

Almost four minutes later, she came back carrying a glass of water and an industrial-looking phone with a long cable trailing behind it. She sat down at the far side of her bed, facing away from the camera, tapped numbers into the phone and put it to her ear.

I could only see the back of Imogen's neck and jawline, but it was enough to tell she was talking to someone, speaking into the phone and then listening. After a little while, she turned, looked straight at the camera in surprise and silently mouthed, *Jesus, how many?*

She listened for a second. Her mouth made all the shapes for ... *whoa. Hang on, I'll write that one down.* Cradling the phone in the crook of her neck, she reached and made a note. *Nine, four, five,* her lips were saying, then she turned away from the camera again so I couldn't see what came next. Almost straight away, she turned back and I caught ... *now I'm thinking about it.*

I lifted up my hand to the monitor, the palm flat.

Imogen waved at the camera. Her lips made, *I'm waving at them.*

She listened, still waving, and replied, *I'm doing it right now.*

I waved at the screen.

Imogen smiled.

You're lovely, she said to the camera without a sound, then she turned away and carried on talking into the phone.

'Yes, I am,' I said to myself.

Before very much longer, Imogen-on-the-screen finished her call. My wife took the phone from her ear and pressed a button. With only a glance towards the camera, she stood up and walked out of shot.

· II ·

Lockwood of the *Tribune*

And so to my account, which truly begins with the arrival of a letter. In light of the Great Exhibition and this keen public interest in all things mechanical, I was to find myself approached in writing by a Mr Isaac Lockwood of the *New York Tribune*, a newspaper at that time running regular reports from the crowded machine halls of that great glass palace just previously described.

Neglecting formalities for the preservation of ink and time, the letter read as follows:

Sir,

I write to you today on account of a most peculiar undertaking having lately come to our attention.

In recent weeks we have been furnished with no small number of communiqués, and each of these detailing the construction in New England of a most curious and improbable mechanical device by one Mr. John Maxwell Spear, spiritualist.

Although I may state quite categorically that the machine in question has no hope to function — indeed, that it shall produce nothing at all save embarrassment and a considerable financial impediment is the cast-iron belief of all here at the Tribune — it is nevertheless our intent to commission a body of writing upon the thing and its architects, and in this way, provide our readers with an amusing counterpoint to our many articles on genuine mechanical endeavor.

If you should have a mind to undertake such a work for us, I'd be much obliged of a response by return.

I was half standing to leave the room, when she suddenly reappeared.

Close up this time, she leaned in towards the lens, smiled and mouthed *go out*.

Then she was gone.

By anyone's reckoning, it had become time to get dressed. Wandering through to the kitchen, I balanced my mug on top of all the other pots, then poked around inside the washing machine. Nothing helpful.

I looked around the kitchen, taking in the pile of dirty plates in the sink, the remains of cooking, curry pots, jammy bread crusts, fish-and-chip papers, baked beans tins, empty Pot Noodles.

Written on the fridge door in multicoloured magnetic plastic letters, there's an old message from Imogen:

St y Alert: Entropy Wants th s Kitch n.

Just before we went to bed, I'd plucked the 'a', the 'i' and the 'e' out of their respective words and arranged them at the bottom of the door, making it look like they'd fallen down in a heap. I remember lying in bed the next morning and hearing her call out *oh, how we laughed* as she opened the door to get milk for her tea.

Do you know why time works the way it does?

It's all down to entropy.

To see why, I'll need you to imagine that my kitchen is the universe. Or, if you'd rather, you can imagine your own kitchen is the universe instead – it doesn't really matter. But pick a kitchen.

So. There are only a relatively small number of ways for this kitchen to be tidy. Only a relatively small number of ways for the boxes to fit in the cupboards, the bowls to fit on top of the plates, the bottles to stand up in the fridge door, all those things. Relatively small, I mean, against the countless billions of different ways the same kitchen can be messy. If the Rice Krispies are *anywhere else* but in the Rice Krispies box, the kitchen is messy. If the milk bottle is *anywhere else* but standing upright in the fridge (with the milk still closed? The Winter Garden burned down? The pleasure boats all run aground? Not at all! So what pilgrimage is this, what compels this sea of humanity to this great glass illuminatory in the park?

Why, what else but the machines!

Over one hundred thousand Americans, myself included, have thus far attended the Great Exhibition, and yet more, arriving from all states and stations, build on that lofty tally daily.

Squeeze through the marvelling crowds as best as you are able, and there on display may be discovered a vast spectrum of new mechanical devisements: from Mr Burt's typewriter to the latest refinements to Mr Faraday's electrical dynamo, from the great mechanical loomings of the cloth trade, to a machine for sewing devised by one Mr Singer, and even to Mr Walter Hurt's ingenious 'safety pin'.[1] Oh so thoroughly do the mechanical achievements of today outstrip those of yesterday, that upon wandering those great glass halls and avenues, even the well informed and mechanically minded shall repeatedly find themselves with no option but to revise and revise again their understanding of mechanical principle and application. Indeed, even they may quick find the phrase 'whatever next' becoming a wide-eyed refrain.

Though much of what follows may prove disturbing or incredible (or some combination thereof, as it was, and still remains, for me), the only indulgence I beg for now is that we might at least agree upon the following: this is a world where a telegraph message may travel a thousand miles in an instant, where many tons of goods are transported across our great nation under the power of compressed steam and where men may be carried aloft in vast balloons to sail the currents of the air.

Already, this is a time of marvels.

---

1 For those unable to attend the exhibition, I would suggest Horace Greeley's book *Art and Industry* by way of thorough and illuminative compensation.

in it), the kitchen is messy. If one or more of the bowls are on the worktop, on the floor, on the table, smashed in the sink, *anywhere else* but stacked neatly away in a cupboard – then the kitchen is messy. You get the idea. Messy is more likely than tidy. But in order to see the full picture, we need to see how much more likely messy really is.

To get a good look at the massive improbability of tidiness compared to messiness, let's empty all the plates, cups, bowls, food, drinks, cutlery, cloths, sponges, towels, powders and cleaning products out of our kitchen, then put just a single item back in – the butter. Now. Let's say the butter can be in maybe five hundred different places around the empty kitchen that we would call 'messy' and maybe five places we would call 'neat'. So there's a one in a hundred chance that the butter is somewhere we would describe as neat. Let's move up to two items – the butter and a butter knife. Assuming the butter knife has the same number of messy and neat positions as the butter, the chances of them *both* being in a place we could call 'neat' goes from one in one hundred to one in ten thousand. At three items – the butter, the butter knife and a slice of bread – the chances of all three being in a place we would describe as 'neat' are now one in a million.

Already, *messy* is a million times more likely than *neat* – and this in a kitchen with only three objects. Three. Now go ahead and put back all the many hundreds of other objects into your ordinary, everyday kitchen and you start to get some sense of just how very unlikely *neat* is versus *messy*.

Of course, the universe is a lot bigger than a kitchen, and made of a lot more things. And those things are made up of things, which are also made up of things, all the way down to a basic, atomic level. There's also an added complication – the universe does not have the benefit of someone coming along once in a while to tidy the place up. Taken together, what all this means is that when a thing – the butter, the butter knife, a brick, a stone, a screw, an atom – happens to move to a new position somewhere in the universe, it is a countless

Now. Given the singular nature of this tale of mine, and the unenviable position in which I find myself with regard to its telling, it would be a very good thing, I think, if we were to begin our journey together on somewhat firmer ground, in the hope that we might find ourselves a little common footing and, if you are in a gracious mood, I might yet be awarded some modicum of your trust. To this end, let's hold back our visit to dark and misty Lynn a while, and turn our gaze instead to the clear glow of a grand, well-accepted and thoroughly modern belief, a belief carried by me, as it is carried by many modern peoples, and not simply those of education or privilege, but by all who have eyes to see and ears to hear the truth of it. The belief I refer to, is this:

THESE ARE MOMENTOUS TIMES, BOTH FOR THE
UNITED STATES OF AMERICA, AND FOR THE WORLD.

We have been given to live at the dawn of a great age of invention and industry. This is, and increasingly shall be, a time of widespread upheaval, swift change and accelerated progress unlike any seen before, and, though great aspects of this change shall doubtless socially and culturally manifest, it takes neither a greatly wise nor insightful man to proclaim that the driving heart, the steaming, smoking, clanking, clattering, belching heart of this new age, is the machine.

Oh, how deep America's fascination with gear and pulley, with steam and valve!

Look now – there is New York's Crystal Palace, proud New World child of Old London's original, and open almost a year. Doesn't she gleam and shine some? And the crowds! So many people, and – look – still more coming all the while; each hour brings a fresh procession, a new column of eager visitors, so many that when the sun strikes the palace just so, then – yes – the grounds come full a-bloom in a spring meadow of opening parasols!

But what do they all here, this army of squeeze-eyed fellows, hat-tipped gents and ladies with their shades? Are the promenades billion times more likely to move into a 'messy' position than into a 'neat' position.

Without someone around to tidy and fix it up from time to time, the kitchen and the house around it would progressively get messier until the whole thing fell apart. Everyone knows this happens to old houses because they've seen it – uncared-for structures fall into disrepair and collapse. This is common sense. *Why* it happens is simple: because there are countless billions of messy situations for the things that make up the house – bricks, beams, nails, lintels, joists and all their atoms – to be in, *any* of which would cause it to fall down, and only a handful of neat situations where the house stays standing.

This ever-increasing messiness is called *entropy*.

But here's the thing. We wouldn't say 'the house fell down due to the gradual movement of its component elements from a low-entropy state to a high-entropy state' (at least, most people wouldn't). We'd say – the house fell down *over time*.

Entropy is what drives time forwards, and only forwards. It's the reason you can't un-stir the milk from your coffee, the reason you can smash but can't un-smash a glass vase, and the reason that if you did smash a glass vase then fixed it really well, somebody might say, 'It looks almost as good as new.' People get old and die *over time*, things get lost *over time*, stuff gets broken *over time*. Time as we know it is simply the inevitable sliding of all things from order towards disorder and meaninglessness.

This all seems a little bleak, I realize, but these basic principles need to be added in here, and added in near the beginning, in order that they're available later, when we need them.

It's also important, and maybe even heartening, to say that there is a single speck of scientific fairy dust to be found among the gloom and collapse of the Laws of Entropy: time is driven by probability, and probability alone.

What I mean is, there are no laws of physics specifically saying that a kitchen can't shift from a 'messy' to a 'neat' state by sheer chance. It's just that such a shift is so astonishingly, incredibly, mind-of day most amicably together, and you would, in all likelihood, leave with a good enough impression of me, or certainly no very bad one, for I am all for the meeting and the getting by with people as a general rule; yes, though all of this is true, it is nevertheless an immutable and inescapable fact that my position, one might say obligation, as historian in this matter is a deeply unfortunate thing.

To this, we might only suppose that the three grand old ladies of the cotton mill, the Fates – dour and industrious by all reputation – must, in actuality, possess a humour of the blackest sort. For how else might it be that an *author*, and an author such as I – a man whose early biographical tales were oft unfairly accused of whimsy or romance, and whose later romantic efforts dismissed entirely – yes, how else might it be, I say, that such an author might find himself sole witness to events as remarkable and disturbing as those which occurred in the town of Lynn, Massachusetts, in the Year of Our Lord 1854?

I come before you now, a man granted a solitary peep at things hitherto unguessed, yet so nearly am I bound by Providence that all testimony in the matter shall likely come to naught. But what else to do but lay out my story regardless? What else now but to hope for a stranger's curiosity, maybe even understanding? For who ain't been made a joke of by them three old Spinning Jennies, one way or another? You tell me that.

And so – if it happens that you have chanced upon these words of mine as a bundle of old pages in an attic or writing bureau; or else – if my luck's come a little better – as a book in one of those out-of-the-way places in Boston or New York that might afford it a nook of shelf, and, in time, a dusty nightshirt and a spiderweb cap too; well, however it is that you've come to look over this page – do not return it to its pile, or its box, or its shelf, but grant me the small enough indulgence of reading on, at least a little while longer. For just as the moon passing through the heavens makes bewitched courtiers of the trailing tides, so – I am now sure – there are far stranger bodies in motion beyond the human sphere, and their pulls and wants can neither be guessed at nor measured.

It could be that this story has chosen you.

bogglingly, unimaginably unlikely, compared to 'neat' to 'messy', that for practical purposes we say it doesn't ever happen. But it *could*. You'd have to watch countless billions of kitchens for a countless billions of years to glimpse even the beginnings of something like that, but – it could happen, in theory.

How would that feel?

I have to imagine that the overwhelming sensation would be that something magical and impossible had happened, a visit from the fairies. But also, wouldn't there be a nagging sense that you had somehow travelled back in time?

Cleaning the kitchen in a kind of trance, entirely absorbed in the act of ordering and restoring, I took a deep satisfaction in matching up the plates, cups and pans, and in vanishing each set behind cupboard doors and drawer fronts. I'd just finished mopping the floor and was pouring grey water into the toilet bowl when there was a knock on the front door.

Danni Greyson from the flat upstairs stood in the doorway, her arms full of post. All of it for us, and all of it delivered to her flat by mistake at various times over the last three weeks.

I knew the letter was from Andrew the moment I saw it.

A small, simple, handwritten envelope buried in a printed, logoed and plastic-windowed heap – a singular item among automatically generated statements and notifications. My name and address written in small, neat black capitals, finished with a perfectly aligned first-class stamp.

I picked it up and turned it over a few times. The letter surprised me. I hadn't heard from Black since before Imogen and I were married, and I suppose that – without thinking very much about it – I'd come around to the idea that I probably wouldn't hear from him ever again. There hadn't been any falling-out to speak of, but things had become difficult for us – difficult for Andrew especially – and time gradually swamped the little boat of our friendship, until one morning I realized it had sunk from view altogether. The world

Spring
March–May 1854

1

Declaration

The tale I set down in these pages is truth from first word to last, though few may happily be convinced of its veracity, should it ever find print.

Indeed, it is well past possible and nearer a certain, bankable thing, that I myself would credit not a sentence, point or period of what is to follow, if I were in your place, reader, and you were in mine. But – since each man gets his pick of only one place, and since the good Lord has never granted a swap (at least, none that I ever heard of) – it is to nowhere but the witness stand for me now, and to the judge's seat for you. I can only say again, Your Honour, all that is to be reported herein, however outlandish, however distressing, both in actuality and by implication, is relayed with the utmost solemnity and faithfulness. It is all true. That, and I would trade seats with you in a moment if I were but able.

Onward then – with role firmly fixed and no possibility of retreat, I'll come straight at the barb, the catch, the stumbling step that shall make this most difficult task of mine a nigh-impossible one. For, having no sooner met, and leaving no time for you and I to become more comfortably acquainted or better settled in our respective roles, I find that I must straightway risk whatever small trust as you might have in this account of mine, for having most sincerely pledged that you'll hear nothing but the truth from me, I'm at once beholden to give you the very best reason to doubt it.

Though I am, I should like to think, a trustworthy enough fellow; though I have never stolen and do not fight, at least not as a rule; though I am neither gambler nor cheat; though if we happened to meet in the wider world, I've no reason to doubt that we could pass the time moved on, and what was once a living thing in the present tense became quietly pressed flat into the past.

The postmark told me that the letter had been sent three weeks earlier. I ripped it open, feeling a stab of anxiety. Small talk, pleasantries, just saying hello – it wasn't Andrew Black. This meant that something was happening, or had happened, and I was only finding out about it now.

Inside, a single Polaroid picture and a small folded note.

The picture showed a black spherical object, resting on what I took to be Andrew's workbench. He'd placed a ruler next to the sphere, and though the Polaroid was a little fuzzy, it seemed to indicate the object's diameter at around ten centimetres. I struggled to make out much more, partly because, as I say, the Polaroid was slightly blurred, but also because the sphere was so utterly black. The most diffuse crescent moon of light touching the thing's left side, and an equally faint shadow on the bench to its right, were all that gave it away as three-dimensional.

The object – whatever it was – looked as black as a hole.

And it bothered me.

I don't write that lightly. I've thought long and hard about whether to include my reaction here at all, but the facts are the facts. I didn't like the picture when I first saw it, and I don't like it now. As to whether we should set any store by this, whether it means anything – that's another matter altogether.

I put down the Polaroid and unfolded Andrew's note.

Only nine words, each written in the same precise, practised hand:

Philip,
What do you think this is?
Andrew Black

Steven Hall

THE END OF
ENDINGS

GRANTA

GRANTA

A WORLD INTACT

Adam Foulds

ADAM
FOULDS

1974

Adam Foulds is a poet and novelist from
London. He has published two novels,
The Truth About These Strange Times and
The Quickening Maze, and *The Broken
Word*, a narrative poem set during the
Mau Mau uprising in Kenya at the end
of British imperial rule. He is the recipient
of a number of literary awards, including
the *Sunday Times* Young Writer of the
Year, the Costa Poetry Prize, the Somerset
Maugham Award, the South Bank Show
Prize for Literature, the Encore Award and
the European Union Prize for Literature.
The Quickening Maze was shortlisted for
the Man Booker Prize in 2009. He was
made a Fellow of the Royal Society of
Literature in 2010. 'A World Intact' is an
excerpt from his new novel, *In the Wolf's
Mouth*, published in 2014 by Jonathan
Cape in the UK and Farrar, Straus and
Giroux in the US.

A nd here was a world intact, like a dream of his childhood. After years of war, not a sign except the intriguing sight from the train of numerous unfamiliar young women in the fields, land girls brought in presumably from Birmingham or Coventry, silently labouring. In London there were shelters, sandbags, militarized parks, blacked-out windows and gun emplacements. Here, nothing. Trees washed through with sunshine and birdsong, the smell of the ground breathing upwards through the thick moist heat. As Will started out, his feet remembered the exact rise and fall of the walk home from the station. How perfectly his senses interlocked with the place. He knew that when he rounded this corner, yes, here it was, the peppery smell of the river before he could see it. He could picture the dim bed of round stones, the swaying weeds, the surface braided with currents. *A full-fed river.* Behind his left shoulder, away up for a couple of miles, was the rippled shape of an iron-age hill fort where he'd played as a child, battling his brother down from the top. Everything here was still clean and fresh and in place, the countryside sincere and vigorous. It was as though he were walking through the first chapter of a future biography, with his kitbag on his shoulder.

Will decided to avoid the village and headed down through the wood. According to his father this was a recent planting, maybe only a hundred years old. It was still coppiced, which gave this section a peculiar regularity. The evenly spaced, slender trees always made him think of stage scenery. When the wind died the coppice had an indoor quiet, the quiet of an empty room.

'And where do you think you're going?'

Startled, Will turned to see his younger brother, Ed, wearing his hunting waistcoat, his open shotgun hooked over his shoulder.

'For God's sake, Ed.'

Ed smiled. They shook hands.

'You didn't hear me, did you?'

'Can't say that I did.'

'Makes a fellow wonder who's been in training and who hasn't.'

Ed was much given to stealth. He loved hunting and had a

straightforward aptitude for it that Will sometimes envied, often mocked. Ed would appear suddenly in a room, quiet in his body, his senses splayed around him, then smile and go out again without saying anything. Father had been in a way similar, although sharply clever, a quiet grammarian indoors but a sportsman outside, hard-riding, red-faced, breathing great volumes of air, his hair sweated to his head. A mere schoolmaster, he'd been invited to join the hunt after the last war when he'd returned with a medal, with *the* medal. It was outdoors that Will was allowed glimpses of what he took to be his father's mysterious heroism, that undiscussable subject. There was a kind of calculated rampaging, his movements very hard and linear. Ed had a different quality. He was less reflective, less troubled by thought, simply a live moving part of the world of trees and creatures and water. Will wasn't sure how he himself would be described. He wasn't a natural sportsman although he was efficient and strong enough. He always noticed the moment of commitment, the threshold he had to cross between thought and action, his mind instigating his body. He didn't think he should notice; it made him feel slightly fraudulent. His movements were effective but too invented. He was playing a part.

'Why aren't you fishing?' Will asked. 'I can't imagine there's anything left to shoot. I thought the woods would be stripped bare with rationing having everyone setting snares and popping their shotguns.'

'Ah, but for them wot knows the old woods like I does.' Ed opened his waistcoat to show, hanging inside its left panel, a rabbit, teeth bared and eyes half closed. 'And,' he said, reaching into his front pocket and carefully lifting out a bird, 'there's this.'

'You little tinker. A woodcock. When everyone else is working on the nth permutation of bully beef.'

Will took the bird from his brother. Its head, weighted by its long, narrow bill, hung over his fingers on the loose cord of its neck. The small body was warm, the plumage still shining with the airy burnish of a living bird. Will's senses were lighting up, home again after weeks of training grounds, weapons drills, diagrams, distempered huts and dismal food. 'That's a very generous homecoming gift,' Will said.

'It isn't any such thing,' Ed said and took the bird back, refolding its wings to fit into his pocket.

'All for you then. You going to sell it on the black market?'

'No.' Ed was impatient. 'I'll give it to Mother. You'll probably eat it tonight in a pie.'

'Did she send you out to meet me?'

'Er, no. How could she if we didn't know you were coming?'

They walked out of the wood, the shadowy trees gently breaking apart to reveal the river, there with the sun on its back, the fields glowing beyond.

'Yes, yes.'

'Pleased to be home?'

'I won't be back for long.'

They turned away from the riverside and up a rise to come out into the lane. Either side of them as they walked back to the house the hedgerows were lively with small birds, the verges starred with the blues and purples of wild flowers.

As they entered the front garden, Will called out, 'Ma! Mother!' They rounded the side of the house and came in through the back door. Immediately he was inside, dropping his kitbag down beside the boots and walking sticks and umbrellas, Will felt himself claimed by the familiar aroma of the place. It was a combination of many things – carpets, dogs, wood, the garden, the damp in the cellar – too subtle to be separated. It was more a mood, a life. It contained his school holidays, his father's presence, his father's death. A world intact.

'Oh, Mother! Where art thou?'

He found her in the kitchen, leaning over the table with palms pressed flat either side of the newspaper.

'Surprise.'

'Oh, crikey, yes. It's this one. Here he is. William of Arabia,' she said, lifting her spectacles and fixing them on top of her head before reaching her arms towards him, and waiting. That annoyed him, the quick flash accusation of emulation. As though T.E. Lawrence were the only man in the world to learn Arabic, to be a soldier. He walked towards her and she took hold of his shoulders with hands that were scalded red. She must have just been busy in the sink. He looked into that emotional round face, her eyes moist and diffuse with poor sight, her heavy cheeks hanging. She pulled him forwards over the long incline of her bosom and kissed him vividly on the temple.

'So you've survived training?'

'Outwardly I seem fine, don't I?'

'Near enough.'

'Some chaps broke significant limbs with the motorcycle training.'

'Motorcycles?'

Hearing the voices or scenting him, perhaps, the dogs came shambling in. Will bent to Rex first; the King Charles spaniel squirmed down onto its haunches and whisked its feathery tail. He rubbed the soft upholstery of its ears. Will had a voice he used for the dogs: clear, enthusiastic and mocking. 'Look at you. Look at you. Yes, indeed.' Teddy, the black Labrador, his large mouth loosely open, panted and bumped against Will's legs, trying to insinuate his sleek head under Will's hands. 'Oh, and you. Yes, boy. Yes, Teddy. Oh, I've missed you too. Yes, I have. I have.' Squatting down now, Will combed his fingers through the rich, oily fur at Teddy's nape. He felt the upswept rough warm wetness of Teddy's tongue against his chin.

'Don't overexcite them, darling.'

'They're dogs, Mother. They overexcite themselves. You do. Yes, you do. Pea-brained beasts. They're just pleased to see me again.'

'Broken limbs on motorcycles, you said.'

'Off motorcycles. Up a hill as fast as you can, whizz round then down again likewise. They disconnected the brakes to make it more difficult. Intelligence, Mother. Not your usual soldiering.'

'No. It doesn't sound like it . . . Ah, would you look at that?'

Will glanced up to see Ed laying his kills on the table, the woodcock's wings dropping open, the rabbit stiff and grimacing.

'Number two son brings great treasure.'

The predicted pie appeared for supper. The fine dark meat of the woodcock, with its flavours of dusk and decaying leaves, and the clean tang of the rabbit were both impaired by a horrible margarine pastry. They ate economically, without candles or lights. Through the windows floated a soft lilac light. It hung in the room, almost as heavy as mist, and made the striped wallpaper glow with dreamy colour. Will realized how tired he was at the end of his training, at the end of a lot of things, and posted now, although Mother was yet to ask, off to the war finally. She spoke as though overhearing his thoughts.

'You know I had hope the war would have finished before you got dragged into it.'

Will sat up. He was horrified. 'But you wouldn't want a fellow to miss his chance.'

'I think I could cope.'

'A man wants to fight,' Ed said solemnly.

Will laughed. 'And how would you know?'

'Boys.'

'Look, it's my duty, isn't it? It needs to be done. It's what Father would have wanted.'

'I'm not so sure you know that about him,' Will's mother said quietly.

'Why wouldn't he?'

'You're his son.'

'Precisely. I know that. All somewhat academic, anyway. I've been posted.'

His mother looked up at him, her pale eyes watery, a rose flush blotching her neck. 'Have you?'

'Yes.'

'And?'

It wasn't what he'd wanted. It was not what he deserved, with his Arabic and ambition. He had been warned by one NCO during training, a sly and adroit cockney who seemed to be having the war he wanted, who had friends in the kitchens and spat at the end of definitive statements. 'You need blue eyes,' he'd said, smoking a conical hand-rolled cigarette, 'to get a commission. Take my word for it. You'll end up in the dustbin with the rest of them.' There was a look for the officer class and Will didn't have it. Five feet nine inches tall, he had dark hair and dark eyes, a handsomely groomed round head and a low centre of gravity. This was unfair. In his soul he was tall, a traveller, a keen, wind-honed figure.

The man who sat at the last in a sequence of desks Will had visited, the man who decided Will's future, considered the paperwork through small spectacles and made quiet grunting noises like a rootling pig. Finally he looked up. 'All very commendable. Languages. I'm putting you in for the Field Security Services.' The dustbin.

Will pinched the bridge of his nose. 'If I may, sir, I was hoping for the Special Operations Executive, you see, I –'

'The duty to which we are assigned', the man interrupted, as though finishing Will's sentence, 'is where we must do our duty.'

And so Will had humiliated himself precisely in the way he'd told himself he never would.

'Sir?'

'What?'

'Sir, I'm not sure I should mention this, but my father, you see, in the last war . . .'

'Yes?'

'Distinguished himself. He was awarded the VC. I –'

'Oh, excellent. Jolly good. You should try to be like him.'

The personnel of the unit Will was assigned to was like a saloon-bar joke. *An Englishman, a Welshman and a Jew* . . . And lo and behold his commanding officer was tall, a wistful blond, younger than Will by a couple of years, an Oxford rowing Blue, perfectly friendly, unobjectionable and unprepared. To Will he said, 'And suddenly we're soldiers. All a bit unreal, isn't it?' But they weren't soldiers. Not really. The only danger Will could perceive with the FSS was spending all of the remainder of the war guarding an English airbase doing nothing at all.

Will considered how much of this to tell his mother as she asked again, 'And?'

'You needn't look so worried. I'm not going far just yet. Port protection sort of thing. Security.'

'Isn't that police work?'

Ed, leaning low over his plate, looked across to see Will's reaction.

Will felt an urge to throw his drink in his mother's face. He pictured the water lashing out from his cup and striking. It was a thought he had now and then, in different company, just picking up his cup and hurling its contents into the face of whoever it was who had provoked him. He wouldn't ever do it but in those moments the vision of it was so clear and fulfilling that he had to resist. 'It is what I've been assigned to do until I am posted abroad.'

After supper they listened to the wireless, angling their heads just a little towards its glow and chiselled voices, their eyes vaguely involved in the carpet or what their hands were doing. Often Mother was sewing, her needle rising and sinking. The dogs slouched around the room, lay down and got up again. Will called Teddy to him and patted his smooth, hard head. The wireless made Will crave action and involvement with a feeling akin to hunger, an emptiness and readiness in his tightened nerves. He was very alert. He'd had years of this now: battle reports, a burning, piecemeal geography of the war, its leaders and chaos, victories and defeats. And propaganda, of course. You couldn't really know what was going on, but Will, with his intelligence, deep reading and cynicism, made shrewd guesses. The reports on the wireless were so charged with possibility and vibrant with what was never said or admitted about the battles, the terror and exaltation. The mere cheering of victories didn't come close to what Will supposed the reality must be. The war was large and endlessly turbulent. There was room in it for someone like Will, for his kind of independent mastery. He could make elegant and decisive shapes out of the shapelessness. He wanted in. *By it and with it and on it and in it.*

When the news reports gave way to dance-band music, Will got up to go into his father's study.

The room had its own stillness. The book spines. The vertical pleats of the heavy blue curtains. The solidity of the desk with its paperweight, mother-of-pearl-handled paperknife, the blotter and wooden trays. Behind Will, the sofa on which his father had died.

Somewhere in a drawer in this room was the medal his father never took out. The room's composed silence was like the silence of Will's father himself. He had always raised a hand halfway to his mouth and coughed quietly before he spoke, preparing himself to do so. Sometimes Will felt as though the empty study might do the same, clear its throat delicately and say something neat and short, something devastating. A terrifying rupture of his reserve had presaged Will's father's death. He'd come back from the hunt after being unhorsed. He'd landed badly, apparently, and sat down to dinner looking pale with a deep red scratch trenching his cheek just beside his nose. There was a small notch taken out of his forehead. Ed asked what had happened.

'What do you bloody well think happened?'

'Darling . . .'

'What are you leaping into the breach for? Damnfool question. And I have a pounding headache. Christ.'

He'd leaned over and vomited onto the carpet right there at his feet. They all sat there waiting through the noise, the wrenching up out of his body. Teddy ambled over afterwards and sniffed at it.

Father sat up straight and gulped water. 'Don't just all gawk at me like that. I'm obviously ill. I'm going to lie down.'

He stood up, swayed and stalked out to his study. Half an hour later, Will's mother found him dead on the study sofa. Dead and gone having hardly ever said anything at all to his sons.

Will read along a shelf. Something fine and sharply enhancing of his intellect. Lucretius on the nature of the universe? Why not? It had that fine brilliance and fearlessness as a description of the world, bright bodies in space. Distinctive also. Let the other fellows always be quoting Cicero and Virgil. And reading Latin would keep his mind active. Will would have this and his Arabic poetry. The Lucretius was a squarish, green-covered volume. Inside he saw his father's pasted ex libris, signed with his fastidious, vertical pen strokes. *Henry Walker, 1921.*

He began reading it that night under the low, sloping ceiling of his boyhood bedroom, intending to remember and look up the words he didn't know.

In the morning he drew the curtains. A neutral light, white and even. There was none of the gorgeous lustre of the previous day and this was almost a relief. The world was a realer place, more practical. Then he noticed in the glass of one pane of the window the twist of bubbles. He'd forgotten about them, or felt as though he had but if asked at any time he could have sketched their exact distribution, rising up through the clearness. They had been a small magic of his childhood, catching the light differently, sparkling a little. As a child he'd almost felt them inside himself, a sensation of excitement spiralling up in his breast. And they connected his room to the river, as though his windows were formed from panels of the river's surface. That river there, brown and steady, rather workmanlike today. The bubbles in the window filled him, even before he'd gone, with a grand feeling of nostalgia for this house and the landscape and his childhood. It was poetical at first but gradually he became aware of a dark outline around that emotion, a constriction, and realized that it was fear. His life, unexciting as it may have been so far, was still a detailed, complicated thing. In its own way, for him, it was precious. It would be a lot to lose.

He turned away and examined the small bookshelf in this room, painted with creamy white paint that showed the tracks of the brush. *How to . . . Boy's Adventures . . . Alice. The Wind in the Willows.* Ah, yes. He realized that it had been in his mind since his return. *A full-fed river. By it and with it and on it and in it.* He'd loved that book as a boy, with its small engrossing illustrations, darkly cross-hatched and tangled-looking like nests holding the forms of the characters. Sentimental, of course, but he decided to take it too.

At breakfast Will told his mother that he was off that day to his posting and she fell silent. They chewed through their rough and watery meal of national loaf and powdered eggs – here, in the countryside, they were eating powdered eggs – and after that she disappeared. Will was used to interpreting her silences, particularly those of the stricken widow period, and he knew what she was saying. A stiff, stoical farewell was all that was required, but instead she would force him to think of her, helpless and alone in this pristine place in the middle of England that the dark, droning bombers had swept over on their way to flatten Coventry. She would be here all the while, imagining him blown to bits. This thought demanded that he imagine his death also and that was entirely pointless and unhelpful. Typical. Her determination never to make a scene often resulted in strange, cramped, unresolved situations like this. Useless woman. A boy going away to war without a goodbye from his mother.

Ed walked with Will towards the station, putting on a flat cap when light rain began to fall from the low unbroken clouds. The dismal, factual light looked to Will like something issued by the War Office. They walked together through the quiet coppice with the dogs snuffing at the ground and there they parted with a firm handshake. Will thought that Ed may have held on to his hand a fraction longer than necessary and said, 'Let's not be silly about this. I'll probably be back before you know it. There'll probably be some administrative foul-up resulting in delays.'

Ed put his hands in his pockets and called the dogs. 'It's all delays for me.'

Will smiled. 'Nice for Mother, though.'

Ed hitched an eyebrow, saying nothing, then called the dogs again. They gathered, breathing, at his feet. Will petted them a final time and Ed turned to go, the dogs following after in a wide swirling train. Will watched his brother vanishing and appearing through the trees, slightly hunched, the rain pattering on his cap. Ed was heading home, sinking back into his place. Then Will turned himself and headed towards the station, out into the world and the war, and he was glad to be going. ■

IF YOU ARE OVER 40 and feeling aggravated by all this youthful talent, turn to Professor David Bainbridge for consolatio he can prove that the middle-aged human is the very pinnacle of the species

'A welcome corrective to the widely held notion that being middle-aged is ghastly'
India Knight, *Sunday Times*

Portobello
www.portobellobooks.com

THE BEST OF YOUNG BRITISH NOVELISTS

Nadav Kander

I.

8.

9.

13.

16.

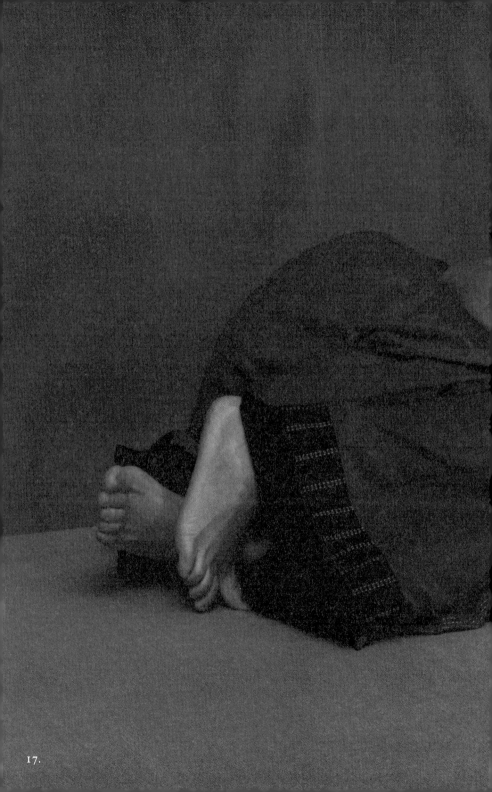

20.

1. ADAM THIRLWELL

2. KAMILA SHAMSIE

3. EVIE WYLD

4. ROSS RAISIN

5. BENJAMIN MARKOVITS

6. NAOMI ALDERMAN

7. NED BEAUMAN

8. JENNI FAGAN

9. DAVID SZALAY

10. TAIYE SELASI

11. JOANNA KAVENNA

12. ADAM FOULDS

13. NADIFA MOHAMED

14. XIAOLU GUO

15. STEVEN HALL

16. SUNJEEV SAHOTA

17. TAHMIMA ANAM

18. HELEN OYEYEMI

19. ZADIE SMITH
(based on a photograph © Dominique Nabokov)

20. SARAH HALL

Nadav Kander

Nadav Kander grew up in South Africa. He began photographing at an early age and moved to London in 1982. In 2009, he was awarded the Prix Pictet for his *Yangtze – The Long River* series, and he was also named International Photographer of the Year at the 7th Annual Lucie Awards. His work is featured in several public collections including the Photographers' Gallery, London, the Franks-Suss Collection and the V&A Museum. He has exhibited internationally at venues including the Musée de l'Elysée, Lausanne, the Museum of Photographic Arts, San Diego, the Museum of Applied Art, Cologne, the Kennedys Museum, Berlin, the Photographers' Gallery, London, the Palais de Tokyo, Paris and the Herzliya Museum of Contemporary Art, Israel. A new series of photographs, *Bodies. 6 Women, 1 Man*, is published as a monograph by Hatje Cantz in 2013. Kander lives in London with his wife and children.

GRANTA

THE MAGAZINE OF NEW WRITING

SUBSCRIPTION FORM FOR US, CANADA AND LATIN AMERICA

Yes, I would like to take out a subscription to *Granta*.

GUARANTEE: If I am ever dissatisfied with my *Granta* subscription, I will simply notify you, and you will send me a complete refund or credit my credit card, as applicable, for all un-mailed issues.

YOUR DETAILS

MR / MISS / MRS / DR ....

NAME ....

ADDRESS ....

....

CITY.. STATE ....

ZIP CODE .... COUNTRY ....

EMAIL ....

☐ Please check this box if you do not wish to receive special offers from *Granta*

☐ Please check this box if you do not wish to receive offers from organizations selected by *Granta*

YOUR PAYMENT DETAILS

1 year subscription: ☐ US: $48.00 ☐ Canada: $56.00 ☐ Latin America: $68.00

3 year subscription: ☐ US: $120.00 ☐ Canada: $144.00 ☐ Latin America: $180.00

Enclosed is my check for $ _____ made payable to *Granta*.

Please charge my: ☐ Visa ☐ MasterCard ☐ Amex

Card No. ☐☐☐☐☐☐☐☐☐☐☐☐☐☐☐☐

Exp. ☐☐☐☐

Security Code ☐☐☐☐☐☐

SIGNATURE .... DATE ....

Please mail this order form with your payment instructions to:

Granta Publications
PO Box 359
Congers NY 10920-0359

Or call 845-267-3031
Or visit GRANTA.COM for details

Source code: BUS123PM

GRANTA

YOU DON'T HAVE TO LIVE LIKE THIS

Benjamin Markovits

BENJAMIN MARKOVITS

1973

Benjamin Markovits grew up in London, Oxford, Texas and Berlin. He left an unpromising career as a professional basketball player to study the Romantics. Since then he has taught high-school English, worked at a left-wing cultural magazine and published six novels, including a trilogy on the life of Lord Byron. Markovits has lived in London since 2000 and is married, with a daughter and a son. He teaches creative writing at Royal Holloway, University of London. 'You Don't Have to Live Like This' is an excerpt from his new novel, about a group of university friends who get involved in a scheme to regenerate Detroit.

Robert had a room on the same floor as mine freshman year, but I noticed him for the first time in the dining-hall lunch line. I was waiting for a plateful of baked ziti when he struck up a conversation with the guy behind the counter – this tall, kind of rickety black guy, maybe fifty years old, who wore a dirty white hat and an apron with his named stitched onto it. Robert introduced himself, like a gentleman.

'Willy,' he said. 'Is that your name? Do you mind if I call you Willy?'

'Go right ahead,' Willy told him, and Robert stuck out his hand.

'Robert James.'

He had to reach over the food counter and Willy, who clearly felt uncomfortable, wiped his dirty sweaty palm on his apron for about a minute before taking it. I remember thinking, it doesn't matter if you call him Willy, he'll still call you Sir.

The reason we started hanging out is that Robert saw the squash racket sticking out of my backpack. In those first sunny weeks of September, I used to bounce a ball everywhere around campus – to and from the library and dining hall, sometimes on the way to class. As if to say, none of this big shot Ivy League bullshit means much to *me*.

When Robert couldn't sleep, he'd knock on my door. (I never turned the lights off till two in the morning.) There was something touching about the way he hunted for company in the small hours. Sometimes I wondered if he couldn't sleep without a girl in his bed. Even freshman year he had plenty of girls.

'Hey, Marny, Marny,' he said and tapped at my door. (Marnier's my last name, pronounced in the French fashion, which my college friends refused to do. So I got called Marny. Greg is my Christian name, the name I was known by in high school, but at Yale only my professors used it.) 'You up, guy? Want a game?'

There were steam tunnels in the college basement that opened out onto squash courts. Nobody could hear us. The temperature, even in winter, topped ninety degrees, and we could play as late as we liked.

'How come you don't sweat?' he asked me once.

'Because I'm not running.'

It felt sweet sending this strong handsome kid all over the court. Robert rowed stroke in high school and sat on the bench for his varsity basketball team, but he wasn't especially quick on his feet.

Squash is a sport I happen to be good at. My father and I had a weekly game at his downtown club, starting when I was thirteen. The Racquet Club in Baton Rouge has first-class showers. My father always took his time in the locker room afterwards, standing around in his towel and talking to some of the guys. It took me four years to beat him, but after I beat him once I beat him again and again.

I beat Robert, too, but he didn't mind much. Somehow he always looked like the kind of guy who won. There were a few freckles to go with his almost curly hair (what I thought of for some reason as sailing freckles) and his skin was sandy and reddish. Everything about him looked in proportion. You know, shoulders broad, but not too broad, strong hands but feminine fingers, a straight classy nose.

His room-mate, Charlie Denby, was also pretty, a little taller maybe. They liked going around together, they liked being seen. Charlie played baseball, and I guess he was the real deal – the East-Coast, blue-blooded, prep-school, George Bush kind of Yalie, which is what Robert looked like to me. Most of the girls they hung around with were what I thought of as fraternity girls. It seemed like every weekend another couple of blondes showed up at their door. I used to daydream about the world he belonged to, where the men are composed and amusing, and the women have a good time.

The kids I knew in Baton Rouge were nothing like Robert and Charlie. I was the kind of kid Robert and Charlie wouldn't have sat with at the lunch table in the school cafeteria.

My friends and I played a lot of Dungeons & Dragons. In seventh grade I moved out of my brother's bedroom into the backyard extension, built out of the old garage. It had its own door to the garden and on Saturday mornings kids used to leave their bikes outside and walk straight into my room. We battled orcs, ogres, dragons, goblins, demigods . . . with poleaxes, two-handed swords, shurikens and magic spells. There would be six or seven boys sitting around with dice, pieces of paper, pencils and home-made maps. We kept the curtains closed and the lights on.

My parents began to worry about me, my mother especially. 'You seem like a reasonable human being,' she liked to say. 'You don't look violent.'

I was kind of scrawny, blue-eyed and fair in the face but black-haired. My brother, who was five years older, belonged to a completely different physical type. He played tight end on his Pop Warner football team and might have started in high school too, except my mother wouldn't let him. When we were kids he used to sit on my chest with his knees on my puny biceps, trying to make me say stuff I didn't want to say. 'Dungeons & Dragons is gay. Say it.' If I refused, he'd kneel up on his weight until I squealed.

My friends eventually graduated to more sophisticated games like BattleTech and Risk, but when I was fourteen or fifteen I realized that the real thing (war, I mean) was much more interesting than any fantasy. I started reading Churchill's memoirs and Sandburg's life of Lincoln. Probably my favourite battle of all time is the second El Alamein. Tank strategy in the Sahara turns out to be highly complex, and I checked out from the public library all the biographies of Lumsden and Montgomery I could lay my hands on. But I also had a soft spot for Nelson at Trafalgar and Meade at Gettysburg.

I didn't wear fatigues around school or sign up for ROTC or anything like that. In most ways I was a pretty average nerd. Military history was just my nerd specialty. I got good grades. I played the trumpet in band. The only weird thing I did, apart from read books about war, was collect lead soldiers. My bedroom was full of these guys, arranged in actual troop formations on the windowsills and in my closet and on top of the chest of drawers. They freaked my mother out. She couldn't understand why I spent so much time on what she called tiny metal dolls.

My childhood was happy and suburban. I used to ride my bike to elementary school and when my brother and I were small we sometimes set up a lemonade stand in the front yard. When I was older I made six bucks an hour mowing lawns in the summers. My parents paid for everything else, but I had to pay for my 'war shit' myself, my father said. Yard work in the heat of a Louisiana day was the only kind of suffering I put myself through as a kid. I probably dreamed about war because I wanted to know what I was made of – under the gun.

My mother hoped I'd grow out of it, and I guess I did. Two weeks before the start of freshman year, I wrapped the soldiers in cotton wool and packed them in shoeboxes. I didn't particularly want to go to college, but my parents made me.

'What do you want to do with yourself then?' my dad asked.

'Don't know,' I said. 'In your day I might have got drafted.'

'Not if you went to college, you wouldn't.'

He was a journalist and union organizer; a tolerant, social, easy-going guy. Even as a kid I could tell that women liked him. But he didn't know what to do with his son's obsessions.

'I don't understand,' he said. 'You want to enlist?'

'Mom would never let me. Besides, I'm too chickenshit. Guys from my high school have enlisted. Not my type. Anyway, it doesn't have to be war. I'd be just as happy gold-rushing or homesteading or something.'

Instead I went to Yale and majored in history. But the feeling didn't go away – that there must be a better test of who I was than middle-class American life.

When I got to college I wasn't really ready for the chances that came my way. I didn't even know what they were. Something in my personality would have to change to make room for girlfriends, that much was obvious. But I didn't realize until later that my classmates were checking out more than the opposite sex. They were looking for the kids who might cut a figure in the world one day: future senators, millionaires, newspaper editors, hotshot lawyers. I was lucky to stumble upon Robert James the way I did. By the time of the Yale–Harvard game, he was known by name (usually his last name) even among the upperclassmen.

This became clear at the tailgate party. The fields outside the Yale Bowl were crowded with parked cars. Thousands of students made their way between them, turning the grass to mud. Guys showed up with folding tables and cooked hot dogs on throwaway grills, which they served with ketchup and mustard bottles stolen from dining hall. They rolled out kegs of beer from the backs of their pickup trucks. You could sometimes grab a drink or a bite from strangers on your way past, but it was better to hang out with people you knew – if you could find them. The stadium itself, low and large and crumbling, loomed incongruously over us like some Roman coliseum.

Eventually I ran into Robert. He and Charlie were putting on a show. They mixed cocktails in a fruit-juice blender and served up Irish coffee and jello shots, while Robert (this was one of his tricks) made crêpes on a battery-powered hotplate. He leaned over the griddle in a stiff white apron, with his sleeves rolled up to the elbow, in spite of the bitter cold, showing off those rower's forearms, from which the fine sandy hairs stood on end.

There was a steady roll call of 'Hey, Robert', 'What's up, James', 'Robert James!', 'Mr James!' as people stopped to eat and drink by the back of Denby's Dodge Ram. But Robert called me over and introduced me, and I stood around breathing mist with all these meat-faced East Coast prep-school types and thought, Well, I'm here.

Once I spent a day at the beach with him. I came in to lunch while Robert and a few of his crowd were still sitting over their dirty trays; he made some room and I joined them. They were wondering what to do with themselves, on a bright, windy, not very warm, early-spring Tuesday afternoon. Some girl had a seminar she wanted to cut and needed an excuse. Charlie thought he knew a guy with a car.

'Let's go to the beach,' she said, with the lazy enthusiasm of a girl among boys, taking pleasure in the way she's being paid attention to. She was shorter than most of the girls Robert hung around with, short and skinny, with hard curly brown hair. A birthmark or burn scar blurred the skin under one of her eyes; not unattractive. I think she was a gymnast, or rode horses, or both.

We wasted about an hour trying to rustle up the guy with the car. His kid brother was in town, doing the college tour with his parents, but they had taken the train in to New York for the day. Charlie was sure his friend hadn't joined them. We kept calling his room on one of those campus phones, standing in the street in the cold sunshine.

Eventually, Charlie said, 'Fuck it,' and we made the trek out to Silliman to knock on his door. It turned out he was just asleep. When he came out in his underpants he was still too dopey to protest, and Charlie took the keys from him.

'It's probably been fucking towed anyway,' he said. 'I was supposed to feed the meter.'

But it hadn't been towed, and the five of us got in the car, which was one of those Buick sedans with a bench front seat. There was Charlie, Robert and me, and the curly-haired girl, Nell. The fifth kid was some prep-school wrestler type named Bill Russo, a high-energy guy, on the short side.

I don't remember much about the afternoon. I'm not sure why I went with them, but I'd never been to the beach in New Haven – which was rocky and bleak, and kind of fairground deserted – with an old carousel and a clean white lighthouse. It was cold as hell in the wind, but somehow the sand in the sunshine felt warm enough to sit on, and I remember Nell laying her scarred cheek against it and saying, as she dug one arm into the sand, 'This is what you need to solve the spare-arm problem. You know, when you're lying in bed with someone.'

Most of the afternoon I tried not to talk to her exclusively, which means I didn't say much at all. Robert kept making apologies for me, making fun of me. 'Don't expect Marny to say much. He's an intellectual.'

'I thought maybe you were on the squash team,' Nell said. 'I always see you bouncing one of those balls.'

'That's just a front,' Robert said.

Nell was the daughter of some federal court judge in Connecticut, a moderately well-known reactionary figure. But she didn't care anything about the law and kept flipping between majors. Her latest idea was that she wanted to be a vet. She loved horses and was trying to discover if she could stomach taking biology.

'I expect it doesn't matter anyway,' she said. 'I'll probably just marry some rich asshole in the city. I don't really care so long as he makes enough dough to buy me an apartment on the East Side, and a weekend place somewhere, it doesn't have to be the Hamptons. Upstate is fine. Somewhere I can keep a horse. What about you?'

'What do you mean?'

'What are you into, Marny?' she asked.

'Tank manoeuvres.'

By the time we got back, it was almost dark – the light coming coldly over the college rooftops was a milky blue. Dining hall was about to close, but Charlie had a box of magic mushrooms in his room, and everybody went up to his place to eat them.

Except me. I got a wet plate of pasta and tomato sauce from the canteen kitchen and ate it while the student staff cleared up around me – bussing trays, wiping tables and upturning chairs. That night, before going to sleep, I masturbated, feeling very ashamed, but at the same time trying to call up an image of Nell's face against the sunny sand. What shamed me, oddly enough, wasn't the idea that Nell might find out – about the use to which I had put the thought of her – but that Robert would. I practically heard him saying, 'I present you to a nice high-class girl, and this is what you do to her.'

As it happens, I set him up with his only serious college girlfriend. Or introduced him, anyway.

Every year there was a party before Spring Break called Screw Your Room-mate, where the girls ask out the guys, but not for themselves, for a room-mate or a friend. It was a combination of blind date and practical joke. Maybe a week after our day at the beach a girl came up to me outside dining hall and said, 'You're Greg Marnier, right?'

'Yes.'

I didn't recognize her. She had a mild pretty face, and yellow and brown hair, tied up in a bun on her head. There was snow on the ground now. Blizzards sometimes blew in as late as April, and she wore a thick green woollen sweater and a hand-knitted scarf and leggings and a miniskirt with high boots. She asked me if I wanted to take some girl called Beatrice to the dance.

'Which Beatrice?' I said, but I knew which one she meant. We had a philosophy seminar where we both talked a lot, though I hadn't spoken to her outside of class – except once, to finish an argument. This was a couple of days before. Neither of us backed down and my feet got wet in the snow before she went off to lunch.

'Castelli-Frank. How many do you know?'

'Just her.'

'Well?'

'Do you think she wants to go with me?'

'I don't know, but she mentions you sometimes. You really get on her nerves. I mean that in a good way.'

'It doesn't sound good.'

'Look, she likes you, OK? Do you want to go or not?'

'Yes,' I said. 'OK. I like her, too.'

This cost me a lot, saying yes. I was nineteen years old and had never been on a date – I'd never been in a sexual situation. All that pressure building up since puberty came out in weird anxieties. About contraception, for example, and sexually transmitted diseases. Really what worried me was the idea of contamination; even sharing food made me uncomfortable. I knew that I had to deal with these feelings, and the dance seemed a good opportunity. I was also extremely excited and spent the next week working on my philosophy paper, since it was somehow connected to Beatrice.

But then she came up to me after class and said, 'Are you doing anything Saturday night? Because there's this stupid dance and I want to set you up with my room-mate.'

'I think I met her,' I said.

'She's prettier than me.'

Beatrice was tall, almost as tall as me, and red-headed – more striking than pretty. She had a short upper lip, which pulled a little on her expression; even when she wasn't smiling she looked amused. In class she dressed like a grown-up, in dresses and low heels, and sometimes took her shoes off under the table and sat with her feet on the chair and her chin on her knees. Maybe she was pretty, but there was also something harsh or masculine about her voice. Her forehead seemed a little prominent; she tried to cover it up with hair.

'I don't know,' I said.

'I'm a big fan of this girl. I like you, too.'

'I don't know,' I said. 'No. I don't know. Let me think about it.'

Eventually I called up her room-mate and said no, I couldn't go to the dance with Beatrice, and they must have worked it out together, because Beatrice didn't ask me again. But I started hanging out more with Beatrice after that, maybe because she felt like, OK, at least that's clear. She used to read in our college library, and once when I saw her sleeping there I worked until she woke up then asked her for coffee. I said coffee but at the time all I drank was hot chocolate. We walked to a bookstore cafe named Finch's, and when the waiter came around with our drinks, Beatrice said, 'Give me your potted history.'

'What's that mean?'

'You know, your life story.' And we went from there.

Beatrice said her father was the only bad American apple on her family tree, but in fact she grew up mostly in Los Angeles and spent just two years of her life in Europe – at an English boarding school. (I questioned her thoroughly on all that.) Her mother came over to LA to make it in the movies and she landed a few small parts in unmemorable pictures, before marrying one of the industry lawyers and settling down to raise kids.

In her own way, though, Beatrice was an impressive personality. I was beginning to get a sense of what a personality was – that you had to judge people by different rules. She spoke decent Italian and identified strongly with the Italian side of her family. 'A bunch of old socialists,' she called them. But she was also generous with money, which she had a lot of. She asked questions and listened to your answers and asked more questions. She gave small gifts, trinkets, which she either made herself (she double-majored in art) or picked up on her weekends in 'the city'. To me she gave second-hand books. Beatrice was a big bookshop browser, and I still have a first edition of E.B. White's *Here is New York*, which she found in the Strand and bought for me because we'd been having an argument about New York. At that time I was still Southern enough to believe that New Orleans was the greatest city in America.

Probably my best friend at Yale, outside of room-mates, was a kid from Rhode Island named Mike Katz. He spent his freshman year dropping out of the cross-country team; smoked a little at parties, sometimes weed; played pretty fair piano, and sometimes played when drunk on the piano in the common room outside dining hall. Mike had a bony, strong, handsome, Jewish face, large-headed on slight shoulders, and at nineteen he was already losing his hair.

Mike carried a big torch for Beatrice – he talked about his crushes openly.

It was a shock to both of us when she started going out with Robert James. Personally, I liked Robert. For the kind of guy he was, he showed an unusual interest in intellectual ideas, even if he tended to boil them down into something he could digest. He had leftish sympathies. In his own controlling way, he tried to deal honestly with people. But Beatrice belonged in an altogether different league. How she put up with some of Robert's richer friends, and some of his poorer opinions, we couldn't figure out.

Even by undergraduate standards, they had an up-and-down relationship. A few months after they got together, they split up. I don't know why. Nothing that happened to Robert made him look or dress or sound any different, but you could tell Beatrice had things on her mind. Always quick to argue, she started getting angry quicker. Once she saw him waiting in line at Claire's, a cake and coffee shop on the corner of the New Haven Green. Maybe Robert had taken a girl there, maybe he really didn't see her, but anyway, when he kept his shoulder turned, she called out loudly, 'Don't turn your back on me. You saw me. I didn't blow you so two weeks later you could turn your back on me.'

I wasn't there, but I heard about it from Walter Crenna, who was.

'Did she say that?' Mike said. 'God, did she really say that? What did he say?'

'I don't know. I was at the cashier. I had to pay for my cake.'

Walter was a friend of Mike's – a heavy-footed, tall, awkward, lit-magazine type. I was friendly with him, too. He had a sweet tooth and ate like he talked – slowly, with pleasure. His face was still baby pink and smooth (I think he hardly shaved), and his sexuality was what Mike called 'indeterminate'.

By Christmas Beatrice and Robert were back together. In the spring she persuaded him to take an art class. There was something genuinely charming about the way he lugged the gear around – oversized paper pad, easel, paints – and set up openly in the middle of the quad. You could see him mixing his paints, taking his time. It struck me as a public declaration of love – he knew perfectly well he was no good. People stopped by to look at his work, which was not only bad but childishly bad. Still, he battled with perspective manfully, the way a father might, assembling a crib for his baby out of duty.

A lot of girls stopped by, too. They could see he was being sweet.

I think Beatrice and Robert spent part of the summer together, sailing the waters around the James family place near York. She came back the next fall a little more in love than she was before – she liked his father.

Mike still refused to believe she could see anything in Robert, in spite of the fact that he was friendly with Robert, too. They used to go running together every couple of weeks, out to East Rock and back, and Mike loved putting on the burners at the end, coasting away from him.

'What do you talk about?' I asked him once.

'What do you think we talk about? Beatrice. I point out to him that he's no good for her. I ask him when he's going to give a few other guys a shot.'

'Is that really what you talk about?'

'Mostly we talk about making money,' he said.

Junior year, over Thanksgiving, Beatrice's parents came into town and took a bunch of people out for turkey dinner at the most expensive restaurant in New Haven, the Grand Union Cafe. Mike and I both got invited along, and afterwards in his room I tried to explain to him what Beatrice was doing with Robert James. Mike was drunk and I wasn't – a lot of our late-night conversations happened that way.

'What do you think of her mother?' I said.

Mike was lying in bed, on his elbow. When he was drunk and tired he sniffed a lot and blinked his eyes.

'You see,' I went on, 'she wasn't what I expected. She looked a lot more conventional – pink combinations, that little handbag. And the dad, too, what did you make of him? A real lawyer dad. He called her Trixy. He thinks what he's got is an all-American girl. What I mean is, it struck me that Beatrice – to a certain extent – has been – I don't know. You know, you get to college and you realize, OK, this is my chance, I can pretend to be what I think I am. That's all I mean. I'm not saying she's a phoney. But still, for a girl like that, a boy like Robert James has a lot of attractions. He really belongs somewhere; he's the real deal.'

'Listen,' Mike said, 'I don't give a damn about Beatrice any more. I wouldn't kick her out of bed, but that's not the point. The point is – these guys, guys like Robert, they get what they want. They get the money, the real estate. They win elections. You haven't got a clue. You have no idea what guys like Robert end up with. But they're not supposed to get girls like Beatrice. That's what bugs me about the whole thing. At least not in college. When he's five years out and sitting on a million bucks, I don't care who he screws. But in college, guys like us are supposed to stand a chance.'

'I don't see him making a lot of money,' I said. 'To make money in his world, you probably need brains to spare. And Robert uses everything he's got. That's what I like about him. He's one of those guys –'

'Listen, Marny. You think everything is brains. Nobody gives a shit about brains. With his looks and connections, Robert is smart enough.'

'Is this some Jewish thing against him?' I asked. 'Because if it is, I don't buy it.' And so on.

In college, my closest friendships came down again and again to the same arguments; this was a conversation Mike and I had in one way or another for four years.

He saw us all as classic examples of particular types. Robert was the great Wasp, a millionaire-in-waiting, a future power broker. If he didn't run for office himself, he'd pull the strings behind some centre-left senator or governor. Walter, he figured, would end up reviewing Broadway plays for the *New York Times*. He'd settle down in a large bachelor apartment between Columbus and Broadway, in the 80s, with a piano standing in the window for him to play show tunes on during cocktail parties. Beatrice was harder to place. She'd probably marry Robert and divorce him, then move back to LA and have a second career in her forties, producing high-end television dramas. In one way or another, he saw us all playing a part in the culture of the country.

Anyway, I didn't think we were such a remarkable bunch. Most of us were relatively smart, relatively hard-working middle-class kids, who would probably end up landing fairly well-paid jobs in relatively affordable cities and raising families. The most interesting thing any of us *produced* was likely to be the happy childhoods of our children.

My side of the argument got some support when Robert James, in the spring of junior year, failed to get 'tapped' by any secret society. For some reason I didn't understand, he cared a lot about making it into Skull and Bones.

Two days later I got a note from him under my door. It was an invitation to become a member of a new club. This club was going to be everything the secret societies weren't: open, inclusive, intellectually serious. A lot of the people we knew got the same note. Mike, me, Walter, Beatrice (they were still going out). Bill Russo, the little wrestling guy. Mike's girlfriend at the time, Nikki Sanghera.

Nikki was a sophomore humanities major from Solihull, outside Birmingham – in England. None of us could place an English accent, but hers seemed especially wonderful, not posh exactly, but funny and real. She was smart, ambitious, slight, fine-featured and pretty, though probably not very nice. After Mike broke up with her, I went out with her for a month or two (with his blessing), and when that ended nobody saw much of Nikki any more.

So far as I know, Robert's alternative to Skull and Bones met only twice. Once at the end of spring term, junior year. We went to Mory's, the private club, which I had never been to before – Robert had just become a member. There was a door on York Street that was hard to find, and inside there were lots of little rooms with beat-up wooden tables and panelled walls.

At the end of the meal, Robert ordered a Cup – a large urn filled with home-brewed punch. Another embarrassing tradition. Nobody was really drunk enough, but we sang anyway, *Put a nickel on the drum*, all that bullshit, passing the Cup around and drinking and singing. In those days I didn't touch alcohol. One song led to another. *Bright college years, with pleasure rife. The shortest, gladdest years of life. Bulldog Bulldog bow wow wow. For God for country and for Yale.* Walter had a beautiful voice, a little thin maybe but light for a big man and clear as a bell. For a while he was singing by himself: *We're poor little lambs who have lost our way! Baa baa baa!* I don't think anyone considered the evening a success.

Robert had a tough time senior year. Beatrice broke up with him 'for good' a few weeks before Christmas. 'Because he had never heard of Pinter,' she said to me one night; but I'm sure there were other reasons.

She was standing in the courtyard drinking beer when I bumped into her. Every Tuesday night there was a party at one end of the quad, run by a couple of seniors who had rooms nearby. Beatrice saw me walking past and said, 'Do you want a beer? Come on, they're pretty disgusting.' When I shook my head, she said, 'Let me get you a beer.' And then, when I still refused: 'What makes you so superior? Is it some control-freak thing?' She sounded almost angry but changed her tone. 'I don't want to fight with you. Let's get out of here. Have you ever been to the top of the clock tower? I know someone with a key.'

So I followed her into the library and then up the cold stone stairs. There's a seminar room at the top, and next to the stairwell, another door I'd never tried to go in.

'I know the guy who cleans up around here,' she said. 'A student. He always leaves his key behind one of the books. For smokers.'

She couldn't find the key, but it turned out when we tried it a few minutes later that the door was unlocked. There was another staircase behind it, colder and narrower than the first and made of wood, with maybe a hundred cigarette butts underfoot. Beatrice went first. She had on boots with heels and moved awkwardly in the dark. The door at the top was also open, and we stepped out onto the narrow balcony that circled the clock tower just underneath its brassy cupola.

As we stood under the bare winter sky Beatrice put an arm around me. She wasn't wearing a coat, just a wool scarf bundled up around her neck, and I found it disconcerting how close her face was. In spite of her good looks, or maybe because of them, she had quite a forceful, almost male presence – strong bones and broad shoulders. She used to swim in high school.

'What are you going to do next year?' she said.

'I'm not sure. I've applied for a couple of fellowships to Oxford. My brother got one and had a good time over there.'

'Do you always want to do what your brother did?'

'Oh, leave me alone. I've heard that before.' After a minute, I went on: 'What my father did when he graduated is just move to the city he wanted to live in, which is New Orleans. And then he married my mother and ended up staying. Or near enough – in Baton Rouge. If everything else falls through, I guess I could do that.'

'And what city do you want to live in?'

'New Orleans.'

'Because of your father?'

'Look,' I said, 'if you keep giving me a hard time, you can go to someone else for human warmth.'

She let go of me then and stood a little apart. There was not much wind, even up in the tower, but zero cloud cover, and the temperature was somewhere in the twenties. It hadn't snowed in several days, but we could see on the streets below us all the old snow piled up and dirtied between the parked cars. While we were talking, a long way below, students carrying various kinds of bags – backpacks and shopping – came and went through the college gates.

'Oh, it's too cold to argue,' Beatrice said and lit a cigarette. When she had finished, with cold jittery fingers, she breathed in and out and leaned against me again.

'Why did you really break up with him?' I asked.

'I told you, because he had never heard of Pinter. Do you know what his GPA is? Three point two, three point three, something like that. God, I sound like such a snob – I am a snob. But after two years of dating I finally realized he isn't very bright. Does this make me a bad human being? But you don't believe me.'

'No, not really.'

'You think he is very bright?'

'I think he has a kind of efficient intelligence. But that's not what I don't believe.'

'Yes, he has a kind of intelligence. The trouble is, he thinks it is better than *real* intelligence.'

'I'm not sure what that is.'

'Yes you are. It's what you have, it's what I have.'

'The way you put it doesn't make it sound very nice.'

'It's very important to you to be nice, isn't it? I think this is why you don't have many girlfriends.'

In fact, I had just started going out with Nikki, but Beatrice did not know this. I had kissed her for the first time two days before, standing in the street below us, where she had been crying because of Mike.

'Do girls not like nice boys?'

She let go of me again and eventually said, 'This is a very stupid conversation. This is the kind of stupid conversation I had freshman year.' And I could see (I should have seen it before) that she was really quite unhappy, and that her bright sarcastic mood was just the surface of it.

To change the subject, I asked: 'And what are you going to do next year?'

'I don't know. For a while, Robert and I talked about moving in together, probably in New York. Finding jobs. Maybe I'll do that anyway.'

'What's Robert planning?'

'I think he's stuck, and he knows it. He's not as smart as his father is; he knows that, too.'

'Mike is convinced Robert's going to run the country some day.'

'Mike is a little in love with all of us,' she said.

Somehow her saying this changed the tone again. It really was very cold, and Beatrice had begun to look pale. Her lips were blue and the cigarette in her hand shook.

'What am I doing? Let me give you my coat.'

'No, let's go back down,' she said but stayed where she was, so I put my arm around her again and rubbed her side. She was vibrating with cold.

'I don't want to go out in the world,' she added, in the mock plaintive voice of the spoilt pretty girl. And then, in her own voice: 'I thought your parents met in college?'

'They did. They met at U-Dub, in Seattle, which is where my mom grew up. But they didn't know each other very well. Then he moved to New Orleans, and she got a job at LSU, and since she didn't know anyone else, she called him.'

'She called him?'

'My father is very good at making friends. She was lonely.'

'How do you know all this?'

'She told me. She tells me things.'

'And you take after your mother?'

'I don't know what you mean by that. When he's angry, my father sometimes says that she's very good at getting what she wants.'

I had my arm around her shoulder and could smell her, not only her shampoo but her perfume, too. She wore a noticeable scent, and whenever she came to my room, or even passed me in the street, I used to take pleasure in recognizing this scent after she was gone. I remember thinking, if Mike were here, if he were standing like this, he would kiss her. And it's true, I had been sort of in love with her for almost three years. I say sort of, because what made me unhappy about it was mostly the fact that this feeling of being in love had so little to do with my actual relations with her, with our friendship, which was real enough. My sexual feelings towards her were adolescent, masturbatory, not very nice. While in reality I was a pretty good friend to Beatrice.

Finally she said, 'I'm too cold, let's go back down.'

We climbed darkly down the narrow stairs, and when we reached the landing, where the cigarette butts were, the light of the seminar room showed along the edge of the doorway. For a second I thought, in a mild panic, that someone might have locked us in. But the door opened easily; the light inside seemed very bright.

It was much warmer, too, and Beatrice said, 'God, I was getting fucking cold. I kept thinking you were going to kiss me.' But when I tried to suddenly, she said, 'Don't force it.'

Walking through the courtyard afterwards she held my hand. When I got to my room I felt miserable. I thought, I have no idea what I'm doing with my life.

A few weeks after New Year, Nikki and I broke up. We had never slept together. There was one night when we might have, but she had her period, and when I felt her up between her legs, I reached only the odd hard edge of her tampon. All in all, this fact relieved me. Everything was moving a little fast, and Nikki seemed young to me, too. Especially after our break-up conversation, in which she didn't show her best.

What started it off was her announcing over hot chocolates at Finch's that she had gotten drunk a few nights before with Mike. They shared a hotel room too, 'perfectly innocently' she said, with several other people – there was a Student Unions convention in New York, and she hadn't seen him in several weeks, and a bunch of Yalies ended up at the same hotel bar.

'OK,' I said. 'I'm glad you told me.'

'Hello, hello,' she said. 'Is there anyone there?'

'What do you mean?'

'Nothing gets to you, does it?'

'That's right,' I said. 'Everything's fine with me.'

Afterwards, the only thing that upset me about the relationship (and its end) is that I had allowed myself to become intimately involved with someone for whom I had so little real feeling. The relationship made sense only as an attempt to get back at Mike for something, or to get closer to Mike in some way . . . and for several weeks, I had to keep at bay a niggling worry that the problem with me might just be the fact that I'm gay. That this would explain my failure with Beatrice in the clock tower, the intensity of my friendship with Mike, my ongoing curiosity about Robert James. I didn't want to be gay, for several reasons. One of them being that I wanted to sleep with girls. And eventually the niggles went away.

I didn't see much of Robert that spring, which was our last term at Yale. Everybody was busy applying for whatever it was they wanted to do in the fall. Rhodes and Marshall turned me down, but my dad offered to pay my way to Oxford anyway. Mike got into the Yale-in-China programme, mostly to put off law school, he said. Walter was going to take a year out before applying to theatre-studies programmes. Maybe live with his parents in Maine and write plays, or teach part-time at the local high if he got bored. Beatrice won a Shorenstein Center Scholarship at the Kennedy School in Harvard. Her undergraduate major was comp lit, but she had decided to do a master's in international development.

Nobody knew what Robert had lined up. If Beatrice was right

about his GPA, she was also right that he'd have a tough time getting the kind of job he wanted. Just to make it clear, I had no sympathy with the tone she took about his intelligence. Robert, so far as I could tell, was not only able but hard-working and dedicated. On the other hand, all of us that year were getting used to being measured in fairly crude ways. GPA was only one of them, and not the worst. There were LSATs and MCATs and GREs and GMATs. I got out of most of them by going to England. But I couldn't figure out what Robert would do with himself – Mike and I still talked about him a lot.

A few weeks before graduation I got another invitation from him, this time delivered by email. He was organizing an end-of-year dinner with one of his professors, Jerry Liebling, who taught international relations. The email went out to most of the usual suspects: Mike, me, Walter, Bill Russo. Even Beatrice got an invite. I guess they were on speaking terms again. Robert promised everyone free dinner at the Grand Union Cafe.

The reason I couldn't go is that some of my friends had rented a house for 'Dead Week' on the Carolina coast. Dead Week is what we called the week before graduation – the week before the parents showed up – and a lot of students took the chance to get the hell out of town and hole up somewhere by a warm beach.

It was about a thirteen-hour drive to Pauly's Island from New Haven and Mike, Tommy Dietrich, Raymond Shu and I shared Mike's dad's car – a Subaru sedan with manual transmission that nobody knew how to operate. We had to figure it out on the road. Tommy and Raymond were my sophomore-year room-mates. The house was nothing special, just a big under-furnished wooden construction, built on stilts in the sand about fifty yards from the water. It was probably only ten years old, but looked much older, because of the Atlantic weathering. There were maybe as many as a dozen people sleeping in the house at different times. We cooked pasta dinners and went out for crab cakes, that kind of thing. The rest of the day we spent swimming, getting dry, wet, dry again, and playing cards.

At night most of the college seniors met up at Myrtle Beach to get drunk, and one night we drove out there to see what it was like. Pretty awful. Beach bars gave out free T-shirts at the door, with slogans like 'I Chowdered at Jimmy's' sprayed across them. The music was so loud that even at the edge of the surf you couldn't hear the ocean. As it happens, I had an OK time.

Outside one of the bars I ran into Nell, the judge's daughter, who was a little drunk and not very happy, for reasons she was willing to go into; about a half-hour later, in the middle of all those people, we kissed for a bit and nobody noticed or cared. They were all off their heads. I wasn't, and Nell, by the time we kissed, wasn't either. After a while she spotted some of the people she came in with, who were leaving, so she said goodbye.

'That's my ride,' she said. 'I probably won't see you again.'

'I hope you get that horse,' I told her, and she gave me a queer look before pushing her way through the crowds.

On the last night, though the late-spring weather was on the cool side, everybody in the house decided to go skinny-dipping. Most of us were sober; it was cool enough that you felt giggly just standing in the sea air. So we waded naked into the water, which was warmer than the air, and splashed each other like kids. Mike's most recent girlfriend had just arrived – a small, pretty architecture major, with short black hair. She wore her glasses even in the water. I splashed her, too.

'Stop it,' she said in a grown-up voice, which made me feel suddenly ashamed. So I left her alone. Her name was Alana; she and Mike had started going out during Spring Break senior year and broke up when Mike flew to China. Apart from graduation weekend, I never saw her again. But for a minute she really put me in my place. It felt like everything that had happened to me in college, everything I had learned to be comfortable with, had produced this jerk standing naked in the water, splashing his best friend's girlfriend in the chest.

The next morning we got in the car and drove those thirteen hours back to Yale.

I heard about Robert's dinner party from Walter. Even in college he was an excellent, old-fashioned, small-town kind of storyteller. You needed time to listen to a Walter Crenna story. But Mike and I both had a big appetite for Robert James gossip, and we also felt bad about missing his dinner – we wanted to hear all the details.

What made the whole thing so strange was this Liebling guy who supervised Robert's senior essay. He was something of a fixture in college life. Every night around six he appeared in dining hall, picked up a tray of food and sat down by himself to eat it. Whenever he thought a student was looking at him, he smiled, a little blindly behind his glasses, which were too small for his big eyes. It was hard to imagine a more unlikely mentor for Robert James.

Liebling, as the older man, should have presided over dinner, but Robert played host. He had booked the private room, which wasn't easy to find – you reached it by a staircase next to the kitchens, and Robert kept doubling back to make sure nobody was lost. The guest list was made up entirely of personal friends, but Robert presented them to Liebling like some kind of cream of the crop.

The point of the dinner was to interest a handful of graduating seniors in a business they were setting up. The original idea came from Robert, which was to sell political information to large companies on a subscription basis. They weren't necessarily looking for poli sci majors, just people with a strong grounding in the humanities and an interest in world affairs. There would also be plenty of part-time work to go around, consultancy jobs, office management positions.

Meanwhile the food kept coming. Robert had taken care of the ordering; there were no menus, no choices.

Liebling hardly said a word. He was sitting between Robert and Beatrice, and Beatrice did a good job keeping him entertained, leaning in to make herself understood. Putting a hand on his elbow. Walter thought she must have patched things up with Robert. Later it struck him that maybe she was trying to make him jealous, but at the time it seemed she was just helping out. It was an awkward meal. Even when they got drunk, nobody had much to say.

'I mean, for God's sake,' Walter told us, 'I'm a theatre major.'

Robert kept trying to draw everyone out, to talk them up. But this was never one of his skills, running a conversation. His manner was dry and economical; he did better at introductions.

Apparently, he talked us up, too. According to him, Mike had won a big grant to study in China. I was going to Oxford on a Rhodes. Then he started bragging to Liebling about Beatrice's scholarship at the Kennedy School. To Beatrice he said, you could probably earn something like forty thousand dollars a year on top of that, just for putting us in touch with the right people there, and spending maybe five hours a week doing research for the company. For some reason, this set her off.

'Come on, Robert. Give it a rest,' she said. 'I don't care about money as much as you do.'

'That's because you don't need to.'

'And I'm not going to the Kennedy School for *connections*.'

She sounded calm enough, but Robert, who had been acting nervous and stiff all night, lost his cool. 'Stop it. You're embarrassing me. And there's no point to it. You made your point six months ago.'

So Beatrice said, 'I don't have to sit here,' and stood up.

Robert started going after her, but Liebling put a hand on his shoulder. 'Sit down, Robert, sit down. Have a glass of water.'

When she was gone, Robert stopped talking for a few minutes and did what he was told. He had a glass of water. His face was pretty red; he'd always had a sandy complexion. But he was also a bit drunk and looked like a young Wall Street type, Walter said, after a bad day on the floor. Liebling made a little general conversation. Have you enjoyed Yale? Do you think you've changed much since you were a freshman? What do you think you'll remember about your time here?

Walter answered, in his serious way, 'I don't think I'll forget this dinner, sir.' Liebling had the decency to smile. It was like he was humouring Robert, for some reason, though Walter couldn't figure out why.

At the end, Robert tried to salvage something from the evening. He stood up and made a speech. 'You all know Professor Liebling,' he began, 'but let me tell you a few things about him maybe you don't know.' And so on. Finally he said (a line he had probably prepared): 'I don't need to tell you what opportunity looks like. It looks like this.'

Walter told us this the night before graduation, when we met up in Mike's room after seeing our parents off to their hotels. Around 1 or 2 a.m. we got hungry again and went out looking for something to eat. There was a diner on Broadway I used to go to, since it stayed open till four, and we ended up there, ordering pizza by the slice. 'At least I won't be one of those guys,' I said at one point, 'who is ever tempted to say that the best four years of my life were these.'

'What do you think he's going to do with himself?' Mike asked.

'You mean Robert?'

'Sure. Who were you thinking about?'

As it happens, Liebling and Robert *did* go into business together. They opened their first office in New Haven, since it was convenient for the university. Robert was the only full-time employee; he was also a minority partner in the firm. They set up an office in Manhattan a year later.

I kept hearing updates from Mike, who even did some work for the company in China. After Robert moved to New York, Mike sometimes crashed on his futon. The flight to China left out of JFK and he liked having a couple of nights in the city to bookend his visits home. Robert had a small one-bedroom apartment in Greenwich Village, with a fire-escape balcony overlooking Chumley's Bar. By this stage he was paying himself something like a hundred thousand dollars in salary. Their monthly subscription rates went as high as thirty grand.

Mike said he hadn't changed at all, that he looked just like he used to in college. Robert bragged that he never wore a tie to work. It was his job to bring in clients, something he turned out to be good at. Just before the dot-com crash, he sold his stake in the company for seventeen million dollars. ∎

TOMORROW

Joanna Kavenna

JOANNA KAVENNA

1973

Joanna Kavenna grew up in various parts of Britain and has also lived in the US, France, Germany, Scandinavia and the Baltic States. She is the author of three novels: *Inglorious*, *The Birth of Love* and *Come to the Edge*; and one work of non-fiction, *The Ice Museum*. In 2008 she was awarded the Orange Prize for New Writing. Her work has appeared in publications including the *New Yorker*, the *London Review of Books*, the *Guardian*, the *Observer*, the *Times Literary Supplement*, the *International Herald Tribune*, the *Spectator* and the *Telegraph*. She has held writing fellowships at St Antony's College, Oxford, and St John's College, Cambridge. 'Tomorrow' is an excerpt from a forthcoming novel.

I went the other day to the loft of a friend's house. It was amusing, how long he'd been storing my stuff. That was because he had a house, a carpeted halogen-lit house, because years ago he'd been virtuous and prudent. Even when the rest of us were busy floundering, doling out beer for rent money, wiping tables clean, chain-smoking in the hope it would convert us into beat poets, Dominic gathered funds for a house on Streatham Hill. We were all living in the area at the time, perfectly placed for the South Circular, and room after lighted room after street after street, we all lived in the same five square miles of terraced Victorian houses, the whine of aeroplanes ritually disturbing our dreams. We lived in the same five square miles but the rest of us lived in fetid little fleapits, our wages palmed over to rat-faced landlords, and suddenly Dominic had garnered his own bricks and mortar.

If you were really lucky you got to live with him.

The rest of us – we just secreted our possessions into his loft. Slowly . . .

You had to be careful . . .

'Dominic, just for a few weeks. Just while I'm waiting to move somewhere bigger/better. Then I'll take it all away . . .'

And then – a few weeks became a few months became a few years and then our hair was streaked with grey and age had clearly started to wither us . . . Custom had somewhat staled us. The custom, especially, of living in rented rooms, even as we withered. Somehow that whole business had escaped us – the business of *Oh yes, I'd love this one, such lovely flooring, and yes, a recently renovated kitchen, and a garden study, of course, I'll pay with cash* . . .

It hadn't quite worked out like that.

Finally, after so many years, Dominic decided that the market wasn't particularly ideal and so he really couldn't flog the house to the highest bidder, there being no bidders at all, and so he had decided to build a loft conversion. By then he was two-thirds bald and he had a wife and three children: Wilfred, Arthur and Lily.

'Such lovely names,' we all said. 'Such beautiful children.' Because he was still storing our stuff.

It had to happen in the end. It was surprising it hadn't happened before. Still it was bad news. Dominic sent out an email, and it said, 'Lo, denizens of my youth', 'walk-on cameos in the drama of my solipsism', or something like that. 'You must now all remove your shit from my loft.'

I was sent a date and a time and told to make sure I had a big enough van . . . I wasn't sure where I'd take it all. I was weighing up the options: in the palm of one hand, I had the dump, and in the other, a storage place in Tooting Bec.

Alas, my bedsit wasn't quite large enough to house the detritus of my former years. Alas, I'd been expecting every month to move somewhere larger.

Somehow I never did.

I presented myself on the doorstep and Dominic, just back from work, loosening his tie, said, 'Oh, hi, how lovely to see you, thanks so much for coming over.'

I said, 'No, no, thank you, Dominic, for storing my shit all these years.'

'No, no, it was no trouble at all.'

A small girl in the background, Lily, crying, 'Daddy, Daddy . . .' So he kissed her.

'How have things been?'

'Oh, good, wonderful. You?'

'Oh, not too bad at all.'

Lily was saying, down below, 'Daddy, we went to the park. Daddy, I ran round and round the football pitch five times. Daddy, I was a horse. Daddy . . .'

'That's great, sweetie. Wonderful . . .'

'Better press on,' I said. 'And up . . . Pull down . . . The rest . . .'

'Let me know if you . . . Yes, Lily, really, I'm coming.'

'Oh no, of course, I'll be fine.'

Up the stairs, the walls filled with paintings, photographs of Dominic's children, his wife Elizabeth, posed on beaches, by monuments, skiing or surfing or generally living it up, then there was an antique barometer prophesying storms, then the stairs opened onto a landing with expensive mock-Regency wallpaper and antique plant pots with foliage pluming out of the tops, and the loft ladder was standing ready.

I merely had to ascend.

I found myself in a place of mildew and other people's stuff. Incoherent piles of suitcases, or I failed to understand their significance. A naked bulb sputtering, so I had to feel my way with my hands. I felt it was imperative not to puncture the ceiling with my foot. Not to send a shower of plaster into the halogen below. So I fumbled carefully, pulling out notebooks, photos, letters, traces of former realities, one after the other.

When I'd finished I found Dominic in the kitchen, Lily at his side. Something whirring in a juicer. He was carrying early-onset midlife pretty well. He didn't look like one of those lawyers who pound themselves mad on a treadmill then lose their jobs and murder their wives. He had a modest gut, just a slight covering of flesh, filling out his shirt a little, just the result of a few too many bottles of quality Bordeaux.

Lily had brown curls, blue eyes; she looked a lot like Elizabeth. I was smiling down at her. Such a pretty fat face, such pretty pink cheeks. I said, 'Do you go to school, Lily?' and she pursed her lips, said, 'Go away, only want to talk to Daddy.'

'Really, Lily,' said Dominic. '*Really.*'

'It's all right,' I said, observing the protocols. 'Really, my daughter's just the same.'

He looked at me, as if he thought that was unlikely, and then we stood at the door, the night all beyond us, cars filing past one by one, so many strangers moving from one place to another, and we said:

Hope it won't be so long next time ... Oh yes ... Thanks so much ... So nice to see you ... All those years ... Hope the conversion looks great ... Oh of course, I'd love ... Yes, maybe. Exactly ... Why not ... Well, thanks again ... Take care ...

I smiled myself off the step. I couldn't really face dumping the stuff in another storage place, so I took it back home with me. I'd sift through it quickly, stow some of it in reassuring files, throw the rest away.

My daughter looks a lot like my grandmother.

I know this because in one of the boxes of personal detritus I found a sepia photograph of a girl half smiling at the camera, a wide gap between her two front teeth. A small putty-like nose, unruly blonde hair, barely combed. For a flash moment I thought it was my daughter, got confused, wondered if there are no individuals at all, just genes like heat-seekers, hunting out warm bodies to carry them, eventually dismissed the thought. My daughter was all the while asleep, on her side of the bed. She was holding a stuffed horse I'd taken earlier from another dusty box.

'What is it?' she had asked, stroking its shabby fur.

'Tom the Greatest,' I'd said. 'It was Aunt Harriet's.'

'It has a funny face. Like it's been squashed.'

My daughter's name is Elska, which means love. Her father doesn't live here any more. It slowly fell apart and so we thought, perhaps, absence might –

Then absence became habitual.

'It was squashed,' I said. 'It was jammed in with a lot of other things.'

'But there's no jam on it at all,' said Elska.

My love.

She sleeps flat on her back, angled diagonally across the bed.

The sulphur lights fizzing beyond the windows. All the frenzy and dissolution and sobriety beyond, the unknowable lives of others. A grand pattern of light and shadow, millions of lives and everything I see just one layer upon further layers of long-buried ruins, rivers under concrete, grassy knolls smothered by city blocks. I can hear bells ringing far away in a nearly abandoned church and engine noise rising and falling, footsteps on asphalt, elliptical cries.

Just the other month there was a riot. The things they didn't rip up they knocked down. I live in a council block, by Victoria Park. If you watch the park too carefully you end up a witness in a murder trial. So I mostly stare out at the orange glow to the west. A clipped half-moon, a neon-stained sky. Sirens hastening towards the scene of another crime.

One thing about this sketchy bedsit, first floor, external steps to the door, so helpful for the masked burglars –

One thing about my pregnable flat, it has a view of the sky . . .

Mark, my friend, woke one night with a knife pressed to his neck. Twelve hours later he was still kicking his heels in a cupboard, his hands tied with his own rope. They'd taken everything. He'd been so scared he'd forgotten his own pin number. So they almost killed him.

One last chance, get it right, or we slit your fucking throat, they said.

Well, that was kind of them, he said later.

This lighted room hemmed in by other people's lives, speech gargling through the walls, the clatter of plates in a kitchen below. My radio seeping into another lighted room, where someone else sits watching the sky. And that, and all of that – it's easy to get bewildered, mesmerized by things you can't hope to understand. It can become your default mode, if you don't keep a check on yourself.

My thoughts drift and then – I get recalled – I bend over the computer and type.

Dear Sir, this is to confirm your order request. You should receive your order in the next week. Thank you . . . V.

Once, you got these bureaucrats in the law courts, buried under mounds of paper. Now we sit in random rooms while the Internet leers towards us. Then we wander away to our offices, we wander to the glittering high-rises of the city. We get a little sick in the head, we wonder where one of us ends and the next begins, which one, who? Standing on a platform, with a thousand others.

Still, we get paid.

I look forward to receiving it – D. Williams.

Let me know if you have nay queries, I type. *I mean, any queries.*

There must be no mistake. Lest something terrible occur. Lest D. Williams becomes even stunned by his own life, how precarious and improbable it is, lest in the silence that follows he finds the rope, ties the knot, kicks the stool from beneath his feet.

Thanks again, D.

D. is still here, it seems.

It was midnight, I crawled towards Elska, buried my head in her fleshy little neck and slept.

I met up with Mark the next day. It was Saturday, I was wheeling Elska towards Victoria Park, noting the black clouds above – but still, there was a smell of spring. Mark waved at his window, came down, shutting the door behind him. He was still living in the flat, the one where he'd almost been stabbed in the neck. For a while after, his neck had a tiny red spot on it, where they'd pricked him with the point of the knife. That had faded and, once he'd repaired the door, he'd thought, why not, I may as well stay here. He lacked the capital for post-traumatic stress.

Mark wiped glasses and pulled pints at the local pub. That was where I'd met him. As the regulars sweated lager into the ether, he said, 'Yes, sir, of course, three pints, yes, sir.' He breathed in lager ether. One evening he said, 'Hello, are you new?'

'No,' I said.

Today he kissed me on the cheek, blew kisses at Elska.

'How's work?' he said.

The sun was breaking through the clouds, so we squinted at each other. Mark shifted his feet from side to side as he talked. He was tall, wiry, so his jeans hung baggily at the back. His hair was brown, straight, falling over his ears.

'Nice morning.'

And yet it looked a little like rain.

We should walk anyway, we said.

The street was lit in patches, cloud-darkened in others.

'Coffee?'

'Or shall we walk now, coffee later?'

'Nothing much to do,' I said, nodding down at Elska. Nothing, and the nurture of a human being. A talking breathing thinking being, who could move her head around and contemplate the view. Who could perceive and interpret and doubt and expect, who could cry, 'But, Mummy, Mummy, why did you bring me out here, onto the half-blackened street?'

Mark had to drop something off in Dalston, should we go there first? Elska's eyes were half shut, against the light, or against the shadows.

Always, I wondered what she thought. And how she saw the faces of the people passing, or the woman hunched over a stick. How she saw the first blossoms on the trees. As she bumped along the pavements.

Mark was walking with his hands in his pockets. He slouched like a younger man. He'd already been for a run.

'Chasing from one thing to another,' said Mark.

I nodded. 'Much better than destitution,' we said.

'A bit of debt never hurt anyone. And it's important not to be greedy.'

'Most of what they tell you to want, you really don't need.'

That was one of the things I liked about Mark. If you said 'they', he never asked you who you meant.

The birds were trilling in the trees. The sun was in Mark's eyes, so he put a hand on his forehead, casting his face into flattering shadow.

He could talk to almost anyone, as a general rule. 'Bar work makes you gregarious,' he said.

He was always picking up waifs and strays, helping them home, loaning them money. Somehow he hadn't succumbed to cynicism and irony.

A great bloated cloud, ushering away the lesser clouds, and it began to rain. Mark refused to share my umbrella. 'Oh, you need it for your little girl,' he said. So he was drenched in moments, his clothes sticking to his skin.

'You're a kind man,' I said.

'Well, that just disproves your bleak prognosis.'

'Of what?'

'Of almost everything.'

'No, no, it's not bleak,' I said. 'That's not it at all.'

'Why don't you tell me what it is, then?' he said. Cocking his head to one side, as if I was about to unskein the whole ball, as if he was about to follow it along the street . . .

'Later,' I said.

'Five minutes later? Or a year later?' he said.

When the rain died down a little, Elska scrambled out of the pushchair, went running in the grass, picking up flowers, soaking her shoes, avoiding syringes, jagged cans, spent cartridges like I'd told her to.

Old Gwenda wasn't at home, so Mark stuffed something through the letter box, wrote her a note.

'I'll go round tomorrow,' he said. 'Fix her Hoover for her, that sort of thing.'

I was smiling at him, so he shrugged his shoulders.

'I know,' he said, 'I'm a fucking saint.'

'You should get an award. You know, at one of those patronizing ceremonies, where lumpen-faced normal people get invited to some glittering prize venue and some shiny celebrity reads a prepared script about the amazing courage of lumpen-faced normal people,' I said.

'Lumpen-faced?' said Mark. 'Thanks.'

'No, no, not you.'

At the cafe, Mark told me how he'd had a good idea. It was something about scintillation.

'The lights?' I said.

'What lights?' said Elska. 'Where?'

'Scintillation,' said Mark. 'People live more quickly because they're bored. Time goes more quickly, I mean. Or it seems to. Because they're not noticing anything any more. If you're noticing everything, your brain slows down time, or it seems to. Because it has to pack so many impressions in, so that's why people say, oh the days go so fast, now I'm old. It's just because they see the same things all the time, they barely notice them. They walk down the street, everything's familiar. Time floods along – because it's empty, not filled with new events.'

'So if you're in prison, time should go quickly,' I said. 'Because you're just confronted by the same thing daily.'

'Ah, but then another law of psychophysics comes into play – because you're presumably waiting to be released, you're willing time to pass, you're watching every minute passing, and thus it slows . . .'

Mark's clothes were still wet. He had taken off his shoes and put them on the radiator. But the radiator was lukewarm, anyway.

It was one of those cafes with mantras on the walls.

Don't dream it, do it.

You are a unique and special person.

Life's there for the taking.

They didn't write:

Life's a bitch and then you die.

Or: *Et in Arcadia ego.*

Or: Because I could not stop for Death, He kindly stopped for me.

They had presumably discussed their options with a brand consultant, worked out what would put everyone off their lattes.

Elska was licking sugar from a spoon.

Elska was living solely in the present, her greatest strength, the wonder gift of childhood. She was living as herself, in herself, without ever thinking about what that meant. She was reforming the world, however she pleased, so when I said, dutifully, even as I thought, well, what matter? 'Oh, Elska, don't eat so much sugar, really,' she said, 'It's not sugar, it's satin dust.'

Of course.

'Of course it is.' I smiled.

'So when you go on holiday,' Mark was saying, 'you feel as if time is going very slowly, or as if it's been replete, and really it's you know, something like – oh, novelty – you've been really conscious of everything that's occurring around you, because it's sort of unusual, so you've been shifted out of, you know, what you usually do, so you've gained a different experience of time.'

'What about people who experience time backwards?' I said.

'Well, who does that?'

'Those people,' I said. 'You know, those people who have some disorder of the brain and they see drops of water going up not down.'

'Well, I mean they're clearly in a minority. Possibly of one. I meant the many.'

'I meant the few, or the lone weirdo,' I said. He smiled at me, his eyes half closed.

He always smiled with his mouth shut. So his chin pointed upwards for a moment and his face went lopsided.

Be Yourself, said the caffeine-slick walls.

Unless You're a Lone Weirdo.

Then Be Someone Else.

That night when Elska was sleeping on the bed, when she was lying across the sheets, when the planes were whining and the street was sulphur-fizzing all beyond and the buildings were lit up so the city looked gaudy and even jovial . . .

That night I lay on the bed and dreamed, woke suddenly, couldn't understand where I was, heard Elska breathing beside me, felt the past breathing down my neck, very deep is the past, felt that once again, and the planes were still whining, so I knew if I had travelled in time then it wasn't far.

The stars receding, the darkness tinged with grey, so I could see dim shapes around the bed, discarded clothes, piles of boxes.

The cry of birds in the eaves – some half-visceral memory of being small, how you felt the world around you, trace recollections, held within the sinew of yourself. Then you are only in the audience, at a psychic lantern show –

The half-desired display – interrupted by a lone sound – on the radio of a passing car –

Deliver me . . .

As the early sun soft-lit the dirty old streets –

Again – ∎

GRANTA

JUST RIGHT

Zadie Smith

ZADIE SMITH

1975

Zadie Smith was born in London. She is the author of the novels *White Teeth, The Autograph Man* and *On Beauty*, which was shortlisted for the Man Booker Prize in 2005 and won the Orange Prize for Fiction in 2006. She is also the author of *Changing My Mind: Occasional Essays* and the editor of several anthologies, including *The Book of Other People*. Her most recent novel is *NW*, chosen as one of the 'Ten Best Books of 2012' by the *New York Times*. She was one of *Granta*'s Best of Young British Novelists in 2003. 'Just Right' is an excerpt from an unfinished novella.

'And your father's in it?'

'Yes, ma'am. He helps my mother and makes the s– the –'

'The scenery? Try to breathe, Donovan, there's really no hurry. I'm sure you'll catch the others in the square.'

Miss Steinhardt sat on the very edge of her desk, working her nails with a bobby pin for the subway grime underneath.

'Now, Annette Burnham told me she went to see the show last weekend, with her mother and baby brother. Liked it a lot. But she said your father does the puppets, too – and you, too, isn't that right?'

'Oh. Yes, ma'am.'

'Don't call me ma'am, Donovan, we're not in the South. The things you kids get from television.'

'Yes, Miss St–' began Donovan, although he had neither an idea of the South, being Greenwich Village born and raised, nor much conception of television, which he was not allowed to watch. It was from his mother – whose father had been English – that he had received the strange idea that *ma'am* was a romantic form of British address, suitable for ladies you especially admired.

'Anyway, that's fine,' said Miss Steinhardt and looked over at the door until the boy had stopped wrestling with her name and closed his big wet mouth. 'Well, I'd say it's an unusual pastime for an eight-year-old. If I were you, I'd use it. Always best to use what you have.'

'Ma'am?'

'I'm sure the class would be interested to hear about it. You could bring in one of the puppets.'

'But –'

'Yes, Donovan?'

Miss Steinhardt moved one of her stolid Mary Janes over the other and readjusted the long tartan skirt. She looked directly into the pale but not unbeautiful face: a long nose and bright green eyes, full, almost womanly lips and a lot of dark hair, cut into a pair of slightly ludicrous curtains on either side of his narrow face. A boy who might have some hope of growing up into a Robert Taylor type – fine cheekbones, for a child – if it weren't for this absolute lack of purpose that revealed itself in every pore of his being.

'I already got the pictures from the paper. I was planning on doing –' Donovan looked pleadingly at his teacher.

'Breathe, Donovan. It's not an interrogation. You're always in such a panic.'

'The tower, in Chicago. The one they've been building. They just finished.'

'Sears?'

Donovan nodded.

'Oh, well, yes, Sears would be fine,' said Miss Steinhardt, and wondered at the child, for she knew S was the letter of his particular difficulty. She returned to her nails. Donovan, finely attuned to the moment when people grew bored of him, picked up his book bag and made his way out onto Sullivan Street, into Washington Square.

Lit by a bright full sun, the arch looked more than usually like its Roman progenitor, and the boy found the leaves made a pleasing crunch underfoot, and some wild man in the fountain was talking of Christ, and another stood on a bench singing about marijuana – for the great days of the Village were coming to an end. Another obvious thing was that his mother must never hear of his class assignment. He swore this solemnly to himself on Fifth Avenue, as boys will, before walking as slowly as could be managed back to the mews. At that charming row of cottages he stopped and clutched a replica Victorian lamp post.

'Donovan? What are you, cracked? Get in here!'

Irving Kendal stepped out of their little blue home and took up a spot in the middle of the street. He packed a wad of tobacco into a pipe and peered over at his only son.

'Get in here. Hanging off that thing.'

The boy stayed put. It had recently come to his attention that his father's W came out like a V, that his H had too much water in it, and that everything he said came from another era.

'Who're you meant to be? Gene Kelly?'

Worse were the clothes: a broad-check three-piece suit in yellows and browns, cut to create the illusion of height, with widely spaced buttons and trouser legs that kicked madly at the knee. In the cottage next door, Donovan could see Miss Clayton in her elegant black-and-red kimono, standing at the window with her Maltese, Pablo, in her arms. She looked from the father to the son and gave the son a warm look of sympathy. It would be a fine thing to walk straight past Irving to go drink from Miss Clayton's SodaStream and listen to her old bebop records, or sneak a look at the nude in her bathroom, or throw a beanbag around for Pablo to snap at with his harmless jaws. But such visits had to be rationed, out of loyalty. 'Four bedrooms, is it?' said Polly, if Donovan happened to visit the apartment of a friend with means. 'Well, I can see how you would have enjoyed that. Naturally. I know I would. Probably wouldn't want to come home at all.' Or: 'A SodaStream! Well, that's what disposable income means, I guess – not having anybody but yourself to dispose it *on*. But was it *deliciously* fizzy?' These conversations, much dreaded, always left Donovan with a free-floating sensation of guilt, all the less manageable for the indeterminacy of its source.

Now Polly emerged, barefoot, despite the autumn chill. Donovan waved; his mother mimed her incapacity. In her left hand, she gripped a long piece of green velvet attached to a stake, held high to keep it from dragging on the ground, and in her right, three coloured feathers, each a foot long. Flying over to him, velvet streaming like the banner of a medieval princess, she moved with her toes pointed, so that what might simply be 'running' in another woman looked like a series of darting *pliés*.

'Just when I need you, darling – the whole of the forest has come away from the blocks. It'll need something better than glue – maybe tacks – and a whole new set of ferns from some very evergreen thing – it's of the utmost importance that it look lovely for Tuesday – Oh, Eleanor Glugel came by just after school and told me all about it and I think it's an excellent opportunity for the show, really excellent. I've been dying to talk to you about it – what took you so long? I had to listen to Glugel rattling on about her grandmother's tattoo for half an hour – that's what she's bringing in, to show – or tell – if you can believe it – her own grandmother.' Polly shuddered, and indicated a spot on the underside of her own delicate wrist: 'What an uplifting subject! Oh, but don't we all already *know* the world is full of horror? Do we *really* need to hear about it all the livelong day? There's no romance in that child whatsoever. No clue of the magic of storytelling. I'll bet you a dollar she wears a girdle already.'

All of this poured right into his ear, as Polly's lips happened to be exactly level with it. She pressed his hand; he pressed back. She was perfect – an elf princess who had sworn allegiance only to him. Yet sometimes he wished that she could see, as he did, that theirs was a steely bond, not as easily broken as she seemed to imagine – one which he would never, ever give up, no matter how many four-bedroom apartments or soda fountains he came across in his life. Who else could make him agree to appear before his classmates in a pair of long johns, a nightshirt and a droopy hat with a bell on it? What larger sign of fealty could a knight offer a princess than his pride?

But the next morning Miss Steinhardt made a further announcement: the children were to work in pairs, encouraging the values of compromise, shared responsibility and teamwork, so lacking in these difficult times. She gazed in a pained sort of a way out the far window, in the direction, the children could only assume, of the difficult times. Thus would a small public school in the Village, in its own little way, act as a beacon for the world. It took a few minutes for Donovan to recognize in this new directive the last-minute reprieve for which he had not even dared to hope. 'Me and you!' cried a child called Donna Ford, grabbing the hand of another child called Carla Woodbeck, who flushed happily and replied, 'Yeah, us two!' and in another moment the room was filled with similar, urgent cries of allegiance, requested and answered, all around Donovan, like a series of doors shutting in his face. Reduced to trying to catch the eye of Walter Ulbricht, he found even Walter Ulbricht avoiding him, apparently holding out for a better option.

'Part of my point,' said Miss Steinhardt, in a queer wobbly voice that silenced her class, 'is we don't always get to choose whom we work with.' Miss Steinhardt had spent yesterday at her grandparents' home in Brooklyn Heights, watching tanks cross the Suez Canal. 'Line up please as I call your names.'

The pairing was to be achieved alphabetically, as if a third of the class wasn't coloured and Walter Ulbricht didn't have a port wine stain eating half his face. A second flurry of anxious voices went up; Miss Steinhardt ignored them; the double line was achieved; the bell rang. In the hall, Cassandra Kent fell in step with Donovan Kendal. They walked out like this, onto Sullivan, neither holding hands nor talking, yet clearly walking together. Once again he passed through Washington Square Park, as he did daily, but the fact of Cassie Kent transformed it: the leaves were not merely crunchy but entirely golden, and the fountain threw up glorious columns of water, over and over, an engine of joy. Whatever it was that glistened in the wide skull-gaps between her tight plaits smelled of a vacation somewhere wonderful.

'Let's do yours,' said Cassie. 'The tower. Since you got it all figured already.'

'Oh. Well, all right.'

'S-S-Sears?' she said, somehow not unkindly. 'Now, how tall is it, anyway?'

'A thousand four hundred and fifty-one feet high,' said the boy, as they went under the arch. 'And this is eighty feet, maybe. Then if you –'

'Eighteen times taller,' said Cassie, without pausing. 'I'm mathematical. Wanna play?'

They took a left and sat on two stone benches under the shade of a sycamore tree, in front of a game Donovan had never before played in his life. Cassie drew a ratty plastic bag from her satchel and emptied a small pile of plastic chess pieces onto the concrete table. Donovan tried to concentrate on her instructions. All around them, the men the Kendals usually took the long route round the park to avoid gathered close. One of them was completely topless and had something like Saran Wrap wound tightly round both shoes. Another had only a handful of teeth and wore a broken gambler's visor to keep the winter sun out of his eyes. He appeared to know Cassie.

'Hey, boy – you ready?' asked the visor man, of Donovan. He knelt down by both children and planted his rusty elbows on the table. 'This girl 'bout to school you.'

Donovan's plan was to watch each of Cassie's moves intently, hoping to follow the logic of the game, and, from there, recreate this logic in his own woolly mind. But where she moved her pieces ruthlessly over the concrete table, with an eye only to their strategic use, to Donovan these were noble kings and queens, and those were the castles in which they lived; here were the advisers they trusted, and there the minions waiting in lines outside the castle wall – and no amount of explanation from Cassie about the rigid rules that were meant to dictate all their movements could stop the boy from instinctively arranging his pieces by rank or relationship.

'Can't win anything, playing like that,' said Cassie, abducting Donovan's queen, who had rashly stepped out of her chamber to stroke a favoured white steed. 'Can't even get started playing like that.'

By the time she had his king surrounded, not too long after they'd started, she was sat up on her own heels, laughing and clapping her hands.

'Donovan Kendal,' she crowed, jabbing a finger into his sternum, 'you got no place to turn.'

'But couldn't this Cassie whoever-she-is just learn the lines?' Polly wanted to know. She was holding a tube of glue unwisely between her teeth. Her son passed the paper doily of Grandmother's cap and the cardboard face of the wolf, to be affixed to each other, a task that had to be redone almost every week. 'I mean, we could certainly do with another pair of hands.'

'But turns out it's got to be just two kids together. Just me and her. Teacher said so.'

'Well, all right, but I still don't see why that should –'

'She's a coloured girl,' said Donovan, hardly knowing why, but in its way, the intervention worked; for reasons of consistency it was now impossible for Polly to speak ill of the project. Anyone who knew anything at all about Polly Kendal knew she held the idea of 'Racial Integration' almost as close to her heart as she did 'The Power of Storytelling' or 'The Innocence of Children'. Once upon a time – on what was back then a rare trip downtown – she herself had been caught up in the drama of 'Racial Integration', in the form of a large, excitable crowd pushing through Washington Square towards Judson Church. Being, by temperament, 'a lifelong seeker', she'd joined this crowd, finding herself, a few minutes later, three pews back from the podium listening to the young Reverend Martin Luther King Jr give a speech. A lively story for coffee mornings and parent–teacher conferences. 'His eyes! The only word I can find for them is "limpid". Limpid. I could see them looking straight at me: this kooky, sixteen-year-old scrap of a white girl from Brighton Beach. I mean, naturally I stood out. And I'll tell you something else and I'm not the least bit ashamed of it: whatever he would have asked me to do, I would have done it! I would have done anything!' But as it happened the Reverend King had not asked the teenage Polly to do anything. Her practical involvement with the civil rights movement ended with that sermon, leaving behind only a residue of enthusiasm.

'Why *shouldn't* the children of Harlem get the equal chance to hear our stories?' she asked Cassie two days later, as the child pulled a rattan chair to a circular table covered by a fringed gypsy cloth, missing only a crystal ball. 'Telling someone a story is a way of showing love. Don't they deserve love?'

'I love everybody!' said Cassie happily, and accepted the breadstick that was passed to her. 'But: if I am attacked, I will defend. You play chess, Mr Kendal?'

'Me?' Irving lowered his newspaper. 'Nope. Not my game.'

'I play.'

'You do?' Polly stopped stirring her spaghetti sauce and took a second, anthropological look at Cassie Kent. There were the girls in pigtails who skipped and sang by the fountain, and then there were the grubby old men hunched over the stone tables by the far west gate, but the two groups had always been quite separate in her mind. 'At school, you mean?'

'In the park sometimes. Whenever, wherever. I'm pretty good, too.'

'I'll bet you are!'

'I beat Donovan good.'

'Cassie, do you know Donny never brings any of his friends round to see his poor maw and paw,' said Polly, putting her hands on slender hips and delving into her small trove of theatrical accents. 'So I'm real glad he thought to bring you round to see us.'

'I was gonna show-and-tell my chess . . . but when you think about it, there ain't that much to show.'

'Of course, *our* show is up and ready to go, any time . . .' began Polly slowly.

The train was coming back down the line, and Donovan, tied to the track, did his best to divert it: 'But that's not – you can't teach a person to do that in just a few days. Puppets are a real craft,' he said, quoting Polly back to Polly, which seemed to calm her; she stopped biting the spoon and put it back in the pot.

'Well, that's very true. It *is* a craft. Not everyone can pick it up just like that.'

'There's a war on,' said Irving loudly, and flicked a finger at the front page. 'Somebody should show-and-tell about that.'

Cassie examined the photograph: 'They your people over there?'

'Hmm?' said Polly, with her back to them all. 'Oh, no, not mine. Irving's. Technically. I mean, he doesn't have any relatives over there or anything.'

'*Technically?*'

The door caught on the usual tile and failed to slam; Polly did not flinch. Polly, Cassie and Donovan listened to Irving leave the cottage, and – such was the silence of the mews in those days – strike a match against an outside wall. Polly returned placidly to her sauce.

'Of course, in the end,' she said, with a contented look on her face, 'we're all one people.'

'This is a scale model,' said Cassie, holding up a cardboard tower in front of the class, and Donovan read the scale off a piece of paper, and then Cassie said the name of the architect, and Donovan told them the population of Chicago, and it all passed off without a hitch. But in the hallway, afterwards, when they should have been simply congratulating each other, Cassie announced her intention to soon visit the Polly Kendal Puppet Theater.

'But – it's two bucks.'

'I'm not in the poorhouse – we got two bucks!'

'It's just for little kids,' tried Donovan, gripped by the horrible confirmation of a private fear – that all roads led back to his mother. 'You're too old. And it's on a Sunday. You'll go to church, won't you?'

'I'm *coming.*'

'It's not two bucks, that was a lie,' said Donovan, turning red. Having put his hand up inside Pinocchio every Saturday for the whole of the previous year, he had been unable to rid himself of a feeling of deep identification. 'If you really want to know it's only fifty c–'

Most adults at least would keep looking into his face when he was in trouble, smiling kindly, until the word, whatever it happened to be, was completed. Cassie, like all children, only said, 'What? *What? What?*' and groaned with impatience. She walked ahead. When he caught her up, she turned on him: 'Man oh man, can't you *stop* that?'

'Yes,' said Donovan, feebly, but perhaps that was just another lie. A man called Cory Wallace had assured the Kendals that their son could be easily 'cured' of his peculiar trouble, but he did not seem to be a proper doctor – he had no certificates on his wall and his office was next to a Chinese restaurant down on Canal. Still Polly had 'faith in his sincerity'.

'Donovan Kendal,' said Cassie, sighing and putting her hands on her hips like somebody's mother, 'you tire me out. Wanna see my titty?'

They were within spitting distance of their classroom; it did not seem a viable prospect. But in the turn of the stairwell, Cassie pressed herself against a wall and pulled her pinafore to one side. Donovan stared dumbly at a breast no different than his own except that the nipple was slightly larger and the skin a deep and lovely brown. He put his palm flat against its flatness. They stood there like that until a footstep was heard on the stair. 'If I was a hooker,' whispered Cassie, pulling the fabric back over and looking serious, 'that would be ten bucks easy.' After which they walked to the exit and parted without another word.

Matters developed, in spasmodic order. One morning before school, she conceded an utterly chaste kiss, two closed mouths pressed against each other while Cassie jerked her head violently back and forth, as perhaps she had seen people do in the movies. At an arbitrary moment, she pulled away and primly flattened her pinafore against her chest. 'Don't think I've forgotten,' she said, 'I'm coming to that show.' That same afternoon, in a restroom cubicle, she showed him her 'ding-a-ling' – a confusion of black folds that parted to reveal a shockingly pink interior. He was permitted to put one finger in and then take it out again. After which it was hard to see how he could refuse her.

Black folds, green velvet. Donovan peering through. He could see Cassie sitting with the adults on the fold-up chairs, her feet up by her bottom, hugging herself. 'Please remember,' said Polly backstage, drawing the heads of her crouching husband and son towards her own, 'I don't want to see Goldilocks *or* the bowls until I've dismantled the woodshed. You were much too quick with that, last week, both of you – but you, Irving, in particular.' Irving thrust his hand violently into Papa Bear: 'Don't tell me what to do. I know what I'm doing.' Donovan rang the little bell, and the church warden dimmed the 'house lights' and Goldilocks's hair got caught on a nail, and all this had happened before, many times. In a sort of dream, Donovan got off his knees and walked round the front to invite all the little believers to join him in the Land of Nod. He was sure enough that he said his lines (carefully written by Polly, free of the dangerous letters), and sang his song; he could hear the children yelling, and knew the brown smudge of the wolf must be behind him, appearing and disappearing, in rhythm with their cries. But all he could see was

Cassie's upper lip pulled tight into her mouth, and the deep crease of her brow. Somehow, he got through the half-hour. The house lights went up. Polly was by his side once more, all in black, a tiny piece of punctuation, and she was saying My Husband Irving and My Son Donovan and they were all three holding hands and bowing.

'Cassie, you came!'

Polly reached both hands out to the girl. Cassie kept her own in the back pocket of her jeans.

'I'll tell you what: would you like to come backstage? There's a box of tricks back there.'

She led the girl behind the velvet to where Irving sat on the floor, smoking a cigarette, placing props and puppets into open shoeboxes. He held up the wolf and placed it on Cassie's hand.

'You try – move it.' Cassie moved it slightly to the right. Grandmother's cap came unglued and fell away. She handed it back to Irving.

'This god*damned* –'

Polly rescued the wolf from her husband before it could be flung, and placed it back with its cap softly in a box marked 'Bad Guys #2'.

'Why all the puppets so raggedy?' Cassie asked.

'Well . . . if they look home-made, I suppose that's because we make them ourselves.'

'Thought you meant puppets like puppets,' said Cassie, turning to Donovan. 'Like Big Bird or somebody.'

Polly stepped in: 'Well, that's really not a puppet. That's a grown man in a bird suit. Which is fine – if you like that sort of thing. But it's really not puppetry.'

'Puppets got arms and legs and bodies,' Cassie persisted, pointing to Goldilocks at rest. 'That's just a cut-out cardboard face. It ain't even got more than one side.'

Polly put an arm around Cassie and led her back out into the hall. 'I hope we see you again,' she said, speaking over Cassie's head to the fleeing families. 'We do a charity show in the Bronx, and in Harlem, once a month, paid for by your generous contributions. Do please leave what you can in the bottle by the door. We've been doing this show in this spot for almost six years! But not everyone's as fortunate as our children of Greenwich Village.' She put a hand on top of Cassie's head. 'It's a wonderful opportunity for the children up there.'

'I live on Tenth and 14th,' protested Cassie, but Polly had moved on, and was now accosting her small audience as they tried to take their leave. And how did you come to hear of the Polly Kendal Puppet Theater? A friend? An advertisement? The unlucky few looked up rather desperately; more fortunate, dexterous women had already managed to wedge their children back into their coats and were halfway down Hudson by now. So which was it: 'Word-of-mouth' or 'Publicity'? It took a moment to understand that the latter category referred to those little four-by-six cards, poorly illustrated and printed, that were to be seen in every cafe, dive bar, jazz den and restaurant beneath 14th Street.

'On the first of the month, we go to the November cycle: *The Musicians of Bremen, The Three Little Pigs* and *Cinderella.* Tell your friends!' Across the hall, Donovan lingered, half hidden by the stage curtain, trying to choose between a number of things to say. He was still preparing the sentence, checking it for what he thought of as 'snakes', when Cassie Kent simply ran past him, into the church, down the aisle – and was gone.

The Kendals were alone. Shoeboxes were numbered, sealed and placed in a suitcase in their correct order. The three-sided 'stage' was flattened and care taken to fold the green velvet into a clean square. Irving switched off all the lights and collected a handful of dollars from the jar. Polly sat lightly on the closed suitcase and pressed its brass clips down.

'What happened to your little friend?'

Donovan pulled the nightcap off his own head and held it in both hands.

'But, Donny . . . why would you even want to spend your time with a girl like that? Oh, I'm sure she's nice enough – I don't want to put you off her if you really *like* her, but she seemed to me to be so clearly – well, she has so little, oh, I don't know: fancy. Imagination. Whimsy. Trust me: you don't want that. Irving has no imagination whatsoever and look how hard that makes just about everything. A sense of imagination is so much more important to me than what colour someone happens to be or how much money they have or anything like that – if that's what you think you're standing there frowning about. The only thing I care about is what's going on in here,' she said, and thumped her narrow chest, but Donovan only looked at his shoes.

'Listen to me. Why do you think she doesn't like you? Because you have a little problem sometimes when you speak? Because you're skinny? Don't you see that if she had even a scrap of vision she'd see what a first-class kid you are? But she's got no vision to speak of. I bet she's going home right now to turn on that idiot box and just *vegetate*.' Now his mother performed a funny mime – eyes crossed, tongue tucked in front of lower teeth – and Donovan found it impossible not to smile.

'All she does is watch TV,' he confided, and let the cap drop to the stone floor where he worried it with his foot a little. 'All weekend. She told me one time. Her mom doesn't care what she does, she really doesn't care one bit,' he added, employing a little imagination, 'and they never read or anything. The whole family thinks reading's a big waste of time. She's never heard of Thor or the Sirens or anybody!'

'Well, there you are.'

Polly bent down, picked up Wee Willie Winkie's nightcap and, with great tenderness, brushed the godly dust off it and placed it back on her son's head.

'People find their natural level, Donny. You'll see when you're older. It all works out.' ∎

GRANTA
THE MAGAZINE OF NEW WRITING

Best of | G |

Best of podcasts
Best of new fiction, non-fiction and poetry
Best of the stories from our archives
Best of literary news on Twitter, Tumblr, Facebook or via our newsletter

granta.com

THE
RESERVATION

Sarah Hall

SARAH
HALL

1974

Sarah Hall was born in Cumbria and currently lives in Norwich, Norfolk. She is the author of four novels: *Haweswater*, *The Electric Michelangelo*, *The Carhullan Army* (published in the US as *Daughters of the North*) and *How to Paint a Dead Man*; a collection of short stories, *The Beautiful Indifference*; original radio dramas; and poetry. She has won several awards, including the Commonwealth Writers' Prize for Best First Novel, the Betty Trask Award, the John Llewellyn Rhys Prize, the James Tiptree, Jr. Award and the Edge Hill University Short Story Prize, and has twice been recipient of the Portico Prize. She has been shortlisted for the Man Booker Prize, the Prix Femina Etranger, the Arthur C. Clarke Award for science fiction, the BBC National Short Story Award and the Frank O'Connor International Short Story Award. 'The Reservation' is an excerpt from a novel in progress.

It's not often she dreams about them. Through the day they are elusive, keeping to the tall grass of the Reservation, disappearing from the den site. They are fleet or lazy, moving through their own tawny colourscape, sleeping under logs: missable either way. Their vanishing acts have been perfected. At night they come back. The cameras pick them up, red-eyed, heads lowered, muzzles darkened, returning from a hunt. Or she hears them howling along the buffer zone, a long harmonic. One leading, then many. At night there is no need to imagine, no need to dream. They reign outside the mind.

Now there is snow over Chief Joseph, an early fall. The pines are bending tolerantly; the rivers see white. In backcountry cabins venison stocks and pipes are beginning to freeze. Millionaires' ranches lie empty, their thermostats set, their gates locked. The roads are open but there are few visitors. The summer conferences and powwows are long over; only the casinos do business with tourists, with stag parties and addict crones, in neon reparation. Soon the pack will be gone too, north, after the caribou, the centre will close for winter, and she is flying home to England.

Her first visit in six years. The last ended badly, with argument, a family riven. This time she is being called upon to entertain a rich man's whimsy. And her mother is dying. Neither duty is urgent; both players will wait, with varying degrees of patience. Meanwhile, snow; the Chief Joseph pack are scenting hoof prints, foraying from the den, the pups have grown big and ready, any day now they will start out; the tribal councils are meeting in Lapwai to discuss scholarships, road maintenance, the governor's hunting quota; the Hernandez comet is low and dull in the east, above survivalist compounds.

The night before she leaves Idaho she dreams of Binny. Binny is sitting on a wooden bench in the wildlife park outside the bird huts, wearing a long leather coat and smoking a rolled cigarette. She is dark and short-haired under a green cloche hat. It is Rachel's birthday. This is her birthday choice – Setterah Keep – a ruined

Victorian menagerie in the woods of the Lowther Valley. They have walked round the boar enclosure, the otters, the peacocks, to the owls. Binny likes the eagle owl. She likes its biased ears, the fixed orange tunnels of its eyes. She sits quietly and smokes, watches it beating clipped wings and preening. She is all bone and breasts under her coat: a body better out of clothes. Not yet pregnant with Rachel's brother, not yet disintegrating. Her green nylon trousers tingle with static when Rachel leans against them. The stocky haunched bird prowls across the pen towards its feed, and gullets a mouse whole, up to the tail.

Rachel hates owls. They are like fat brushes. They sweep and swivel their heads and have sharp picky beaks. A ridiculous shape for a thing. When she goes inside the huts to see the lunar white one, the darkness hurts her head. It stinks of lime and feathers and must. Outside she sits on the bench with Binny and kicks the ground. *Are you bored, my girl?* Binny says. *Go back to the otters then. Take some ice cream.*

Binny likes everyone to have freedom. She likes the man in the sweet kiosk. He makes her laugh by asking are they sisters. *Go on, my girl*, she says. *Have a good look round. Be brave.* On the way to the pool Rachel unwraps a mint choc chip and licks the gritty dome. The otter pool has a green-stained moat that moves like a river. Otters paddle round it on their backs, eating fish heads. Their fur snugs the water. They chitter to each other. She goes to the snake house where there are bright bugs clinging in glass tanks. The snakes move slower than time.

Binny is still talking at the kiosk, leaning in. Best to leave her alone and go exploring. It's OK to go quite far. Rachel knows all the ways around the village where she lives, and the drove-tracks over the moors. She walks past netted parrots squawking at each other, past the toilet block, over a bridge over a stream, to a burnt creosote gate. There's a sign: she can't read because she's not yet in school. Through the gate and into the trees. Wooded pathways, with arrows pointing. *Be brave.* The trees are very quiet. Brown needles stream between trunks. Her steps make tiny silky squeaks. Fork to the right. Fork to the left. Arrows pointing. At the bottom of the ice cream there's a chocolate stub. Once it's gone she's more aware of where she is.

Here. Beside a fence built tall and seriously, up into the trees. The wire is thick, knotted into diamond holes. Pinned to it is another sign; red writing. Maybe it's the end of the park. Maybe there is no more. She reaches up and takes hold of the wire. She slots the tips of her shoes through and lifts herself off the ground. On the other side are bushes and worn earth. A bundle of something pink with bits of ragged hair and buzzing flies. She leans back, bends her knees, and sways and rattles the metal. Emptiness beyond. Flickering leaves.

Then it comes between the bushes, as if bidden. It comes forward, long and grey, paws lifting, moving fast but not running, the definition of a word she has not yet heard. *Lope*. It is perfectly made: long legs, sheer chest, dressed for coldness in wraps of fur. It comes close to the wire and stands looking, eyes level with hers. Pure yellow gaze. Long nose, short mane. A dog before dogs were invented. A god of dogs. A creature so fine she can hardly comprehend it. But it recognizes her. It has seen animals like her for two million years. It lifts a heavy paw. Yellow eyes, black-ringed. The fence has almost disappeared and she is hanging in the air, suspended like a soft offering. Any minute it will be upon her.

In sleep, Rachel has stopped breathing. Her brain's electrical state is unknown. Snow is falling on the cabin roof; the computer in the office is winking slowly, storing emails and enquiries and data; elk season is open. Her British passport is in her jacket pocket. Her mother is dying a long way away. The den has been abandoned and the pack is moving single file through the white Bitterroot terrain. She is not breathing. In the dream it stands looking at her. Pure yellow gaze. A mystic from the Reservation once asked her to describe the feeling of contact with them. What did her heart feel? *I don't know*, she said. *I don't believe what you believe.*

Pre-erotic fear. Her heart smells bloody. She un-clutches the wire and steps to the ground. Its head drops. Eyes level again. She holds still. It stays still. Then it releases that extraordinary jaw. Inside is a lustre of sharpness, black-ridged gums, and a spooling, buckling tongue. In her brain an evolutionary signal fires. *Move. Now.* She steps back and walks carefully along the fence, up on her toes. It crosses paws, its body folds round, and it walks parallel on the other side. Long and grey. Close to the wire. One watching yellow eye. She stops. Slowly she turns round and walks the other way. It swaps feet and follows, head tilted inwards, following. Again she stops, turns and walks away. Again it turns and follows. She stops. *What are you doing?* she shouts. *What are you doing?* Its ears prick up, rotate a fraction. Its head drops again. She turns round and begins to run along the wire, kicking hard on the slippery forest floor. She runs fast, over leaves and broken branches. But it is faster, there at her side, then in front, running with her. She stops, turns and runs. It turns and runs with her. She turns and runs and it runs with her. *What are you doing? What are you doing?*

But already she must know. The layers of sleep are falling away, the radio alarm is blaring, a rock song from the eighties. Her shoulder is cold outside the heavy covers. Her brain is restarting. That creature of the outer darkness, of geographic success, myth and horror, hunted with every age's weapon, stone axe, spear, sprung-steel trap and semi-automatic, was playing.

Five a.m., Mountain Time. Kyle will drive her to the airport before daylight. She lies under the blankets and listens to snow dispatching softly from the roof and the branches. In 1981 the Licensing Act brought an end to the worst exhibitions. But even a century before they must have known the enclosures were too small, pens almost, dementing places. After coffee and a shower, when she is properly awake, she phones Binny and reminds her what time she will be arriving. *Yes, Thursday. Yes, by dinner time.* Then, unusually, she tells her about the Setterah Keep dream. *No*, her mother says. *That wasn't a dream. There were wolves in the park. Don't you remember? One of them got out. They closed it down.*

The earl is not at home when Rachel arrives at Pennington Hall. She has been warned by his secretary that he is unreliable, that he keeps only some of his appointments. The prerogative of wealth and eccentricity. The drive from London has taken eight hours; congestion around the airport and the north orbital, an accident south of Kendal, all lanes halted until the air ambulance could set down on the carriageway to collect the shattered motorcyclist. As ever, the county's interior routes move sluggishly: compact drystone lanes and dawdling sightseers. A landslide on one of the mountain passes has resulted in road closure, so she must turn back at the barrier and take the longer lake road into the western valleys.

The fells rise, carrying dead bracken on their slopes the colour of rusting iron. Granite juts through, below gathering cloud. She sets the wipers to intermittent, but the rain is either too heavy or too fine, the rubber blades screech or the screen goes blind. The GPS becomes blank. She buys a road atlas from a village shop. This is not a part of the district she knows – her home village is on the other side of the central peaks. She is extremely tired by the time she reaches the road to the estate, nauseous with jet lag and service-station coffee. But she's alert enough to notice the beauty of the place, September's russet left in the trees, wet light on the hills, and to note that the lake would be a good territorial boundary, were this still wilderness. It has not been wilderness since the primeval forest was felled. She lowers the window and inhales. Moorland, peat, ferns, water and whatever the water touches. The myrrh of autumn. She's become used to spruce and sagebrush, the occasional rancid vegetable smell of the paper mill downriver from the Reservation. But the aroma of Cumbria is immediately recognizable: upland pheromones.

She pulls up at the gate of Pennington Hall, reaches out and presses the intercom. There's a crackle and then the gate opens silently. The drive is long and newly gravelled, oak-lined. She passes a tree so old and obese with bark that its lower branches are sagging almost to the ground. Wooden struts have been built underneath to prop them up. Beside the driveway a handful of spotted deer graze. They raise their heads as she drives by but do not move.

In the rain, the red-stone manor looks patched and bloody. Ivy is growing shaggily up the facade, but for a building of its size and age it is far from dereliction. The crenellations are intact, the windows expensively replaced. It seems Lord Pennington has not suffered hard times, death duties or insurmountable taxes. The building is clearly not a casualty of democratic change like so many of the countryside's aristocratic behemoths. Possibly the garden and house are open to the public, or a lucrative tea room is hidden somewhere behind the maze, bulbs and plant cuttings for sale, the usual schemes. Or the earl's business portfolio has been skilfully updated and he has accounts offshore. She parks on a gravel apron to the side of the tower, gets out and stretches. The air is moist and cool. Rooks clamour in the trees nearby.

The main door of the hall is a dense medieval affair, shot through with bolts, siege-proof. On either side sit two stone lions, lichen mottling their manes. She pushes the bell and there is a ferrous donging within. A woman answers: middle-aged, plump inside her herringbone suit. She is auburn-haired, unadorned by jewellery or cosmetics, extremely English-looking, an England seventy years gone. She would suit a rabble of hounds at her feet, a shotgun crooked over her elbow, and Rachel has no doubt the complete incarnation has at some stage existed. The woman introduces herself as Honor Clark. The secretary, through whom all correspondence has been exchanged, and the person responsible for booking the airline tickets and hire car.

Really sorry I'm late. The flight was delayed. Snow in Spokane. We were sitting on the runway too long – they had to respray the plane. I almost missed the connection. Then the drive up . . . I hope you haven't been waiting long.

The apology is irrelevant. Honor Clark shakes her head.

He isn't here. I don't know where he is at the moment. The Land Rover's gone, which doesn't bode well, but at least it means he's on the estate. Somewhere. I'm leaving in an hour. Do you want to come in?

Rachel checks her watch.

Ah. Yes, OK. Thank you.

She follows the woman across the threshold, down a corridor hung with portraits of stags and Heaton Coopers and a few tasteful abstracts, to a vast drawing room containing an elaborate suite of furniture, a Bauhaus chair, glassware cabinets, bookcases and a huge stone fireplace. The grate is unlaid but the room is warm. The secretary holds her hands up as if fending something away.

I can't offer you dinner, I'm afraid. The housekeeper's already gone home and nothing's prepared. Thomas has an event in Windermere tonight so he's dining out. We have no guests this week.

I'm fine.

As I say, I doubt he'll be available before he has to go out.

OK. But I did have an appointment. I should probably wait.

The secretary nods and lowers her hands.

You said you didn't need a hotel so I haven't booked one.

No. I'm staying with family.

You're local? I don't hear an accent.

I've been away quite a while.

I see.

At the direction of Honor Clark, Rachel crosses the room and sits on the chaise longue. Lambent Chinese silk, in near-perfect condition. Her trousers are badly creased. The sales tag inside the waistband is irritating her lower back but she has failed during the course of the flight or the drive to tear it out. She has not worn slacks for over a year, not since the Minnesota conference, at which she delivered the keynote speech, drank too much in the hotel bar with Kyle and Oran, argued with the chairman of the IWC, slept with Oran again and left a day early, not disgraced exactly, but en route. In the bars and restaurants of Kamiah, which the centre workers frequent at weekends, the dress code for both men and women extends no further than boots and jeans. She hasn't showered since leaving the centre yesterday morning; any trace of deodorant is gone. She has never been received at this level of society before, in any country. Even beyond the warp of altered time zones, the event feels deeply uncanny. Honor Clark moves to the sideboard.

OK. Well. I'll set you up. Would you like a sherry?

Yes, all right.

Sweet or dry?

Dry?

The secretary lifts one of the cut-glass decanters, unstoppers it, pours out a viscous topaz. The rugs under her sensible heels are intricately woven, plums and teals, each one no doubt worth thousands. Rachel's cabin in the centre complex has flat-pack cabinets and linoleum floors. There are fading plastic coffee cups with the Chief Joseph logo. The entire cabin would fit, if not into this capacious, silk-wallpapered room, then certainly into the wing. It feels as if a kind of Dickensian experiment is taking place, except there will be no charitable warding, no societal ascent. Her intended role has not yet been defined. A consultant? A named advocate? A class of specialist suddenly called upon in times of extravagant ecological hobbying? A delicate bell-shaped glass is placed into her hand. Honor Clark heads for the door.

I'll come back before I go. I have to make a few phone calls and finish up. If he arrives I'll send him to you. But, as I say, it's unlikely. You'll be all right in the meantime?

Yes. Fine. Thanks.

And the woman is gone, back into the panelled dimness of the manor corridors, back into her officious oubliette – whichever chamber of Pennington Hall she arranges the abortive comings and goings of the earl from. The sun shifts from behind a cloud and the drawing room is filled with glimmering Lakeland light. Rachel sips the sherry, which is crisp, salty and surprisingly enjoyable. Not a trace of dust or mouldering cork. She finishes the drink then stands and crosses the room. Beyond the tall windows, the estate extends for miles. It is the largest estate in England. Little of the acreage has been sold off, quite the opposite. Thomas Pennington owns most of the private woodland in the region, farmsteads, all but the common land. On the horizon, the fells roll bluely towards bald peaks. At the bottom of the sloping lawn, at the lake edge, is a wooden reiki platform – perhaps one of the earl's alternative hobbies, certainly safer than flying microlights, which famously almost killed him, and killed his wife. The lake surface reflects complicated weather. On an island near the opposite shore is a red-stone folly, an architectural match for the hall, and towards this a tiny boat is rowing, leaving a soft V on the cloudy surface. The coast is fifteen miles away, ugly and nuclear. Maps of the estate have been sent to her. Diagrammatically, spatially, the argument is easily made; it is one of the few places such a project is viable. He already has permission, obtained through the correct channels and a new game enclosure bill, though no doubt there were strings pulled, or wheels behind wheels. Work is already underway on the barrier. The money seems limitless. What he does not have, what he wants, is her. The native expert.

She takes her phone out of her jacket pocket. The signal is low, barely a single bar. Binny has rung but left no message – she hates answerphones. There are two texts from Kyle. *Left Paw radio transmitter kaput, possible dispersal. Trustafarian volunteer quit. Owe you 50.* Then, off duty: *How's merry old England had any warm beer?* She types and sends a reply, but it fails to deliver. Kyle will be out trying to track the young male. The disappearance is not unexpected. There's a text from one of the local rangers, married but persistent. A mistake over the summer. Another white night. She deletes it without reading.

Hanging over the lake are fine slings of rain. The boat has made it to the island and is moored. She walks the circumference of the room, pauses at an adjoining door, then opens it. The library. Assuming no intrusion – is she not somehow entitled while she waits? – she goes inside. There is another cold fireplace, elaborate and deeply recessed, classical scenes painted on the tiles. The shelves are fitted, floor to ceiling, with glossy hardwood. She browses the contents. There are leather-bound antiques, hardbacks of contemporary novels. Below are illustrated wildlife encyclopedias. An impressive row of first-edition poetry volumes: Auden, Eliot, Douglas. A large Audubon folio. What evidence does she expect to find? Tomes of the occult, perhaps? Fairy tales? Has she imagined him to be a Gothic fetishist? A Romanticist with a liking for exotic pets? Who is this man who has expensively summoned her across thousand of miles?

On the mantelpiece is a heavy bronze of the Capitoline she-wolf, the infants Romulus and Remus on their knees suckling beneath her. Or has Rachel suspected, as soon as she knew whose name was attached to the project, that this landed British entrepreneur, known for causing trouble in the House, for sponsoring sea eagles and opposing Defra culls, is deadly serious about his latest venture? Isn't that why she is here? Not for Binny, who is simply benefiting from this stranger's buck. She goes back into the drawing room, sits in the chaise longue, leans against the plush upholstery and closes her eyes.

After forty-five minutes Honor Clark comes back into the drawing room, wearing a brown raincoat, belted at the waist, and carrying an oxblood lady's briefcase. She has a headscarf knotted under her chin. Rachel wants to ask, do the shops in the county still sell such items? Are these fashions depicted in the country magazines?

We're going to have to scratch, she says. Can you come back tomorrow?

The tone is vaguely triumphant. Clearly, clerical intuition and rescheduling are a normal part of her job description, and it is not within her remit to apologize for the errant earl. The airline ticket from Spokane was business class; Rachel's hire car is a BMW. Any additional expenses are being covered during her stay; all she has to do is submit receipts. If the man himself is disorganized, disastrous or mad as a bag of wasps, little else in his sovereignty seems to be. Rachel stands.

Sure. Tomorrow. What time?

Let's try eleven. He has t'ai chi from nine until ten.

As she crosses the room, the tag in her trousers scratches her lower back again. She reaches in and snaps it from the plastic frond, crumples it and puts it into her back pocket. She has a week's leave from the centre, during which time her soliciting benefactor can put in an appearance or not, as he so chooses. He can dream of fields of unicorns or invest in the reanimation of sabretooth DNA, if the prognostication visits him. It will make no difference either way. Her obligation ends after their first meeting. She will not take the job. But, foolish or time-wasting though the courtship may be, it has at least given her the means to come home.

R achel? Is that you?
You look smaller, Mum.

It's true. Since her last visit, Binny has shrunk considerably. She leans in the doorway of her care-home apartment, a stoop-lump on her back under the quilted gown. Her hair is almost gone, her scalp as white and dull as shell. Her hand on the door frame looks petrified, like a lump of driftwood, out of proportion with her thin arm. On her face there are brown flaky cancers. Her descent since the last visit, when she was still able to lob a vase at the wall, has been steep.

And you look like an American. Lord! You're not a bloody citizen, are you?

Not yet, no.

Good. Cause you can't change something like that, my girl.

Binny unclutches the door. They embrace. She holds Rachel fiercely, a grip far exceeding her frail demeanour, a grip reminding her daughter just how long she has been gone. From under the quilted gown comes the reek of sweat and ammonia, and a masking perfume – not the Paestum Rose Binny once favoured, gifted by suitors and worn in the wen of her thighs, but something sweeter, cheaper, a scent that will cover sins. They release each other. The yolky eyes of her mother look her over.

Lost a bit of weight too. You're not living on hamburgers and fries then.

Most of the time I am.

I did teach you to cook.

There's a slur when she speaks, a damp collection in one corner of her mouth. The stroke, three years ago. Somehow Rachel has managed not to register the impediment much during their phone calls. Binny is trying to look her daughter in the eye, but her vision is shot, and she has lost her height. Yes, you taught me, Rachel thinks, because you never lifted a pan, and Lawrence was always hungry.

I hate cooking. You know that.

I suppose you just drive through those places in your car.

Sometimes.

Her mother appears to be stalled in the doorway, as if she wants to turn round but her body won't cooperate; first she must will it. This can't really be Binny, Rachel thinks, the toxic, striking Londoner who charmed and upset the northern villagers with her brassy left-wing talk and her new looks. Binny: the woman who broke up several marriages, casting aside the borrowed men as soon as they were hers, or keeping them as lodgers. Who ran the post office as if it was a social club, giving out cups of tea, stacking the tiny entrance hall with controversial items – frosted cornflakes, condoms, the *Guardian*. Who raised a young daughter alone. Or, rather, let the daughter raise herself alone on the moors. Communist in the Tory heartland. Self-declared red-blooded sensualist, whose second child, Rachel's half-brother, left home at fourteen rather than argue with the men frequenting the house. And now: this impotent, leaking ruin.

It's a dire impulse, one Rachel had not truly anticipated. Regret. Or pity. The desire to return this sick-smelling, degraded woman to those years of virility and, yes, notoriety. Return her to the postal cottage, the hoo-ha and scandal in the village, the old red Jaguar always breaking down on country roads, and the caravanner's wardrobe. Even though it would mean all the rest too. The arguments. The name-calling in school. Other women banging on the door. Not bringing boyfriends home because they would stare and stammer, ask embarrassing questions, then be ardent upstairs in Rachel's bedroom and not understand why.

Binny moves from her position in the doorway, without catastrophe, and shuffles inside.

Come in then. Hope you've eaten. Dinner is liable to be an atrocity. They think we can't tell sirloin from slop. You'll want to sit next to Dora – she's the only one with any noodle left.

The same wit. The same vim. The old personality locked in a tomb and struggling to get out. But it sounds like a practised line.

Dora. Got it.

Rachel picks up her bag and follows her mother into a small sitting room, the temperature of which is subtropical. The green leather armchair, which was her mother's chair in the cottage kitchen, is the only recognizable item from the past. She has never visited Willowbrook before. It was Lawrence who moved Binny in and cleared out the cottage; it is Lawrence who takes care of things financially. There will not be time to see her brother. She has not emailed him for a while, though Binny has probably kept him in the loop about the visit. Her mother is struggling out of the gown, inching it down over her shoulders, her hands more an incapacity than any use. She resists Rachel's help.

Get off now. I can manage. You have a seat. You look done in.

Binny shuffles into the bedroom and comes back a few minutes later wearing a blue winged jacket, an astoundingly conservative garment. She has on a smear of burgundy lipstick and a string of beads. Is this the usual effort for dinner, Rachel wonders, or is it being made for the prodigal's return and introduction? Binny moves slowly towards the chair, leans over it and sits.

We can catch up later. Go and get changed. They'll be serving in a minute, so let's get it over and done with. Then you can tell me what Lord Muck wanted. And who you're screwing. Not that wet one who works with you, I hope. He sounds like a prevaricator. The other sounds far better – Carl, is it? Put your stuff in there.

I'll just wear this.

Well, do something with your hair. It's sticking up like a loo brush. Why did you cut it all off anyway?

In another small adjoining room a narrow bed has been made up. Willowbrook allows guests to stay for a week, free of charge. When Rachel goes into the bathroom the smell of urine is overwhelming. There's a grey wig with improbable nylon curls in a wicker basket on top of the toilet cistern. The towels are stained with talcum. The walk-in shower has a seat and a safety handle, an alarm bell nearby. There are boxes of incontinence napkins. Flags of the future. It is all laid down, in the genes. Back in the little spare room she unzips the side pocket of her bag and takes out a spotted feather, which has survived the trip uncrushed. Her mother is hunched awkwardly, on the edge of the armchair.

Here you go, Binny. I think it's from a hawk owl.

At dinner, the cogent residents make a fuss over her, asking her about work. It is apparent they think she is some kind of veterinary, though her mother must be perfectly capable of explaining. They ask whether she is married or has any children. No, and no. Oh well, she is young, someone says. Her mother snorts.

She's nearly forty!

Isn't that how old you were when you had me?

Laughter from the other ladies at the repartee, the mother–daughter spat. Does she have a boyfriend? they ask. Rachel shrugs. Pissing in tandem is how the centre workers describe relationships, like the urinary markings of the breeding pairs. Despite the residents' clear enjoyment of that which is slightly naughty, this observation would not be an appropriate addition to the dinner-table conversation. She must watch herself. Amid these leached desiccated beings, she is already feeling too burlesque, too alive. The woman to her right, Dora, a tiny wobbling creature, informs her that Binny is a very popular member of the Willowbrook community, one of the fun personalities, a good card player, a huge flirt. Dora pats Rachel's arm and name-drops as if she will recognize the people being spoken about. While the ladies cluck and gossip around her, Binny remains silent, pushing apart a piece of fish, trying to lift the skin away. There's the soft clicking of dentures and the scrape of cutlery as the meal progresses. The meal progresses painfully slowly. Though the food is boiled and blanched, flavourless and easy to digest, the exercise of eating still seems too rigorous for most.

Rachel scans the table. Almost every resident has a box of divided pills next to their place setting. Her mother's medication is for high blood pressure and the ruined bladder. She has not taken Herceptin for fifteen years. Her left breast is whole; the right was never reconstructed. The surgery heralded the end of an era for her mother; either she lost interest in men, or they in her. She notices very few men at the home, but longevity is not their strong suit. Opposite her is a woman in a gaping blouse, her chest crêped, her face vacantly concentrating on her fork. She is helped from time to time by an orderly or a neighbour, her attention brought back to the peas and the present. There are a couple of empty chairs at the table. The health of whoever is missing is openly discussed. Such-and-such has fallen, broken a hip, been hospitalized, has a bowel obstruction, isn't expected to come out.

Rachel is past hunger, and so tired that cruelty begins to creep in. The scene, the knotty hands and flaccid jowls, the bagging and slippage of bodies, begins to look grotesque. The tablecloth is stained with sauce. They spill. They tremble. They are ghouls that have passed over the borders of worthwhile existence. It isn't natural. They should be assisted. Last year she and Kyle performed an autopsy on Finestrau, the old male, who was killed by the pack's young adoptee, Tungsten. The collar was still signalling without moving coordinates; they got to his body quickly. He was fresh on the slab, slack, his hind legs gristle-edged, the penis retracted. On his forelegs were old scars. The bite marks in his neck were not survivable. But this is humanity's demise, she thinks. We eke it out, limp on, medicate, become increasingly compromised. For us there will be no status fights, no usurping, no healthy death. Decay continues until the end. Mercifully it might come quickly or during sleep.

Afterwards, she and Binny get ready for bed and squabble about who will use the bathroom first. Her mother raises a twisted finger towards the door.

You look like the walking dead. Bloody well go in there now.

I'm fine. I have to spend days on end awake, when I'm in the field.

You're my guest and you'll go when I say, my girl.

My girl. She is too tired and loses the argument. She showers and cleans her teeth. An orderly hovers by the door. The folding bed is hard and narrow, bowed in the middle, but after a moment or two the room stops kiltering, the static in her ears quietens, and she is unconscious. All night she barely moves. In the morning she is woken by light through the unclosed curtain and the voice of the Polish orderly getting her mother up.

Not much on sheets today, Binnee. Is better. Well done.

Get that leg out of the way, Nedka. Must you poke me around?

Rachel lies on the bunk, looking out of the window at the white sky. She thinks of Left Paw, having dispersed from the pack in search of a mate, climbing over boulders, bounding up off his powerful back legs, crossing the plains and forests, covering miles. Then she sees him splayed in the undergrowth, tongue lolling, eyes slit, blood around the entry wounds. Since the ban was lifted the centre staff are never without worry, even on the Reservation where they are protected. Hunters come for them illegally in planes.

The white unobstructed sky seems unreal. England is unreal, an old imagining, with only a few pieces of evidence to validate it – a passport, a certificate of PhD, memories. Even her mother can't be identified. In an hour, the earl will be taking t'ai chi. She leans over and checks her phone for messages but there are none. She should not have come back, even as a courtesy, or for curiosity, even at the least important time of year. She looks through the window and listens to her mother bossing the orderly. Now that the Chief Joseph pack is nomadic again, Tungsten will be leading the others after the migrating deer, efficiently through the high drifts, each following the same track. The further north they go, the safer they will be. ∎

INTERIM ZONE

Xiaolu Guo

XIAOLU GUO

1973

Xiaolu Guo studied at the Beijing Film Academy and received her MA from the National Film School in London. She has published seven novels in both English and Chinese. *A Concise Chinese–English Dictionary for Lovers* was shortlisted for the Orange Prize for Fiction. Her other novels include *UFO in Her Eyes* and *20 Fragments of a Ravenous Youth*. She directed the award-winning films *She, a Chinese* and *Once Upon a Time Proletarian*. 'Interim Zone' is an excerpt from *I Am China*, her new novel forthcoming from Chatto & Windus in the UK.

In the beginning there was nothing in the universe. The sky and the earth were glued together and the whole world was a hot and bubbling pool. For 20,000 years nothing changed, until one day a cosmic egg appeared. Inside this egg yin and yang slowly found their balance, and a half-man half-dragon was formed. His name was Pangu …

Kublai Jian writes this on the first page of his new diary, a slender notebook he found lying around on a staff table the other day. He is still in the refugee camp in Lausanne, but in the last few days the ancient god Pangu, the first creature of ancient China, has infiltrated his mind. Jian sees the great creature vividly. Pangu seems to fit well into this alien space, like a vine winding through a lush rainforest. Jian hears people around him speaking in French or German and he feels even more mute and deafened. His own Chinese world has come to an end, so why not think of the origins of things, the beginning of China, the mythical world, before emperors or the cultivation of rice? Before laws, or the worship of gods; before human feet left their prints on the muddy shores of the first lakes …

Everyone is gathering for breakfast and he stands, bored, to queue in the canteen. The other inmates sit or stand around in the boxy white room with sullen expressions, skinny creatures on stick legs. Jian chuckles to himself, as he contemplates his plate of bread and cheese and cup of coffee on the table in front of him, and pictures his ancient ancestor.

After breakfast, the canteen transforms into a classroom for their French-language class. Sitting among the Muslim women wrapped tightly in their scarves, Jian peeks at their naked eyes, wondering what they are hiding. 'Don't stare at me!' He can almost hear the women cursing him in Arabic under their veils. They don't seem to want to be in Europe at all. They sit on the hard benches. Perhaps they are thinking of nothing, have nothing but fragmentary images of their previous life looping in their heads: a shady corner of a clay house, hens pecking in the dirt, an old plum tree on a dusty road, fish bones thrown towards a stray cat, the afternoon sun blazing down.

The French class is the only thing Jian likes about being here. The teacher, Monsieur Georges Godard, has admirable patience for the elder foreign students and the mentally disarranged. Useful phrases Jian has learned to speak this week:

'Asile de réfugié', and 'Je suis venu de Chine'.

Monsieur Godard asks everybody in the class to change the last word according to their country of origin and to say the phrases out loud.

'Asile de réfugié. Je suis venu de la Somalie.'

'Asile de réfugié. Je suis venu de l'Angola.'

'Asile de réfugié. Je suis venu de la Libye.'

'Asile de réfugié. Je suis venu d'Egypte.'

'Asile de réfugié. Je suis venu de la Syrie.'

2

In the library that evening, Jian reads his Russian novel, Grossman's *Life and Fate*, looking up now and then at the scrawny Africans reading their Qurans, which they flip through with grimy fingers, snot dripping from their noses. They look like they are crying, he thinks, as they mumble their prayers. Their god is not his god Pangu. Man makes gods in his own image. And in his case the gods had Mongol faces. They were there from his early childhood, the years he spent with his maternal grandparents before they passed away.

A brief, blurred memory of his mother comes to him. She was in the kitchen, standing in front of a small mirror. She used a heated iron poker to curl her hair. The burning smell floated into his nostrils. Then his father's image sneaks in, like a black crow in a bright garden, squawking. The squawking man-bird sticks in his mind. In this foreign, in-between space, Jian chooses to confront it rather than shoo it away.

The memory of one of the last times Jian was with his father now presents itself as a lucid picture. Can this really be him, this smiling nine-year-old boy running down the narrow alleyways of Beijing? The summer sun hits hard, singeing the poplar trees and melting the asphalt roads. Dogs are sleeping in the shadows of the trees, as are old people from the Hutang Quarter, sitting there like sacks of rice. It's a relentless August, the summer holiday of 1981. Jian's mother had died a few years before, and his grandparents are visiting relatives out of town. He has been left home alone throughout the summer.

On the day of the annual conference of the Beijing People's Representatives Congress, for whom Jian's father was an administrative secretary, he decides to take his son into the office with him. As the chime tolls from the Dongcheng Bell Tower behind his father's office, hundreds of delegates start arriving in the conference hall with their dark shiny suits and their hot shiny faces. Jian's father orders him to keep quiet and stay in the kitchen, where the chefs are clattering about preparing tea and food. It is a scorching day and Jian's cotton shorts cling to the backs of his thighs. He does his homework and waits. And waits. Two hours later Jian is bored to death. He sneaks past the guard tasked to keep an eye on him, and escapes through the Congress gate. Wandering in the sleepy hutang, the boy feels the freedom and aimlessness of a stray dog. He sees a gang of older boys riding their bikes and longs to join them. They welcome him into their game. It's the usual war story played out so often on the streets of Beijing: Chinese soldiers versus American soldiers in the Korean War. Jian is told to be a Korean peasant standing on the sidelines. But he refuses. He's bored and hot and desperately wants to take a side in the conflict. He takes on the role of an American soldier and the boys turn on him: he becomes everybody's target. This game of war becomes violent and Jian is badly beaten up, punched in the face so hard that he bleeds. There's a cut under his eye, which forms a scar like a sickle moon he has forever after.

At dusk, with his clothes and trousers torn and his face bloody, young Jian stumbles back to his father's office to find him in a rage. Silently he orders Jian on the back of his bike, and rides home without uttering a word. His father enters the house, places the keys carefully on the kitchen table and, without a sound, picks up a steel ruler. Suddenly he grabs his son, and shouts: 'You want me to open up that scab under your eye? Here it is!' His father raises the weapon, anger in his face, and seems about to bring it down upon the cringing boy. But instead of the expected blow, nothing happens. A look comes over his father's face: a fixed stare, like a frozen image from a Communist banner, except in this case there is a cruel coldness in his eyes. Grasping his son, he takes him to his room and closes the door. He locks it and leaves him inside. Jian is locked in all night.

A week later, Jian remembers, his grandparents returned and resumed their role in looking after him. His father left Beijing. He went out on assignment for Xia Xiang to survey the political minds of the countryside and rarely came back to the city. After the episode with the steel ruler, Jian barely saw his father, or received any letters. He spent his teenage years with his grandparents, and had regular nightmares about his father returning home.

A year or so later, when Jian hadn't seen his father for nearly nine months, a wave of gossip spread through his school about his father having a new wife and starting a new family elsewhere. His father never came home to see his son. Jian felt he had been locked in a room again, only this time it was permanent, and this time it was a larger room, a world in which his father would never set foot again. His father had sent him into exile. ∎

BOY, SNOW, BIRD

Helen Oyeyemi

HELEN OYEYEMI

1984

Helen Oyeyemi is the author of *The Icarus Girl* and *The Opposite House*. Her third novel, *White is for Witching*, was awarded a 2010 Somerset Maugham Award, and her fourth, *Mr Fox*, won the 2012 Zora Neale Hurston/Richard Wright Foundation Award. 'Boy, Snow, Bird' is an excerpt from a new novel of the same title, published in 2014 by Picador in the UK and Riverhead in the US.

I

The morning I turned twenty-two I put twenty-two dollars in cash into an envelope addressed to Mr Frank Novak and mailed it to Mia's address in Worcester. It was the sum total of the money I stole plus interest. Mia was to mail the envelope to a friend she had in New York, who'd drop it into the rat-catcher's letter box and make him wonder if I was around. I didn't enclose a note, though there were a few things I'd have liked to say. Restraint is classier.

Over at the bookstore, Mrs Fletcher asked me if I thought it was shaping up to be a good year for me. It was the closest thing to 'Happy birthday' I was going to get from her, so I took it with a neutral smile. We were sitting in her office, dealing with her correspondence. She went through a folder of letters I'd already opened for her, scrawled responses at the top or in the margins, and I turned those responses into letters.

Thirteen-year-old Phoebe was crying next door, because she was reading *Les Misérables* – a trial for all of us, since it was such a long book, and she was liable to cry all the way through it. Sidonie was jeering at Phoebe for crying. 'And just why are you weeping over a bunch of French people from eighteen hundred and whenever?'

'It's too sad,' Phoebe sobbed. 'I mean, it was only a loaf of bread.'

'What's the matter with you? Are you stupid? It'd be less phoney if you cried for every man who's been lynched in Tennessee or Alabama or South Carolina since eighteen hundred and whenever.'

'Don't tell me who to cry for and who not to cry for, Sidonie Fairfax. Dark girl like you talking as though you're the top. You've got a face like a bowl of goddamned treacle. Did you know that, Know-It-All?'

'Treacle is sweet, treacle is sweet,' Sidonie chanted.

'Uh . . . where's Kazim?' I asked Mrs Fletcher, preferring to ask that question rather than reminding her that people were less likely to enter the store if they saw two coloured schoolgirls fighting out front. I already knew how she responded to reminders of that kind: 'Hm . . . I don't care.' Besides, Kazim was my favourite of the bookstore gang – fourteen and tall for his age, his gaze vague behind the thick lenses of his eyeglasses. He drew comic strips about a boy called Mizak, and his card tricks went just a little bit beyond sleight of hand. He'd snap his fingers over a spread pack, say, 'Joker, fly,' and the joker sprang up into his hand. It had to be something to do with magnets. Still, we all exchanged glances. Because, what if it wasn't?

'I suppose I'll have to be the peacekeeper today,' Mrs Fletcher said, and she went out front yelling even louder than Sidonie and Phoebe. I looked over the letters I had yet to answer. I still didn't know Mrs Fletcher's first name. It was beginning to look as if nobody did. Every letter came in addressed to Mrs A. Fletcher.

Having sent Sidonie out to buy RC Cola, Mrs Fletcher returned and asked what she should bring to my dinner party that evening.

'Oh, thanks, but I can handle this.'

She dealt with three letters in rapid succession, writing *No* at the top of one, *A thousand times no* at the top of another, and *OK* in the margin of a third. 'I'm not asking to be helpful,' she said. 'I'm asking so as to make sure there's something there I'll want to eat.'

I handed her the menu I'd been working on for weeks.

'Pear spread and crackers,' Mrs Fletcher read aloud. 'Anchovy ham rolls. Stuffed tomatoes *ravigote*. Potato salad. Chicken à la King. Banana chiffon cake. Peach pie. Post-dinner cocktail: Rye Lane . . . a stupendous blend of whiskey, curaçao, orange squash and crème de noyaux, stirred, not shaken, as recommended by the International Association of Bartenders.'

She leaned back in her chair. 'Why on earth are you putting yourself through all this on your own birthday, Boy Novak? And what's pear spread? Life has changed a lot, you know. You didn't used to get all this food inside food when I was a girl. The other day I was eating a mushroom and found it had been stuffed with prawns. I've got so many misgivings over this craze, Boy. It's flying in the face of nature. A mushroom is a woodland fungus and a prawn comes from the sea. People have got no business stuffing one inside the other. Are the Whitmans treating you well?'

'What?' My mind was on the pear spread. I'd already made it the night before, over at Arturo's. It was sitting in a bowl in his refrigerator, looking radioactive.

'The Whitmans. Arturo Whitman's family. Are they treating you well?'

'Oh. Yes. Gerald keeps issuing orders to Arturo not to let me get away and Viv's very sisterly and Olivia's very motherly and – it's nice.'

She nodded. 'Olivia Whitman looks so young, doesn't she?'

'Yup.'

I typed: *I hope this finds you well*, which was pretty high up on the list of phrases Mrs Fletcher would never include in a letter if she was writing it herself.

She lifted a lock of her hair with a pencil and gave it a baleful stare. This was the first gesture of concern about her appearance that I'd seen from her. She cut her own hair carelessly, with regular kitchen scissors, and it showed. The ends looked like a bar graph. The hair itself was fine, though – rich brown streaked with grey. 'I'm about the same age as her,' she said. 'I just don't know how she does it.'

Olivia made Mrs Fletcher nervous. That was difficult to process. Maybe it worked both ways? I'd recently come across a proverb about not speaking unless you'd thought of something that was better than silence. So I kept typing.

Mrs Fletcher wanted to know if she could ask me a personal question. I gave her an 'Mmm-hmmm' that Snow would've been proud of.

'Do you know what it is you want from Arturo?'

An impressive U-turn, but I didn't look up from my work. 'You guessed right, Mrs Fletcher. I'm a gold-digger. If you know anyone richer and more gullible, let me at him.'

The bell above the shop door jangled – Sidonie or a customer. There was a quiet exchange of words in the next room, followed by the sound of caps falling off soda bottles. Sidonie, then.

'Nobody's calling you a gold-digger,' Mrs Fletcher said. 'Let me explain myself.'

'You don't have to.'

She reached over and took my hand, patted it. 'But if I don't you'll poison me tonight, won't you? I want to be able to enjoy my cocktail, just as the International Association of Bartenders recommends. Listen – I'm not a Flax Hill original, either. I'm from a market town in the south of England.'

'So that's why you talk like that!'

'Well, what did you think?'

'I thought you just went to one of those . . . schools.'

'Oh, good grief. I'm not in the mood for this. Don't interrupt me any more. My husband died nine years ago, and I came here looking for some trace of him. He was my right-hand man for twenty-three years. No children; we married late, liked books and liked each other and that was all. His heart was dodgy – anatomically speaking, I mean – and it killed him. I was all undone. That man. The first time we met, he called me *cookie*. I said, "I beg your pardon?" and he said, "You heard. When are we having dinner?" so I said "We might as well have it now." Then a week later he agreed to marry me –'

'You asked him?'

'I don't mess about.'

'And he never brought you here while he was alive?'

'No. He told me he was a misfit in his home town. But it wasn't true. I barged into people's homes and found him in their photo albums, being carried around on people's shoulders. Homecoming King! People here are nice to me just because I'm his wife – was his wife, I mean. When I opened this store, so many people came by and bought books. Not to read them, I don't think. Well, Joe Webster might read *The Canterbury Tales* one day . . . Anyway, it was a gesture, to help me set up. I'd never seen anything like it.'

I squeezed her hand. From where I was sitting I could see the chess set on her window seat. It was always there; once I asked her if she liked chess and she just sort of hissed and left it at that. The black army faced the white army across their field of chequered squares; the kings and queens seemed resigned, companionable. There was never any change in their configuration. But no dust, either. No neglect.

'I'm only going to say this once, so don't fly off the handle,' she said. 'Flax Hill is home to me because I loved Leonard Fletcher. Not the other way around. Now get back to work; here are customers, and you're behind.'

That day I walked Phoebe and Sidonie all the way home instead of just three quarters of the way. As usual I walked on the outside of our trio, taking the position of a gentleman protecting ladies from roadside traffic. As usual Phoebe's siblings were waiting for us outside the elementary school; three rowdy little girls of indeterminate age and the shortest of short-term memories. Every school day they asked if they could play with my hair, and I let them. Every school day they squealed: 'It's just like sunshine!' and I wished they'd find a new sensation. Ordinarily I stopped when we reached the corner of Tubman and Jefferson – less because there was a tangible change in the neighbourhood and more because that was when we started seeing groups of coloured boys leaning against walls with their arms folded, not talking or doing anything else but leaning. I figured they were the Neighbourhood Watch, and left them to it. So did the white boys who followed us along Jefferson calling out Sidonie's name. We got to Tubman Street and the catcallers evaporated. But that day I kept going because I wanted Sidonie to come to dinner. Phoebe had already excused herself on account of having to watch her sisters while her mother was at work. But Sidonie was an only child, and hesitated. 'Ma probably needs me to help her tonight,' she said. 'But maybe if you came and asked her yourself . . .'

I wavered, needing time to get everything on the menu wrong and then get it right. Sidonie said, 'Hey, you've got a lot to do before dinner time, right? Save me a slice of that chiffon cake; it's going to be in my dreams tonight.'

Phoebe said, 'Me too!' and her sisters joined in. I told them it'd be Sidonie that brought them the cake, and passed the Tubman Street Neighbourhood Watch without incident. Further along Tubman, a mixed group was crammed into a motor car; girls sat on boys' laps, waving transistor radios in time to the music that poured out of them. These kids looked a little older than Sidonie, and ignored us completely. The houses were smaller and newer and better cared for than in Arturo's part of town. The doors were pastel-painted, the front yards were meticulously well swept, and the windows sparkled in the way that only the truly house-proud seem able to achieve. We passed other groups. Boys and girls, singing, wisecracking. Lone, dutiful daughters and sons laden with groceries. One boy with a buzz cut was carrying what looked like a week's supplies for an old lady who called him 'Tortoise' and 'Useless'. His friends pulled faces at him when the old lady wasn't looking, and he grinned good-humouredly. 'That's Sam,' Phoebe said. 'He's my boyfriend. He just doesn't know it yet.' And she and Sidonie giggled.

Then I saw Kazim. He was part of a bunch of boys gathered around an open window, trampling some poor gardener's petunias. There was a green parakeet in a cage inside the living room, and the boys were trying to teach it a new phrase. This is what they were trying to teach it to say: *Fuck Whitey*. The parakeet stumbled backwards along its perch. Sidonie put her hand on my arm to keep me walking, and I did keep walking, but I looked back. The group's main teaching method seemed to be intimidation. They crowded the square of grass beneath the cage, repeating the phrase over and over, all voices together. I heard the parakeet pleading, 'Hey diddle diddle, he-ee-ee-y diddle diddle!' but the boys insisted: *Fuck Whitey, Fuck Whitey*. I saw Kazim and he saw me. He looked away first. He had been laughing until he saw me.

'I guess Kazim's found better things to do than read books,' I said to Sidonie, or to Phoebe, or maybe just to the air. Phoebe and Sidonie looked at each other, and Phoebe said, 'I don't know what you mean, Miss Novak.'

I jerked my thumb at the boys across the way. 'Yes, you do. I saw him.'
Phoebe said, 'Saw . . . Kazim?'

A man about a quarter of a block down opened his window and

issued a warning that he was on his way to end the lives of anyone responsible for creating 'this racket', and the parakeet boys scattered.

Sidonie said, 'That wasn't Kazim.'

Phoebe said: 'I guess we all look the same to you.' She smiled to show she wasn't saying it in a mean way, and ran through her front door with her sisters hot on her heels.

My temples began to throb. It was Kazim, I knew it was him. What did Phoebe and Sidonie take me for, and why had they just closed ranks like that? Were they were trying to tell me that I was on my own if I said anything about Kazim back at the bookstore?

Sidonie stopped at a peppermint-coloured door and said: '*Voilà* – Chez Fairfax.' I didn't answer her, just looked all around me, picturing the walk back down to Jefferson without the girls. All the lines washed out of everything I tried to fix my eyes on. It was like a floodlight had been switched on just above my head. Sidonie said something I didn't hear, then, 'Miss Novak? It wasn't him. Really. Kazim's not a round the way boy. He stays home drawing and doing his wizard stuff. Relax. We all make mistakes.'

I sat down on a wicker bench in the hallway next to a table stacked with *Ebony* and *Jet* magazines, with intriguing text hovering beside the faces of the coloured models on the covers: *Are homosexuals becoming respectable? End of Negro race by 1980 predicted by top scientist.* An older, far less haughty-looking version of Sidonie approached; she was in a wheelchair, and spun the wheels with her arms. I stood, then sat down again, not wanting to stand over her. Elsewhere in the house a television set blared and women talked over it and each other.

'Welcome, welcome,' Mrs Fairfax said, shaking my hand. She said I should call her Merveille, or Merva if I couldn't manage to say Merveille. 'In America I am Merva . . .'

Sidonie must have told her I was a teacher: 'You are so kind to invite Sidonie to dinner. Some other time . . . let Sidonie bring you; you will dine with us, I will give you such a dinner. Does Sidonie behave herself? Is her schoolwork good? Does she read too much?'

Merveille made me drink something so sweet it made my teeth ache; she said it was called sorrel. She was a hairdresser; she worked from home and Sidonie helped her in the evenings. Her husband was a Pullman porter working the train route to Quebec and back. She showed me her appointment book. She had clients all the way up to midnight.

Imagine having a mother who worries that you read too much. The question is, what is it that's supposed to happen to people who read too much? How can you tell when someone's crossed that line? I said Sidonie was top of my class and that everybody liked her.

It was getting dark when I left, and I thought about calling Arturo from a phone box and getting him to come pick me up. But it would take too long. So I just walked fast, with my head down, and didn't raise it again until I got back to Jefferson Street.

Snow kept me company as I embraced the *Joy of Cooking*. She sat up on the counter with an apron over her dungarees and tasted the cake batter and the cream sauce for the chicken. She looked extremely doubtful about the cream sauce, but how sophisticated could her six-year-old palate be anyway?

'Maybe you'll get a mother for your birthday,' she said. I dabbed the end of her nose with a square of kitchen paper, even though there was nothing there.

'Who said I want a mother? Maybe I want a daughter.'

'What kind of daughter?' Snow said, with the air of a department-store attendant, invisible stock list in hand.

'I said maybe. It depends. I might forget to feed and water her.'

'That would be very bad, because mothers have to give their daughters cookies all the time.'

'Oh, like Grandma Olivia and Grandma Agnes give you cookies?'

'Yeah, but then they pat my stomach,' she said, stabbing toothpicks through the anchovy ham rolls. She hit the dead centre of each one.

'OK, so cookies yes, stomach pat no. What else?'

'You have to hide her.'

'Hide her?'

'Not all the time. Only sometimes. Like if a monster comes looking for her, you have to hide her.'

'Well, of course.'

'Even if the monster comes with a real nice smile and says "Excuse me, have you seen my friend Snow?" you have to say "She's not here! She's gone to Russia."'

'I'll do better than that. I'll say: "Snow? Who's Snow?"'

She clapped her hands. 'That's good!'

'Anything else?'

'You have to come find me if I get lost.'

'Lost? Like in the woods?'

'Not just there. Anywhere.'

'Hmmmm. Let me think about that one. It's a big job. Meanwhile, do you think you can get your daddy out of his workroom so he can help you dress?'

She threw her arms around my neck, gave me a kiss and hopped down from the counter. What made her so trusting, so sure of people's goodwill? If I was like her I wouldn't have shrunk back later when Olivia Whitman draped a grey fur stole around my shoulders and said, 'Happy birthday!' It felt expensive; thick to the touch but a lighter weight on the skin than it looked. Mrs Fletcher asked: 'Is that chinchilla?' and gave me a stern look, as if I was at fault for accepting it.

The only thing I felt guilty of was already knowing that it was chinchilla fur – Olivia had worn it the week before, when she took me to see *The Magic Flute* in Worcester. We'd smoked cigars outside the opera house and she'd asked me how I liked the show. 'Isn't it marvellous?' she'd said. I'd said that as far as I could gather it was a tale about a woman who could only be led out of captivity by a man, and that the man could only save her by ignoring her.

'Correct,' she'd said.

'Uh . . . I really like the costumes,' I'd said.

Olivia had switched the cigar from the left side of my mouth to the right side and looked approvingly at me through her opera glasses. 'Yes, the tale is what you just said it is, but it's also about two people who walk through fire and water together, unscathed because they are together. You'll agree that that's not a sentimental interpretation, that that's literally what happens? The trials those two undergo are about being beyond words.'

I'd shivered, and she'd offered me the stole. 'Chinchilla. It keeps you warm.' But I'd declined. Cuban cigars and chinchilla stoles; this was more Mia Cabrini's scene, and I was better off not developing a taste for it.

Olivia stood back, admiring the effect. 'Yes; it never looked quite right on me. But, Boy, you were born to wear this.'

Arturo whispered: 'Poor Viv –' in my ear. Vivian said a stole like that wouldn't have lasted long in her wardrobe anyway, what with her talent for spilling things. But she minded. Of course she minded; here was a fur stole she'd probably grown up coveting and I'd swiped it right from under her nose. Her fiancé didn't even have the good sense to say he'd get her one. Or maybe it was good sense and a healthy awareness of his salary level that kept him from saying it.

All through dinner Arturo and I held hands under the table, like a couple of kids, and that made the dinner quite wonderful, even though Mrs Fletcher kept staring at Olivia as though committing her to memory. It got so bad that Olivia turned to her husband and said, 'Has it happened at last, Gerald? Have I become a curiosity?'

Gerald clinked wine glasses with her and said, 'You were always a curiosity, darling.' And Arturo proposed a toast to curiosities.

2

'I'm sure I didn't mean to make anyone feel uncomfortable,' Mrs Fletcher said the next morning. She put on a pretty good show of being abashed, folded hands and glum headshakes, but I wasn't fooled. When I saw that I wasn't going to get an explanation out of her, I changed the subject and told her about meeting Sidonie's mother and very briefly masquerading as a teacher. She covered her eyes and groaned.

'I wish you hadn't told me that.'

'Oh, so I should've told Sidonie's mother that her daughter doesn't go to school but comes here –'

'– and drinks much more soda than is good for her and associates with disagreeable women and reads novels she's permitted to select without supervision or even orderly thought, yes. Then her mother would have made her stop coming here.'

'Well, exactly.'

'But since you failed to inform Mrs Fairfax of those facts, now I've got to do the forbidding.'

I licked an envelope flap. 'I don't see how that follows, but sure. Let's see how long that lasts.'

Mrs Fletcher still hadn't uncovered her eyes. 'No, really, Boy. This goes for all three of them. They've got to go to school.'

She didn't seem to notice that those were more or less the same words I'd said to her on my first day at the bookstore.

I said, 'Well, this joke has fallen flat. I never met Mrs Fairfax; I don't care for that neighbourhood. Everything's the same as it was this time yesterday, OK?'

She didn't answer.

'Those kids won't know what to do with themselves if you send them away.'

'Oh, rubbish. I know them. They'll mope for five minutes, then they'll go to school and grow up and make something of themselves, that's what they'll do. There are ladders they've got to get up. Ladders made of tests and examinations and certification papers that don't mean anything to us, but Phoebe and Sid and Kazim can't get where they want to go without them. I've been selfish. No more.'

We were busy with customers from opening time onwards, so when Phoebe and Sidonie came by at 2 p.m., I was sure that Mrs Fletcher had reconsidered. She couldn't ban them. She'd miss them too much. They both made a rush at the shelf that had *Les Misérables* on it – Sidonie to confiscate it and Phoebe to snatch it out of Sidonie's way. Kazim came in after them, calling out to the back room: 'What, what, what, did you miss me?'

'Oh yes – very horribly awfully much,' Mrs Fletcher called back. 'Wait there. I'm trying to make this man understand that it's a nineteenth-century first edition he's trying to buy. He seems to think it's an item of clothing, keeps talking about "jackets" . . .'

Kazim sidled over to the cash register and handed me a piece of card he'd folded into quarters. 'When you look at my comic strips you're always saying – and what happened next? And after that? And after that? So I drew this.' I set my elbows on the desk and looked at him, and the more I looked, the less sure I was that I'd seen him in the group gathered around the parakeet. I was afraid to be wrong. I was afraid not to be able to tell the difference between Kazim, who I'd seen nearly every day for the past six months or so, and any other fuzzy-headed coloured boy with eyeglasses.

Mrs Fletcher came out and sent me to the back room to wrap up her customer's purchases. I missed what she said to Sidonie and co. because the man kept wanting to know things – whether I could recommend a good place to eat while he was here, and so on. The kids were gone by the time I got out front again, and I went after them with cake I'd saved from the night before. I'd only brought two slices, but it didn't matter because Kazim was the only one who accepted. Phoebe held out her hand, but Sidonie glared at her and she dropped her hand just as I tried to place the carton into it.

'Ever since we started going to the bookstore I wondered what it was going to be that put a stop to it,' Sidonie said. She and Phoebe had their arms around each other's waists, holding each other up. 'I knew it wouldn't be anything we did. I thought maybe some customer would damage a book and it would look like we were to blame, or Mrs Fletcher would get her sums mixed up one day and think one of us stole, or – any number of things. But no. You did it.'

'We told you it wasn't him.' Phoebe had tears in her eyes. 'It *wasn't*.'

Kazim just eyed his cartonful of cake as if willing it to provide answers. I cleared my throat. The truth wouldn't sound like the truth coming from me. It might even contradict whatever Mrs Fletcher had told them, and Mrs Fletcher was their friend. 'Go to school,' I said, and watched them leave.

A week passed before I could stand to look at the comic strip Kazim had drawn for me. It was about a king called Mizak and his queen, Sidie. Every December a little boy and a little girl approached the throne, the girl 'from above' and the boy 'from below'. Their names were Mizak and Sidie too, and the boy Mizak struggled with King Mizak for the right to the name and the next twelve months of life. The girl Sidie fought Queen Sidie for the same rights. When King Sidie and Queen Mizak were dead, the boy and the girl were dressed in their robes and crowned with their crowns, ageing with preternatural speed every month until December, when the children came again. 'It does us good to fight for life,' Queen Sidie said, and her lips were wrinkles that clung to her teeth. Her words were empty; she and King Mizak were too weak and weary to put up a real fight. It was slaughter, and the boy and the girl were merciless. They said: 'Remember you did the same.'

Kazim used to give me strange looks whenever I tapped a corner of one of his comic strips and asked what was next. He thought it was strange of me to ask. *What's next is what happened before.* ■

John Saturnall's Feast by *Lawrence Norfolk*

'A brilliant, erudite tale of cookery and witchcraft' – A.S. Byatt, *Guardian* Books of the Year.

In the remote village of Buckland, a mob chants of witchcraft. It is 1625, and John and his mother are running for their lives. Taking refuge, John's mother opens her book and begins to tell her son of an ancient Feast kept secret. Little does he know that one day, to keep hold of all that he holds most dear, he must realize his mother's vision – he must serve the Saturnall Feast.

Bloomsbury £8.99 | **PB**

This is Life by *Dan Rhodes*

This Spring,
Choose Art.
Choose Romance.
Choose Paris.
Choose Life.

Canongate £7.99 | **PB**

The Quantity Theory of Insanity by *Will Self*

'If a manic J.G. Ballard and a depressed David Lodge got together, they might produce something like *The Quantity Theory of Insanity*.' – Martin Amis.

From Booker-shortlisted iconoclast and one of *Granta*'s Best of Young British Novelists comes a collection of short stories that tip over the banal surfaces of everyday existence to uncover the hideous, the hilarious and the bizarre.

Grove Atlantic $15 | **PB**

Summer Lies by *Bernhard Schlink*

A conversation between strangers will change lives forever; one night in Baden-Baden will threaten to tear a couple apart; a meeting with an ex-lover will give a divorcee a second chance; holiday lovers will struggle in the reality of daily routine . . . Tender yet unsentimental, achingly personal yet utterly universal, this collection asks what it means to love, to deceive and, ultimately, to be human.

Phoenix £7.99 | **PB**

ZEPHYRS

Jenni Fagan

JENNI FAGAN

1977

Jenni Fagan's critically acclaimed debut novel, *The Panopticon*, was published in 2012 and named one of the Waterstones Eleven, a selection of the best fiction debuts of the year. Her poetry has been nominated for a Pushcart Prize and her collection *The Dead Queen of Bohemia* was named *3:AM* magazine's Poetry Book of the Year. She holds an MA in creative writing from Royal Holloway, University of London, and currently lives in a coastal village in Scotland. 'Zephyrs' is an excerpt from her novel in progress.

He is still half drunk as the bus turns onto the M4. A light above the toilet cubicle has been lit up red for the last hour. There's a man in there and in between bouts of vomiting, he says I die, I die, I die. They appear to be the only two words he knows in English. The motorway is slick with rain and ribbons of light blur past the window: hundreds, thousands of cars. People are leaving London in swarms. Returning to home towns they have not seen in decades. They are queuing at bus terminals, train stations, airports – going wherever they can find accommodation and work.

The river is rising. That's what Cael needs to think about – not his sylphlike mother or the cinema he has just left behind (his family's home), won in a game of poker at the turn of the century – keys prised from a corpse's fist. His mother the moirologist – every sentence delivered like a eulogy – tales of Cael's great-grandmother, a woman who ran her own pub and butchered her own calves in the cellar – hung them up to drain then went upstairs to serve cider. The river is rising and the footage is everywhere, on the front page of papers, in every newsflash. His river. His walking place. All those bridges of light and that bit where great red steel haunches jut out – a place where a bridge should have sat but now just those pillars remain – each big enough to land a helicopter on. Ship masts strung with fairy lights. Trees lit up by fat glowing blueberries. Strange fruit. Pickaxes in the walls to show where men have toiled.

It's an ache. He has locked the doors for the last time and the devil would not accept payment of just his soul. Now, this chaos. Sirens, and thousands of cars, snitches of snatches, fat arms with a gold bracelet driving a jeep, blonde putting on lipstick in her mirror, an old man shouting at his daughter to shut up, four soldiers in a Mini, hundreds of thousands on the move in this strange corporeality.

A man with a thick neck is stood at the front of the bus. He nods at something the driver is saying and then he points ahead, navigating. His bag is bulky. He turns and trudges up the aisle towards the only empty seat left. Shoves his bag in storage and takes down a small rucksack. Sits heavily. Smells of camphor, sweat, deodorant. The man rummages until he finds a giant bag of Thai-chilli crisps, opens them and offers the bag to Cael.

A shake of the head. Legs uncrossed, recrossed. Cael's scuffed Chelsea boots are so old that the stitching has come away. He tucks his hair behind his ear, it's a reflex, his fingers hover where his thick polo neck is bobbled – where he's picked at the cuffs. He's a cuff picker. A cuff picker sat next to a crisp muncher in what appears to be the end of times. Crisp muncher shrugs, he takes Cael's silence as a clear offer of companionship and possibly compliance. Uneasy. Not signing up for jackshit, mate. If anything happens. Crisp muncher watches him, a sidelong stare – he should just have accepted a crisp. A salty-spicy aroma permeates recycled air.

Cael brushes a bit of nothing off his jeans, finally opts to give the staring man a wide smile. Expects a response he does. Sat there with his crisp poised, chins florid. The wide smile confuses him. Cael can see confusion in the man's eyes, a kernel of uncertainty. Who is who in times like this? It's a valid concern. Cael stops his grin abruptly (just the same way as he proffered it) and turns to look out of the window.

The Internet is up so Cael scrolls through his phone and it's all about Jesus – he's everywhere. *Jesus hides out at Elton's. Jesus saves the ugly first. Another hooker and Jesus. He's black! He's Asian! He dresses as Elvis! He IS Elvis! He's Elvis's Dead Twin Jesse. The river is rising and he WILL NOT TURN IT INTO WINE.* Inch by fucking inch, barriers being reinforced. *Triple Red Alert, legally it's only the* – a blue ball rotates at the top of the screen.

A woman in front of them flicks on her reading light and the man next to Cael tuts. He tuts more – he might as well stand up and roar TUT MOTHERFUCKER TUT-TUT FUCKING TUT! The woman reads on. Next to her is a little boy. He stares, his eye in the gap between the seats. Pale blue eyes, almost no eyebrows.

Another drink, trying to see something out the window – some sign, too late for looking now though, all that time sleeping in his projectionist booth and getting up to shine a light in the dark. Selling old cinema posters. The signs. Sets of chairs. A popcorn stand. The price of light! The price of fucking light these days – unbelievable – what they want for light is a kidney – the firstborn – and heat? This bus is warm though, the engine humming and his hip flask half empty, trails of orange, yellow and white fly past the window, a violent beeping, Little Chef burls past, a garage forecourt, a multiplex cinema. Crisp man is on a roll now. Cael tries to tune him out but his voice just gets louder.

So then it was the oil rigs. Ten years, a stint in Thailand, don't like the flying, don't trust planes, don't fucking trust them – how do they stay up? Can you tell me that? No, you can't. Sinister shit. Don't like trains. Fucking planes though. Steel fucking sharks. Circling. Fucking circling. Buses – you can trust a bus, don't you think you can trust a bus? Solid fuckers buses are – do you want to SHUT-THE-FUCK-UP?

The man is up then, banging on the toilet door and the bus driver glances back and the passengers stare straight ahead hoping there will not be any violence. Crisp man sits back down. The retching at the back of the bus has gradually begun to abate, and now there is just an occasional whimper. The bus driver shifts in his seat – his sunglasses like bug-eyes in the rear-view mirror. The little boy is asleep now, his mouth open, his mother still turning pages.

Crisp man eyes Cael – the Chelsea boots, faded jeans, roll-neck, longish hair curled behind one ear. He shakes his head, now apparently disgusted by his choice of comrade – betrayed even by Cael's apparent indifference to him. Cael rests his feet on his old brown suitcase on the floor, his coat is folded neatly on his lap, ready to use as a pillow. At the fringes of the motorway there is countryside – vague shadowy outline, old watermills, chimneys. In his suitcase is the urn. It's a fitting place as any to be dead. Ashes to ashes. He wonders if they actually give you the deceased's ashes or just some random dead people that they have cremated? All of them in there together. A crematorium austere and white and inhuman, with plastic flowers and a grate underneath the incinerator to catch metal hips and teacup hearts. He has the urn. A key. An address he printed off last week. He has the original programme from opening day at Babylon in 1902 – it was presided over by a lesser-known royal. There is a small chic audience in the picture too, all dressed up for a Saturday night in Soho, all smiling.

At a roundabout there appears to be a table set up. Right there in the middle. Place mats. Flowers. Just a glimpse of it and Cael wondering who would dine in the middle of a roundabout while car headlights blare by – the dinner guests would have to wear sunglasses – it could be on one of those programmes on telly – they could call it 'Dinner on Location'. He slips the hip flask out of his pocket and takes a drink – a welcome burning in his throat – peaty, honeyed, smoky, the whisky warms him and takes away from the smells on the bus: rain, vomit, sweat from the man sat next to him.

I got a second place to rent out then, got some tenants, dirty – had to tell them, left their nappies on the stair they did, stacks of them, piles of shit. Could have rubbed their fucking faces in it. Should have. Fucking cunts. Need the money but. My missus. She goes to Brussels for lipo and that, lipo on the brain she has. New tits. New nose. Had her sagging moaning face dragged up around her ears. I own it though. Me. I own her fucking nose.

Cael unwraps a bar of chocolate. He's never owned someone else's nose. Not someone else's sagging moaning face, certainly not, nor their nose. Not even an eyelash. The roads are sparser now. Sleep, a heaviness, a fug that he falls into, a density to it that means it's a struggle to rise back up to the sound of an engine which drones louder and louder. That drone becomes everything. It is unbearable. Waking. Falling. Night lights flicked on shine down on passengers' features. Road signs and roadworks outside the window.

Cael wakes up as Crisp man walks away with his bag on his back – the bus is pulling into an all-night diner car park – the doors hiss open.

The black cab is cold. Cael shows the address and pulls his coat tighter around him – shoves his fists deep into his pockets and realizes his mouth is dry. The driver doesn't say anything. They drive out of the city – across a different bridge where tiny orange lights on either side indicate that there is land. The cab turns onto country roads with no lights on them at all – then hulks of buildings appear – industrial units – then some trees and they turn in between two tall wooden gates. Cael pays the guy and watches the cab lumber off. He turns round and the shock of how cold it is slaps him back into life.

The caravan park is in total darkness down here but lit up behind it is the mountain range – seven peaks and the middle two are on fire. Right up the top sparks fly up and out, flames bite at the black like a vengeful halo. Nobody is up. None of the residents here are coming out to see it, so it must be normal. A garden of gnomes, ruddy-faced, malevolent, one launches a fishing line, another waves, and Cael walks on, past a charred building, a *Shop Closed* sign. It's hard to tell if the fire is travelling up or down. It's a Zen riddle – which way does a fire go? Like how big a box is. Marina's wee boy asking him that – how big is a box, Kayell. Well, it depends on how big the box is. Yeah, but how big *is* that, how big *is* a box? It's gone now. This is it. Every step forward causes the road behind him to disappear. One step back and it would be an endless fall. Like that falling man who never stopped falling – he never did stop falling, did he?

Frogs begin to hop along the road, migrating away from a fire that must, realistically, be miles away. It must be miles away. It will burn out by morning. Cael scoops up a frog. Its throat thrums; a clear membrane slides down across the round eyes; it pulses in his cupped hands like a heart. Keep walking on, up through the back lanes looking for the sign. The stars are so clear and the moon is full and each crater stands out starkly – up here it looks so much more like a planet.

Eventually it makes itself seen – the caravan hidden by briars.

No. 9 Ash Lane has a garden so overgrown he has to turn sideways to get along the path without the thistles snarking his coat. The gate is rusted shut. He climbs over it, trudges up three steps that buckle – to a metal door, key in lock, and it opens.

The hallway is one step wide and there is a reek of ammonia. The door in front opens on a shower cubicle and a toilet. To the right, a bed space with a window. To the left, the longer room with a kitchenette on one side. Fucking hell. Fucking Jesus and the saints. Fake wood panelling. Painting of a plough horse. Melted microwave. Scabby sink. Bunker two-cupboards wide. When he switches on the lamp it bathes the room in an orange glow. The carpet is crunchy underneath his boots – like it's covered in small stones.

Cider, that's what this requires. Vodka would be better but he's not got any. But he did get four cans of cider. He takes them out and drinks the first one down in one go. He sits on a flowery armchair and stares back at the plough horse. He gets up to look for a tin opener. A bar of chocolate and a fresh packet of rolling tobacco, another can and a tin of beans. He tries to get the old square television to work. At five in the morning he falls asleep while fuzz flickers light on the walls.

It sounds like a bomber – the sound sputters then roars in again. Cael lurches upright, his heart hammering, thinking of death – the only thought he ever has now when he wakes in the night.

His neighbour's caravan door flaps in the breeze. A BMX bike leans against her porch, a pirate flag on the back of it. The roar is louder as he steps out onto the path and there is a woman hoovering up the road. She is hoovering up the miles between herself and what? Her pyjamas are on all wrong, the bottoms dragging on the ground and the knots of her vertebrae exposed like a fine rope.

The Hoover is ancient, she aims a kick at it and the thing stops pelting pebbles out the back and sputters into silence. Cael's heart drop-kicks as she turns round, her face pale – almost no eyebrows, hair fine, neat, straight, tucked behind her ear. He guesses it is almost white although she is young, or youngish – his age. She is sleepwalking and he is somehow on the fringes of her dream – trespassing. She pads back up her path and into her caravan then out again onto her porch with a rag. She reaches a slim arm up into the sky – and polishes the moon. ∎

ARRIVALS

Sunjeev Sahota

SUNJEEV SAHOTA

1981

Sunjeev Sahota was born in Derby and currently lives in Leeds with his wife and daughter. His first novel, *Ours are the Streets*, was published in 2011. 'Arrivals' is an excerpt from *The Year of the Runaways*, his unfinished second novel, forthcoming from Picador.

R andeep Sanghera stood in front of the green-and-blue world
map tacked onto the wall. The map had come with the flat, and
he'd nearly taken it down – it was too big and crinkled, and cigarette
butts had stubbed black islands into the mid-Atlantic – but he'd kept
it in the end. A reminder of the world outside. He was less sure about
the flowers, guilty-looking things he'd spent too long choosing at
the petrol station. Get rid of them, he decided, but then he heard
someone parking up outside and all thoughts of the flowers flew out
of his head.

He went down the narrow staircase. Straightening his cuffs.
Swallowing nerves. He could see her, blurred by the mottled glass.
She looked to be setting right the chunni on top of her head. He
opened the door and Narinder Malhi stood before him, brightly
etched against the outer night. So, even in England she wore a kesri,
a domed deep green one that matched her salwar kameez. A *C* of
long delicate hairs escaped from under it and curled about her ears.
Behind her, the taxi made a U-turn and went back down the hill.
Narinder pressed her hands together underneath her chin and said,
'Sat sri akal,' and then Randeep took her suitcase and asked her if she
might follow him up the stairs.

He set her luggage in the middle of the room and then straightened
right back up, knocking his head against the bald light bulb. He
reached up to stop it swinging. She was standing at the window,
still in her long black coat, clutching her dull brown handbag with
both hands.

'It's very quiet,' Randeep said.

'It's very nice. Thank you.'

'You have been to Sheffield before?'

'My first time.'

There was a silence and then she gestured towards the cooker.
'My parents used to have one like that. Years ago.'

Randeep looked to where her eyes had gone: a white stand-alone
thing with an overhanging grill-pan. The stains on the hobs hadn't
shifted no matter how hard he'd scrubbed. 'There is a microwave

too,' he said, pointing to the microwave. 'And washing machine. And toaster also, and TV, and sofa-set . . . carpet . . .' He trailed off.

There were only two other rooms. The bathroom was tiny, and the pipes buffalo-groaned each time the taps were turned. The rubbery hand-held shower lay coiled up in the centre of the green-streaked tub like a snake asleep.

'And this is your private room,' he said, opening the second door.

She didn't step inside. There wasn't much to see: a single bed, a rail for her clothes, a few wire coat hangers. Some globs of Blu-Tack on damp loose wallpaper. There was a long, hinged mirror straight ahead which they found themselves staring into, him standing behind her. She didn't even reach his shoulders. It was cold and he noticed her nipples showing through her tunic. She pulled her coat tighter together and he averted his eyes.

'I'm sorry,' he said. 'It's too small. And dirty. I'll look for something else tomorrow.'

'No, no, please, it's fine. It's perfect. I'm really happy with it.'

'Really?' He breathed out, smiled. 'I'm so happy. Do you know there is a bus from the bottom of the hill every fifteen minutes that can take you to work?'

'And that hill will keep me in shape.'

'And this isn't an area with lots of apneh.' Her lips parted, but she didn't speak. 'Like you asked,' he reminded her. 'And the gurdwara's only one tram stop away. I can show you how to use the tram if you like.'

'Thank you,' she said quietly.

'And the flat downstairs is empty. No disturbances. I hope you agree that this flat was a special find. Especially at this time of year, it is not easy. We were lucky.' That 'we' was problematic and knocked him off balance. 'But I should go,' he said hastily. He took up his red tracksuit top from where he'd hung it on the back of the door and zipped it to his chin. He quickly pushed the sleeves up to his thick-boned elbows, for the top was way too short for his arms.

She walked him to the stairs, and said tentatively, 'Do you think you should bring a few of your things and leave them here?'

He nearly blurted out that his suitcase was just outside, in the gennel, but he saved himself. 'I will bring some. But I will telephone you first,' he added seriously. He wouldn't be one of those boys who turned up at a girl's house unannounced and unexpected. Then he remembered about the meter tokens. 'The light.' He pointed down the stairs. 'There is a meter underneath. It takes the pink electric tokens. Not the white ones. The pink ones. There is a shop around the corner. He sells them. I checked for you.'

She nodded, thanked him. But she looked confused. 'Do I have to collect these tokens? Like vouchers?'

'Collect them from the shop, yes. Only be careful you put the cards in straight. Do not bend them. Would you like me to show you? The meter?'

She'd never heard of electricity being pink, or white for that matter, but she was tired from the journey – London was a long way – and just wanted to sleep. 'I think I'll be fine. But thanks for everything, Randeep.'

She used his name, without 'ji' and to his face, which hurt him a little. But this was England. 'No problem. And do not worry. You will not need any for a while yet. I put lots in before you came.'

She thanked him again, and then they stood there staring at each other. She smiled a little and pulled her chunni tighter over her turban and around her head. It made her eyes look bigger, somehow. More beautiful.

Randeep opened out his wallet and held some notes to her. 'Next month's.' He was looking away. He hated having to do it like this. At least when she lived in London it had gone by faceless post. She too seemed embarrassed to take it.

He said goodbye, but halfway down the stairs he turned back. 'Is everything all right? You are not in any trouble?'

She smiled. 'I just need somewhere to rest. I'll be fine tomorrow. Can I call you?'

'Of course you may. Of course.' He smiled, and the smile was quick and easy, and then he went down the remaining steps, turning round at the bottom to nod once up at her. She waved lightly, leaning forward out of the doorway, arms folded. She looked uncertain.

Randeep held his suitcase square on his lap on the bus ride home. Of course she wasn't going to invite him to stay. Had he really expected her to? He spat coarsely into his hanky and worked out a bit of dirt on the brown leather of his suitcase. The leather still gleamed, despite the coach to Delhi, the flight to Manchester, and now three months spent wedged on top of that disgusting wardrobe.

He got off the bus right outside his house and saw the grey-blue light of the TV flickering behind the closed curtains. He'd hoped they'd be asleep by now. He went the long way round the block, stopping off at Hussein Mama's for some of those fizzy little cola-bottle sweets.

'You are leaving?' Hussein Mama asked. The suitcase.

'I was helping a friend move only.'

The TV was still on when he got back. Randeep turned the key quietly and went straight up to his room on the second floor. He sat there polishing his work boots and after that he changed the blanket on his bed. But then the hunger became too much and he took his plate and cutlery from the window and went back downstairs and through the beads hanging over the kitchen doorway. There were flies hovering over the flour barrel and behind the fridge he could see chewed-up chicken drumsticks coiled with human hair. The floor kept sticking to his slippers as he stepped across to the cooker. There was cold saag inside the wok, and half a discarded roti. He used his fork to flick the roti aside and then spooned three dollops of the green mulch onto his plate. Suddenly, behind him, there was the jangling slap of beads against wall and one of the others – Gurpreet, he now saw – came through on bare feet. He'd taken his turban off and his long oiled ropes of hair glistened about his wide back.

'I thought I heard someone. We were just wondering where you were.' He clapped Randeep's shoulder. Randeep flinched. 'Thought you might have made a night of it, heh?'

'I was helping her move only. I don't think I will be seeing her again.'

'Too bad, too bad. Do you want some roti-shoti with that? I can make you some phuta-phut.'

Randeep looked across to him for a long beat, then said it was fine. 'But thank you. I'm just not very hungry.'

'Well, come inside then. Have some fun.' Randeep said nothing. 'Arré, don't be like that. There are always arguments between brothers. I'm sorry, yaar.' Gurpreet extended his hand, which Randeep took warily, and then Gurpreet threw one arm across Randeep's shoulders and pulled him down the hall and into the room.

There were eight or nine of them in there spread across the mattress on the metal trunk or squatting on an upturned blue milk crate or flopped low into a couple of the orange deckchairs someone had nicked from a garden a couple of weeks ago. A TV sat balanced on a three-legged stool in the middle of the room, playing the usual cable-channel piece of desi slapstick. Randeep entered, head low, and sat down on the very corner of the mattress, plate on his lap. Thankfully, no one seemed to notice him enter – too busy laughing at the show. After this morning, he'd half expected everyone to stop and stare. He swallowed down his first spoonful, smiling to himself.

The TV show was all pratfalls and silliness – the kind of stuff Randeep felt he had long graduated from. He didn't say anything, though. Once or twice he even forced himself to laugh along. But it had been a stretch of a day – work, and then a final thorough clean of Narinderji's flat – and soon Randeep felt his lids flickering, and then he yawned loudly. Gurpreet glanced across, mid-laugh. He looked annoyed. Randeep almost apologized, but then wondered what for.

'Here. Have one.' Gurpreet freed a can from its plastic ring. 'It'll keep you awake.'

'Sorry, bhaiji. I don't drink.'

'None of us did. But look at us now. Come on, I'm giving you one of mine.'

Randeep shook his head again. 'I would prefer not to start.'

With terrible slowness, Gurpreet put the can back down on the floor. 'He would prefer not to . . .'

The whole room seemed to tense up. Gurpreet was looking hard at the TV. 'Where's the clicker?' Someone found it, passed it to him. 'Why do you sit like that?' Gurpreet slammed his knees together and pulled himself up straight. He laughed. 'Why do you sit like a girl?'

Randeep cast his eyes down. He wanted to be back in his room, alone. Carefully, he set aside his spoon, avoiding any chink.

'You don't like our food?' Gurpreet asked.

'I'm just full, bhaiji.'

'I made that. For everyone.'

'I really liked it. Thank you.'

Now Gurpreet turned to look at him. 'I saw you flick the roti away. Think you're better than us?'

A couple of the others left the room.

'You don't know anything,' Gurpreet said. 'Stupid little boy.'

Randeep stood and left for his room with his head down, the plate still in his hands.

It was near midnight when the lock catching downstairs woke him up. He was still in his work clothes. He hadn't meant to fall asleep and the scrunch of rough toilet paper he'd masturbated into was still in his hand.

Downstairs, he went through to the kitchen where Avtar was gulping straight from the tap. The back of his orange uniform read Crunchy Fried Chicken. Randeep stood at the entrance, weaving one of the long string of beads in and out of his fingers. Avtar turned the tap off. 'Where is everyone?'

'Asleep.'

'Did you do the milk round?'

'Don't think so.'

Avtar groaned. 'I can't do everything, yaar. Who's on the chapatti shift?'

Randeep shrugged. 'Not me.'

'I bet it's that new guy. It'll be burnt fucking rotis again.'

Randeep nodded, sighed. Out of the window, the moon was full. There were no stars, though. He wondered what his sisters would be doing.

'I asked bhaiji about a job for you, but there's nothing right now.'

Randeep was relieved. He'd only mentioned it during a low moment, needing solidarity. One was enough. He didn't know how Avtar managed two jobs.

Avtar asked him how the thing with the girl had gone.

'Nothing special,' Randeep said.

'Told you,' Avtar said, and he picked up his satchel from where it rested against the flour barrel. He took out his brown exercise book and climbed onto the worktop.

'You still learning English?' Randeep asked, but Avtar didn't reply. Randeep had learned by now that when Avtar didn't want to be disturbed he just ignored you until you went away. Sighing, Randeep let the beads fall through his hands and was turning to go when Avtar asked if it was true that Gurpreet had pushed him this morning in the bathroom queue.

'It was nothing,' Randeep said.

'He's just jealous, you know.'

'I know.'

'You've got a visa.'

'I know.'

Randeep waited – for sympathy? for support? – but Avtar just bent back down to his book, trying out the words under his breath, his pocketknife eyes glinting at the end of each line. Avtar's black spectacles seemed vaguely familiar to Randeep, and as he made his way up the stairs and back into his tiny bedroom, the memory solidified into an image of his own fierce and bespectacled college masterji.

Randeep changed into his grey pyjama suit and then folded himself into a big itchy blanket. He knew he should try to sleep. Five hours and he'd have to be up again. But he felt restless, optimistic for the first time in months. Years? He got up and went to the window and laid his forehead against the cool pane. He looked across the lit city. The dark clouds seemed to be splitting apart and laying the wide sky open before him. She was somewhere in that high settling cloud on the other side, beyond the pinkish blur that he knew was a nightclub called the Leadmill. He wondered if she'd noticed that he'd spent each evening after work cleaning the bathroom and scraping the tiles and washing the carpet. Maybe she was thinking about all he'd done right now as she unpacked her clothes and hung them in the wardrobe. Or maybe she'd decided to have a bath instead and was now sitting watching TV, thick blue towels wrapped around her head and body the way British girls do. He shook the thought away. But he couldn't lose the sense that this was a turning point in his life, that she'd been delivered to him for a reason. After all, she'd called him in her hour of need, hadn't she? He wondered whether she'd found his note yet, the rose-scented card leaning inside the cupboard above the sink. Suddenly, he cringed and hoped she hadn't. At the time, in the petrol station, he'd convinced himself it was the sophisticated thing to do. But now he groaned and closed his eyes and forced himself to remember each carefully thought-over word: Dear Narinderji, I sincerely hope you are well and are enjoying your new home. A new start for us both, maybe! If I may be of any assistance I would be honoured if you would allow me to help in any way I can. And may I be the first to wish you, in your new home, a very Happy New Year. Respectfully yours, Randeep Sanghera, Esq.

Randeep forced his stiff second pair of socks up over the first and then pulled on his oversized black work boots. He stuffed the sides with kitchen towel until they fitted. Then he picked up his rucksack, his hard hat and reflector jacket, and locked the door quickly. He'd overslept.

He and Avtar were the last to come down the stairs. They mumbled a quick prayer over the smoking joss stick and rushed out. Randeep didn't mind being last: it meant they got the nearest waiting point. The street lamps were still on, spreading their sick yellow. The chill as sharp as needles.

'So cold, yaar,' Randeep said, and tucked his gloved hands into his armpits.

They turned onto Parson's Cross Road and waited beside a twiggy hedge outside the Spar. The metal National Lottery sign rattled violently in the wind. Any van pulling up would look like it was only delivering the day's newspapers.

They took out their Tupperware boxes and peeled off the lids. Avtar held up one of his chapattis: a brittle misshapen thing full of burnt holes. 'My cock can cook better than this.'

Randeep spread the puréed chilli gobi around his chapatti, then rolled it all up like a sausage.

A white Transit van stopped in front of them and they climbed into the back and squeezed onto the wheel arches. The van carried on. The others were all in there, either eating or asleep on the blankets that covered the floor. Randeep squashed his bag under his knees, behind his legs. There was the smell of cigarettes. Opposite him, Gurpreet was drawing on his roll-up and looking right at him.

'Did you wear that jacket all the way down the street?' Gurpreet asked, rocking side to side. 'Do you bhanchod want to get seen?'

'I was in a hurry.'

'In a hurry to get us all caught, eh, little prince?' Silence. 'So what was she like, then?' Gurpreet continued. 'Our Mrs Randeep Singh?'

Randeep pretended not to hear. Gurpreet asked again.

'Nothing. Like any girl.'

'Oh, come on. Tall, slim, short? What about . . . ?' He mimed breasts.

Frowning, Randeep said he didn't notice, didn't care to notice.

'And she didn't let you stay?'

'I didn't want to.'

Gurpreet laughed, falsely Randeep thought. 'Maybe one day you will.'

'Leave him alone,' Avtar said firmly, without even looking up from his textbook. Gurpreet stopped sucking on his roll-up and looked sidelong at Avtar.

'Where are we going today?' Randeep asked quickly.

Vinny – their boss and driver – spoke loudly: 'A new job, boys.

We're off to Leeds.' They all groaned. 'Ease up. Or maybe I need to get me some freshies who actually want the work?'

Someone in the back closed his fist and made the wanker sign, a new thing that had been going round the house recently.

The proposed hotel site was directly behind the train station, off the car park. A bright white sign read 'Coming Soon! The Green: a Luxury, Environmentally Friendly Living Space and Hotel in the Heart of Leeds'. But right now it was just a crater. A massive expanse of stripped earth, the topsoil scraped off and piled up to one side in a huge pyramid. But at least all the bushes and trees had been cleared, Randeep thought. Saved them that task for once.

They assembled in the corner of the car park, looking down onto the site. Another vanload joined them. Mussulmans, Randeep guessed. Bangladeshis even, by the look of them. A man approached. His hard hat was all askew on his big pink head. He went straight to Vinny and the two spoke and then shook hands.

'All right, boys,' Vinny said. 'This is John. Your gaffer. Do what he says and you'll be fine. I'll pick you up at seven.'

The van reversed and Vinny left. Randeep moved closer to Avtar: if this John was going to pair them off then he wanted to be with him. But John just began handing out large pieces of yellow paper, faintly lined. Avtar took one, studied it. Randeep peered down over his shoulder.

'These are the project plans,' John said, walking back and forth. 'As you can see there's lots to do, lots to do. But let's just take it one step at a time, yes? You understand?'

'We could do this with our eyes closed,' Avtar muttered. 'What does this bhanchod know?'

'Oi! No, bhaiji!' John said, pointing at Avtar with the rolled-up paper. 'I am not a bhanchod, acha?'

Avtar stared, open-mouthed. And then everyone started laughing.

They put on their hats and grabbed a tool belt and then made towards the footings stacked in neat angles on the wooden pallets. John called them back. He wanted stakes in first.

'But it will take twice as long,' Avtar complained.

John didn't care. 'We're doing this properly. It's not one of your shanty towns.'

So Avtar and Randeep piled a wheelbarrow with the stakes and headed bumpily on down to their squared-off section of the site. 'You put in the stakes and I'll follow with the footings,' Avtar said.

Randeep got onto one knee and held a stake to the ground. 'Like last time?' He glanced towards the plan and then brought his hammer down. He wasn't going to fall for that again. 'We'll both put in the stakes and then we'll both put in the footings.'

The morning went by. Randeep stood and stretched out with both hands to the small of his back. He could feel through his thin shirt how cold his hands were and how the blisters on them scraped against his drenched skin. Avtar used the sharp end of his hammer to get at an itch behind his ear.

'It'll take all week just to do this,' he said, as they both headed off on the long walk for lunch. 'It's as big as one of their bhanchod football grounds.'

Randeep found his backpack among the pile and joined the others sitting astride a large tunnel of aluminium tubing, newly exposed from the dig. Beside them, a sheet of green tarpaulin acted as a windbreak. Randeep slid off his helmet. His hair was sopping.

They ate in silence. Afterwards one or two pulled on their coats and turned up their collars and sunk into a sleep. The rest decided on a cricket match to stay warm. They found a plank of wood – the bat – and several of them had tennis balls handy. They divided into teams of Sikhs and Muslims. Three overs each. Gurpreet elected himself captain and won the toss. He put the Muslims in to bat.

'No slips, but an edge is automatically out,' he said and ran back to bowl.

He was knocked for fourteen off the first over, the last ball screaming for a six. Gurpreet watched it fly above his head and off into the car park. 'Arré, yaar, there's something wrong with that ball.'

'Right,' Avtar said. 'The fact that it is being bowled by you.'
Randeep laughed, but when Gurpreet glowered at him he fell silent.

They needed thirty-one to win but came nowhere near, with Avtar
going for glory and getting caught, and galumphing Gurpreet easily
run out.

'These Mussulmans,' Gurpreet said, throwing aside the bat.
'Cheating is in their nature.'

John approached and for the first time Randeep noticed his
slight limp.

'Bohut good work, men, bohut good work. But come on, jaldi
jaldi, it looks like you'll have it all khetum in no time.'

Randeep stowed his lunch box back into his bag and trudged back
to work. Just another six hours to go.

Vinny was late that evening, not pulling up until seven thirty. They
all piled into the back.

'Some of us have second jobs to get to, yaar,' Avtar said.

'Sorry, sorry,' Vinny said. 'I had to go to Southall.' He was forced
to turn left. 'Crazy one-way system in this city.'

'Is there work in Southall?' Avtar asked, up and alert.

'Hm? No, no. The opposite. I've found another one of you
chumps. You'll need to make some more room back there.'

No one said anything. It was nothing new. They came and went
all the time.

Soon they hit the motorway. Randeep sat rocking on the wheel
arch, chin in hand and staring out at the huge black sky. The moon
was made grey by the grubby window. He was thinking of home. His
mother and three sisters and how they'd be cooking the evening meal
right now. Amandeep shooing the younger two out of the kitchen. But
then he remembered the time difference.

'What thoughts have you sunk into?' Avtar asked.

Randeep shook his head and sighed and Avtar squeezed his
shoulder and said to be strong and to try and not get too down
about things.

Someone asked if Vinny Sahib had heard anything about any raids? Because one of those Mussulmans, you see, he was telling that the raids have started again.

Vinny whistled, shaking his head. 'I've not heard a thing. And why would I? Far as I'm concerned you're all legit, ain't you? You all showed me your papers. Nowt to do with owt, me.'

The van continued on in the slow lane, the tyres rumbling away under Randeep. Then something caught his eye. Some kind of falling outside the black window. At first he thought it was rain but it was too slow and gentle to be that. Then he understood, and leaned forward, smiling. 'Mashallah,' someone said, as Randeep felt the others all crowding behind him, pressing and jostling to stare at the sky, and the globe of tumbling snow around each street light.

He woke in the mornings shivering inside the two blankets. Even through his thick socks, his feet froze on the floor as he stood up and walked to the window and saw the snow that had fallen and kept falling. He washed from an iron bucket filled with cold water, shoulders shaking and Gurpreet banging on the door telling him to hurry the bhanchod hell up. By ten to five he was waiting for the van and jumping on the spot to keep warm and when the van did finally show up he had to help push it back through the snow, his legs already drenched to his knees and the sweat frozen across his back.

The weather had packed tight the ground at the hotel site but he didn't let up. The stakes and the footings took more hammering to secure and several times he hit his hand with the mallet. Gurpreet told him it was his job to carry the barrow back and forth and he tried to keep it steady along the rutted earth but each time the thick concrete slabs spilled over he had to stop and bend and gather them all up again. The sun was weak and brittle, wrapped in gold paper. Darkness came as swiftly as a curtain floating down and when he climbed back into the van he couldn't move his neck and it hurt his arms to lift them. His hands were raw-white with cold, like the frozen claws of some sea creature. At the house he ate alone in his room with his mother's white cutlery and soon he was back in bed, too exhausted to even dream.

By the third week, more snow fell and it lay in total majesty over everything. Randeep stared out the window. He was standing about a foot away from the pane. Any closer and he could feel the chill that somehow blew in through the brown tape he kept double-plastered down the sides of the glass. He turned back to his mattress and the clothes spread out on it. He didn't know what to leave in the flat with Narinderji. The blue shirt with the white collar was a definite, along with the grey tie. And his smart black trousers too. But then maybe he ought to send more casual stuff? British girls seemed to like boys who presented a more laid-back version of themselves. He put down the shirt and in one hand picked up his jeans and in the other an oversized hooded top his mother had bought him a few days before he left. But what if that made him seem too much like those boys who just hang around causing trouble outside the Spar? He picked the shirt up again and kept looking from shirt to hooded top, hooded top to shirt. He then thought how he'd have to leave some of his underwear with her and that sent a mild quake through his brain.

He heard a door sliding shut, like a van's side door, and the downstairs bell being rung. Randeep swiped clear a patch in the window – Vinnyji? – and then went down the first flight of stairs. Gurpreet and the others had edged into the hallway, shushing one another.

'It's Vinnyji,' Randeep called down but no one seemed to hear him. Gurpreet bent down to the letter box and then Vinny's voice came through, asking what was taking them so long and that it was fucking freezing out here. Gurpreet opened the door and Vinny hurried in. He was hunched over and looked shorter than usual and each needle of his spiked-up hair was topped with a bobble of snow. He gave someone his coat and came inside. Behind him followed someone Randeep hadn't seen before.

Randeep joined them all in the front room where as many as could be were seated. Gurpreet sent someone to boil some tea.

'This is Tochi,' Vinny said. 'Starts tomorrow, acha?'

He was very dark, much darker than Randeep, and shorter, but he looked strong. The tendons on his neck radiated out. Twenty-one, twenty-two. One or two years older than him, anyway. So another one he'd have to call bhaiji.

'I've got a spare mattress in the van. He'll be staying in yours, OK, Ronny?' Vinny said. It wasn't really a question but Randeep said he was absolutely fine with that.

They carried the mattress on their backs up the two flights and leaned it against the unpapered pink wall outside the room. They'd have to take out the wardrobe first.

'Wait,' Randeep said, and he took down his suitcase from on top of the wardrobe and placed it to one side.

'Cares more about that fucking suitcase . . .' Vinny said.

They hefted the wardrobe onto the landing and then Vinny said he had to go.

'Have some tea,' Gurpreet said.

Vinny said he couldn't. 'Was meant to be back an hour ago. She'll have the face on enough as it is.' He turned to the new guy and made a star of his hand. 'Five sharp, you understand? These lot'll show you the ropes.' And then he clomped down the stairs in his silver-studded boots and asked someone to pass him his coat.

It was just the three of them left on the top landing: Randeep, Tochi and Gurpreet. Gurpreet folded his arms on the shelf of his hard round gut, slowly, as if establishing dominance. 'So, where you from?'

But Tochi just headed into the room and closed the door. Gurpreet stared after him and then pushed off the banister and went back downstairs.

For a few minutes Randeep waited outside on the landing. He wanted to make a good first impression. He wanted a friend. He knocked, then opened the door and stepped inside. The guy looked to be asleep already, still in his clothes and boots and knees drawn up and hands pressed between them. He'd moved his mattress as far away from Randeep's as it was possible to get in that small room: under the window, where a creeping chill would be blowing down on him.

'Bhaiji, would you like a blanket? I have one spare,' Randeep whispered. He asked again and when he again got no reply Randeep tiptoed forward and folded out his best blanket and spread it over his new room-mate. Downstairs, there were still two rotis wrapped up in foil in the fridge. He heated them straight on the hob. He liked the froggy way they puffed up. Then he spread onto them some mango pickle. He didn't want to join the others in the front room, where he could hear the TV going, but he didn't want to disturb his new room-mate either. So he just stayed there, marooned in the middle of the kitchen because there wasn't a single clean surface to lean on, tearing his chapatti and feeding himself.

By three fifteen he was awake, washed and dressed, and in the kitchen binning the previous day's joss stick and lighting a fresh one. He said a quick prayer, warmed his hands by the cooker flame and then set about getting what he needed: frying pans, rolling pin, butter and dough from the fridge, a cupful of flour from the blue barrel. He tore a small chunk from the hardish brown dough and began warming and rolling it between his palms. He had just over an hour to get sixty chapattis done. About four each, he calculated.

This time he paced himself and rolled out the patties methodically. Four rolls up, turn it round, four rolls more, a pinch more flour, three more rolls on each side and then into the pan it went. He found himself whistling along even as he could feel his upper arms filling with a rich dull ache and a pearl of sweat dripped from the tip of his nose. There was movement around the house: radio alarms, the thrust of a tap. He quickened up and once the chapattis were done and foil-wrapped Randeep dumped the frying pans in the sink and replaced them on the hob with four large steel pans of water, full gas. He added tea bags, cumin and sugar and while all that boiled he took the Tupperware boxes stacked on the windowsill. Each had a name written in felt-tip Panjabi. He spooned in some of the potato sabzi from the fridge then carried a six-litre carton of milk from the shelf and placed it beside the five flasks. One between three or thereabouts.

Gurpreet wandered in. The bib of his dungarees flopped half undone. He was pinning his turban into place. 'All done? Thought you might have needed some help again.' Randeep flushed, but concentrated on pouring the milk into the boiling pans. 'Clean the bucket after you wash, acha?' Gurpreet went on, moving to the Tupperware boxes. 'None of your servants here.' He had cleaned it, he was sure he had, and his family had never had servants. But he didn't say anything. He just watched Gurpreet moving some of the sabzi from the other boxes, including Randeep's, and adding it to his own. He wondered if he did this with everyone or only when it was Randeep on the chapatti shift.

'So where's your new friend from?'

Randeep said he didn't know, that he went to sleep straight away.

'His name?'

'Tochi.'

'Surname, fool.'

Randeep thought for a moment, then shrugged. 'Can't remember.'

'Hmm. Strange.'

Randeep didn't say a word, didn't know what he was driving at, and just stood silently over the pan waiting for it come to the boil again. But he didn't hear Gurpreet leave and then he had the twitchy sensation he was being stared at. He turned round, and Gurpreet was indeed standing at the back of the kitchen and looking right at him with still eyes.

'Bhaiji?' Randeep asked. Gurpreet grunted, then seemed to snap out of it and quickly went out through the beaded curtain. Spooked, Randeep gazed at the beads still swinging but then there was the hiss of boiling tea and he leapt to turn off the gas.

Soon the house was full of voices and feet and toilet flushes and calls to get out of bed. And then they were filing down with rucksacks slung over sleepy shoulders, each taking his food box. A rushed prayer at the joss stick and then out into the cold morning dark in twos and threes, at ten-minute intervals. Randeep looked for the new guy but he must've gone ahead already, so he paired up with Avtar as usual. Before he left the house he remembered to take up the pencil strung and taped to the wall and he scored a firm thick tick next to his name on the rota.

They spent the morning still staking it all out while their foreman, Langra John – Limpy John – and three other white men went tearing out the land in yellow JCBs.

'Wish I had that job,' Randeep said at lunch. 'Just driving about all day.'

Avtar clucked his tongue. 'One day, my friend. One day we'll be the bosses.'

Randeep leaned back against the aluminium tunnel. He closed his eyes and must've nodded off for a while because the next thing he heard was the insistent sound of Gurpreet's voice.

'But you must have a pindh. Was that in Calcutta too?'

Tochi was sitting down against a low wall. Soles of his boots pressed together and knees thrown wide open.

'I'm talking to you,' Gurpreet said.

'My pindh's not in Calcutta.'

'Where, then?'

Tochi swigged long from his water bottle and took his time screwing the top back on. He had a quiet voice. 'Bihar.'

Gurpreet looked round at everyone as if to say now they were getting there. 'Are there many Jats in Bihar?'

Avtar spoke up. 'Arré, this is England, yaar. Leave him.'

'Ask him his bhanchod name.'

Shaking his head, Avtar turned to Tochi. 'What are you? Ramgarhia? Saini? No one cares but him.'

'Ask him his bhanchod name, I said.'

Tochi clapped his boots together, shaking off dust. 'Tarlochan Ramdasia.'

Randeep frowned a little but hoped no one saw it.

'A bhanchod chamaar,' Gurpreet said, laughing. 'They've given us a bhanchod chamaar to work with.'

'Who cares?' Avtar said.

'Only backward people care,' Randeep added, but Gurpreet was still laughing away to himself when John limped up and said they better get a move on.

Randeep had a thousand questions for Tochi: how did he get here? What were his plans? But he could never get him alone for long enough to ask any of them. As soon as they got home from work Tochi would take off his jacket and change his muddied-up boots for some cheap black trainers with Velcro straps and head back outside. When he returned he'd climb onto his mattress and close his eyes. He never responded to Randeep's cheery hello.

'Do you think he's got a visa?' Randeep asked Avtar one night.

Avtar brought his spectacles up to the light, then cleaned them using the hem of his orange uniform. 'When did you last meet a rich chamaar?'

'His parents might have helped him.'

'Arré, don't go asking him about his parents. He's probably an orphan.'

One evening Gurpreet knocked on their bedroom door and said he and a few of the others were going out, so Randeep and Tochi would have to help with the milk run for once. 'You've got Tesco.'

'Where are you going?' Randeep asked and Gurpreet made a fist and pumped it down by his crotch. Then he left. 'He's that ugly he has to pay for sex,' Randeep said.

Tochi was roughly threading his belt around himself. The swish of it sliced the air. 'You'll have to do it yourself.'

'I can't carry all that milk. Do you know how far it is? Can't you help me?'

'Join one of the others.'

'But we can't all go to the same place. I heard some brothers in London were caught last month because one person got all their milk from one shop and the manager got suspicious. Please?'

Tochi said nothing.

'My mamma always taught me to be respectful to those older than me. So I respect you, bhaiji. Can't you help me?'

Tochi sighed resignedly.

On Ecclesall Road the roadworks still hadn't finished and the street was all headlights and banked-up snow. Randeep pulled his tight woolly hat lower over his ears and marched through the stuff. Tarlochan only had on his shirt, which kept belling out with the wind. He touched the side of his stomach a lot, Randeep noticed. And winced each time he did.

'Are you hurt, bhaiji?' Randeep asked. 'Is it the cold?'

Tochi seemed not to have heard.

'Next time I will insist you borrow my gloves,' Randeep went on, loudly. 'You can have them. I have two pairs.' Tochi said nothing. When they passed the Botanical Gardens, Randeep pointed up a side street. 'That's where Avtar bhaiji also works. At the end of that road and turn right.'

'How many apneh work there?'

Privately, Randeep felt 'apneh' was perhaps a little too far, given their backgrounds, but he let it slide. 'A few, but no one else from the house. You looking for a second job too?'

He didn't say anything. Instead he suddenly turned left down a road, his head bent low. Randeep yelled his name, then ran to catch up.

'The police,' Tochi said, still walking.

Randeep turned round, perplexed. He didn't remember seeing any police. 'Arré, that's not the police.' And he explained what a lollipop lady was and then they headed back up to the main road. 'So that must mean you don't have a visa,' Randeep said.

'I guess it must.'

'How did you get here? Ship or truck?'

'On your mother's cunt.'

Randeep stared glumly into a dark coffee-shop window they were passing. It didn't seem to matter how hard he tried.

'Sorry,' Tochi said. He looked annoyed with himself.

'I've got a visa. A marriage one.' Randeep expected a reaction but got none. 'I got married,' he went on, aware he was starting to blather, unable to stop. 'To a girl. She came over to Panjab. But she's here now. In Sheffield, I mean.'

'Why aren't you living with her?'

'She's Sikhni. But I'm not that bothered, if I'm honest with you, bhaiji. I'm going to take some clothes over soon, but that's it. It's just one year, get my passport, pay her the money, get the divorce, then bring my mamma and sisters over. It's all agreed with Narinderji.' And he wished he'd not said her name. He felt like he'd revealed something of himself.

They bought milk, flour, bread, potatoes and toilet rolls and then went back to the house. Others were returning with their milk and shopping too, and it all just got piled into the fridge, all done for another week. ∎

SUBMERSION

Ross Raisin

ROSS RAISIN

1979

Ross Raisin was born in Silsden, West
Yorkshire. His first novel, *God's Own
Country*, was published in 2008 and was
awarded the *Sunday Times* Young Writer
of the Year Award in 2009, the Guildford
First Novel Prize, a Betty Trask Award and
shortlisted for six other awards including
the *Guardian* First Book Award and the
International IMPAC Dublin Literary
Award. His second novel, *Waterline*, was
published in 2011. His short stories have
appeared in *Granta, Prospect, Esquire,
Dazed & Confused*, the *Sunday Times* and
on BBC Radio 3 and 4. 'Submersion' is a
new story.

It comes back in different ways. But this more than any other.

We are out of town, drinking in an empty beachside bar in a small resort down by the coast. The season is pretty much at an end, the bar owner tells us; that is why it's so quiet. I smile politely. Your face is turned away towards the little television set, skewered into a roof beam among old postcards and fading paper garlands. The rain has started up again. It taps and dribbles on the low corrugated roof. This has been a bumper season, the bar owner is saying, owing to the drought. The tourists have come in record numbers to lie on the beach and trek through the forest up to the fertility monument. The governor and his wife were down here for a whole two weeks. A teenage boy died in a jet-ski accident.

'Look,' you say then, your eyes still on the television.

There are always warnings, every year at around this time. Not that anybody ever takes much notice. If it floods, it floods, is the attitude we have always taken. The previous year the rains came late and released a rare, brief joy through our town. Maurice Peake danced in the square. Groups of children ran down to the swollen river to play and smoke and cut channels into van Steerman's soft, wet fields. When the banks overflowed, van Steerman's fields, as they always did, turned into a glistening brown swamp, his parsnips floating up to the surface as pale and bloated as babies' limbs. If it floods, it floods. But we have never before known anything like this.

The bar owner and I turn to look with you at the television. It shows a moving aerial view of our town, or rather the highest parts of it, the rest being underwater. At this stage the head of the rusted cow above the saleyards is still visible, collapsed wooden stalls bobbing all around it. There are people gathered on the roof of the town hall and the hotel, and somebody is clinging, spreadeagled, to the side of the church steeple. It doesn't look to me like the vicar, but it is difficult to tell, never having seen him in that position before.

The view moves over the town to the outskirts, and I notice with some surprise that a tattered 'GIVE THEM THE BOOT' banner covers most of the Mortons' garage roof; it is weighted down with large rocks, as if they have long been expecting the cameras.

'You know that place?' the bar owner asks.

'Yes,' you say. 'We live there.'

I think he gives you a peculiar look at that point, although I can't be sure. The rain begins to pelt harder onto the roof. A dog, which has been asleep on the sand just inside the bar's entrance, walks over as if to join us in front of the television, but instead picks up a gristle of meat from underneath one of the bar stools and slumps onto the floor to chew at it.

A feeling of quiet shame comes over me as I watch those images: here is our town, on national television, a place where people store their junk – fridges, tyres, broken televisions – on their garage roofs; the vandalized statue in the town square that has never been fixed. In desperation, the townspeople are now massing together on top of the dirty buildings, jumping and gesticulating at the helicopter.

The drought that has lasted all through the spring and summer finally ended yesterday, according to the rolling news at the bottom of the screen. The rains intensified overnight and at around ten o'clock this morning the river broke its banks. By eleven o'clock all low-lying areas of the town were inundated with floodwater. The famous saleyards building, despite a sandbag barricade, has fallen apart. So too the post office, the old prison and all the rest of the older wooden structures along the high street. The town hall, however – built from the thick grey stone mined further down the valley – and the supermarket are still standing strong.

'Bloody hell,' the bar owner mutters. 'Bloody hell.'

You don't say anything. You simply watch, and drink occasionally from your beer, the leathery red scars on your forearms clearly visible below the shortsleeves of your shirt. A telephone rings in the back room and the bar owner goes to answer it, and it is at this moment – I can hear distinctly the excited pitch of the news reporter's voice – that he appears.

The helicopter camera has panned down and is following an object that at first looks like some kind of dark box, but as the image grows closer I see that it is in fact our father, asleep in his armchair, drifting down the high street. Instinctively I turn towards you and for a single moment you look away from the television, at me, with an expression not of shock or confusion but rather – as I instantly take it to mean – of accusation.

Our father is drifting now past the barbershop – recognizable only because the top of its pole is protruding from the water. His chair must then snag onto something beneath the surface because it stops for a few seconds, stuck, tugging, as the image holds still and a familiar nausea begins to rise in my throat. The skin on his face is red and peeling; the scalp blistered, hairless. With a sudden rush the chair comes free and races onwards in the current. I have always known that chair as something heavy – its rotten wood frame clung with green hessian matted and spoiled from years of cigarette smoke and television meals – but it appears now light, buoyant. Its charred black shape glides through the water alongside the supermarket until it bumps, spinning, past a lamp post on the corner of Geddes Street. Yet through it all he remains asleep. His head bent forward and his shoulders hunched, arms loosely on his lap, as if it is a Christmas afternoon. And I am struck right then with an awful sadness, or something worse, that here he is for everybody to see. Exposed. Alone. The giddy babble of the presenter talking about him. Only a short time earlier he would have been resting in the living room, watching the television, nodding off. And I glimpse then the TV remote control, deformed and melted onto the armrest.

We set off first thing the following morning. You wanted to return immediately, the very moment the camera left our father for an interview with Freddie Lindsay, the hotel owner, dressed immaculately in a dry suit and a borrowed pair of wellingtons, like a politician at a construction site. I convinced you otherwise. It would be too dark; we would arrive in the middle of the night; there would be nowhere to stay. The roads would be dangerous, impassable. Our mobiles had no reception so we asked the bar owner if we could use his telephone but of course there was no one to answer our calls and, anyway, most of the lines were dead.

So we drive back at dawn. From the winding hill coast road we get our first sight of the flood: we come over a crest and it appears below us as a vast glimmering lagoon, orange and brown in the early light, entirely filling the valley basin.

We pull onto the side of the road to look at it. The surface is broken only by distant clusters of roofs; here and there large patches of scorched forest canopy; the cement works at Eagleford, rising above the water like a castle. I take a photograph with my mobile. You say something under your breath and get back into the car. We argue briefly about what route to take. In the end we decide on your idea of taking the high road along the valley side until we have a better view of the town, from where we can descend to the closest point before the water.

This point, when we reach it an hour later, is on one of the raised fields just north of the town. We arrive to a chaotic scene: an ugly festival of townspeople and news crews packed into the field, the ground slick and rutted everywhere with tyre tracks. We leave the car parked on the road, a safe distance above the pulsing scumline of the floodwater and enter the field with no plan of what we need to do.

As we approach, the drone increases from the four or five generators that have been set up by the news crews. Beside the first of these a man I don't recognize is arguing with a woman in a high-visibility vest because she won't let him use the generator to power up his fridge. 'What the hell's the use of you people being here if you're not going to help?' he shouts as we come by. I follow as you begin to walk purposefully towards a group of tents, their sides streaked with mud, that have obviously been put up after the arrival of the crews and the cars. I can see where you're headed: sitting in the porch entrance to one of these tents is Eddie Tuck from the hardware store. He has a quiet glum look on him that I at first presume to be unhappiness, or pride, but which I realize as we approach is in fact displeasure at seeing us; or me, certainly.

'We need to borrow your boat,' you say before we have even stopped in front of him.

Eddie Tuck shrugs his shoulders.

'Welcome to it. Nothing left to salvage now. Got everything I needed out when the flood came.' He glances inside the tent, where I can just make out Mrs Tuck hanging his limp discoloured underwear onto the tent poles. 'Too late now. Boat's probably carried off anyway.'

He is right, of course. The small boat shed that used to stand a short way beyond the bottom of the field, where Eddie Tuck and his friends used to sit by the river drinking six-packs, has gone. The river itself is no longer there; only the thick veins on the water's skin showing where it now courses underneath.

We walk to the top of the field and look down.

The town appears utterly destroyed. Many of the buildings have gone, and even from this distance the force of the water below is obvious. Parallel to where the river should be, tree branches and humps of detritus course down the high street, and water fills the side roads to a level that must be fifteen feet or more, because it is pouring into the first-floor windows.

From here I can see the missing circle in the forest beyond town, some of the larger cremated trees inside it just about visible. I want to ask you what we should do, if you think it really is possible we can find him, but I hold back.

After a few minutes you start abruptly down the field. You have spotted the news channel whose images we watched in the bar. By the time I manage to catch up with you, on the wet wooden decking behind their cabin, you are involved in an angry exchange with a tall thin man in shorts – although that is probably the wrong way to put it, because the anger is all yours, and the thin man simply stands there with his arms folded, occasionally glancing over to where his colleagues sit on camping chairs beside the generator, drinking coffee.

'How can you film a man being carried to his death and not follow where he went?'

The thin man looks tired, uninterested. 'We aren't responsible for the feed,' he says, twice.

'Then who the fuck is?'

I feel fleetingly that same embarrassment as when I watched our neighbours scrambling among the hoarded rubbish on their rooftops.

'Forget it,' you say, and we leave.

We spend the rest of that afternoon searching for anything we can use to float ourselves through the town. There are fallen trees all along the river, but these are unreachable, and those near the water's edge are too entangled by other trees to dislodge. When finally we do manage to pull free one small hazel, it escapes immediately with the current. We find a wheelbarrow, but it sinks. There are of course the aluminium boats with small outboard motors that the police and fire teams who have arrived from the city are using, but when we ask if we might borrow one for a couple of hours our question is met only with laughter. We ask if a middle-aged man in an armchair has been found and we are laughed at again.

Sometime later, sitting damp and angry inside the car eating sandwiches that we bought at the coast, we consider taking one of those boats. We know, however, that it would be impossible: the ones that are not in use are securely stacked and locked in the emergency services area that has formed at the base of the field, where uniformed men come and go or stand talking in small groups. A kind of segregation has taken place: the police and rescue teams near the water, then the television people a little further up, and at the top, all along the highest part of the field, the people of the town, huddled and gossiping and burning small fires – the same grim determined merriment on their faces as their ancestors probably used to show when they came up here to lynch cattle thieves.

Although we cannot take a boat, something of the stealing idea must stay with you because late that night, after several hours of fitful sleep in the car, we get out and tread quietly to the thin man's news cabin, where we take three planks from the decking and both of their forty-litre water canisters. We hurry these things down to the edge of the water where, by torchlight, we place the planks side by side and bind them using a roll of wire that is in the boot; to each end of the raft we strap an empty canister.

We have nearly completed the raft when Eddie Tuck appears out of the dark, grinning, a beer in his hand.

'Couldn't find my boat then?'

We ignore him, and continue to build the raft.

He is looking directly at me.

'Guess you should've got back sooner,' he says, and leaves.

We sit down on the wood and wait for the light to come up, as floodwater surges darkly in front of us and our backsides begin to itch with damp.

We are about to set out when we realize that we will need something with which to steer, or paddle back. We search around for a few minutes but find nothing.

'We'll have to grab something as we go,' you say, which seems to me like an extremely rash plan, but I say nothing.

The current takes us immediately. The speed of it shocks us both and instinctively we get down onto our fronts. The raft, although buoyant and stable enough that the planks remain an inch or so above the surface, will not point straight and spins uncontrollably so that one moment I am tobogganing head first through the centre of the flow but then the next you are careering round the side of me like a rider on a fairground waltz.

We barrel down the wrecked high street. I am too preoccupied with fear to feel very much about what we are seeing: two lines of bent lamp posts and snapped trees; the first-floor windows of the bank and the supermarket caved in, water lapping at the broken glass; near the town square, a pickup truck beached on top of the bus stop. We continue onwards. It is obvious now that we can have no control over our journey, or its end.

'What now?' I ask.

'We keep going.'

'Where to?'

'We just keep going.'

I have no idea how we are going to get back, or if you even intend to. I don't know how we are going to get food, or drinking water. I know, however, that I can't talk to you about these concerns. When I turn round, you have on your face an expression of such resoluteness that I cannot meet your eyes. I will myself to think only about our father, and not my own safety, but I know that my sense of urgency to find him is being obscured by fear. Perhaps you sense this, and it is causing you to become even more dogged.

We come to the end of the high street, the current slowing into a large pool that rests over the playing field. We drift across it. A filing cabinet comes alongside then overtakes us. Further into the pool you are able to grab onto one of the rugby posts and, from the pile of flotsam that has built up there, pull out a spade.

With this we are able to navigate to the far side of the pool. You take the front position, and the spade, paddling on alternate sides like a canoeist.

It is clear to me now that you are steering towards the house. We pass the filling station, the tops of its two pumps circled by a purple sheen of leaking fuel that trails into the forest, where birds flock in the treetops and splash among the floating debris.

Suddenly I hear my name shouted. I look around in confusion, and the shout comes again. It is van Steerman. He is a short way ahead of us on the roof of his crop barn with Mrs van Steerman and their three children, the whole family wheeling their arms at us. We pilot towards them as their shouting becomes more frantic, and go past. You look up only once. I put out my hands apologetically. 'No room,' I mouth, and point at the planks and canisters of our raft in a ridiculous attempt to demonstrate how they might devise their own vessel, an action that seems to confuse the van Steermans, who probably think I am mocking them.

It has started to rain. Softly at first, but within minutes it becomes a downpour, beating onto the water to create a thick, stinking smoke that obscures the way ahead through the forest, as well as the view behind of the van Steermans waving forlornly on top of their crop barn. After a few minutes the rain subsides but by now we are soaked through and still the smog clings around us, making it difficult to know exactly where we are. Suddenly you stop paddling, letting the spade sink with your hand into the water. You stare blankly ahead through the trees.

'I'm sorry,' I say eventually.

You do not reply.

'I'm sorry.'

'What for?'

You know I cannot bring myself to say it.

'I loved him,' I say after some time.

The motion of the paddling has made your shirt ride up and I can see the livid red scars on your back. I want to grab you by the shoulders, to shake you hard for punishing me, for not allowing me to let out my guilt.

'Here, let me,' I say.

I take the spade from where it dangles in the water and turn the raft so that I am at the front. I see, as I look round, that you are crying. I don't know what to say. I lean back to touch you but all I can reach is your foot, so I grip around your ankle and try to smile as you look at me. Even in your ankle I can feel your body stiffen. I pull my hand back and start concentrating stupidly on my paddling. The sun glows dully through the smog and I realize that I am desperately hot; sweat begins to trickle down my arms and cause the spade handle to grease and slip in my grasp. I grunt with the effort of each stroke, understanding gradually that it is becoming harder and harder to paddle. The water, somehow, is thickening. I stop, and look up to see that all around us the flood is turning into a thick, gleaming mud.

I look at you, not knowing what to do; then I follow as you climb off the raft and begin to advance through the mud. It is dense, and cool, and reaches almost to our knees; we have to high-step over it.

A heavy sulphurous stench now hangs in the air. Mouldering rubbish is caked in place all about us: a mattress, a woman's hat, a sack of onions swarming with flies. I look down at the surface of the mud and I can see that its skin is hardening, baking in the heat so that when we step onto it a soft brown liquid oozes out from the cracks, like a chocolate pudding.

Suddenly you begin to run, slipping, ahead of me, and I yell at you to stop but you will not listen. I try to follow but I fall, tearing the flesh of my palm on something hidden beneath the mud. I stay kneeling in that position and watch as you stop abruptly and turn to look at me. The clothes are peeling from you, revealing the ruined red skin of your body. You are diminishing, your head and limbs and torso shrivelling before me. I cry out to you to come closer to me but you stay where you are and even though the mud is receding I cannot move. My body feels too heavy. I can only watch, powerless, as you disappear.

The mud is drawing back. I begin to see the parched ground and I close my eyes, trying to fight against it, although I know that this is useless, the scene of that night unassailably coming back to me; I can already feel the heat against my eyelids as I stand up and start to run.

A faint orange glow is rising above the forest. An acrid smell in the air that becomes stronger as I run along the hard dry track, panic rising inside me, into the trees. I can hear a strange moaning away to one side and I look round to see a herd of cows, some of them ablaze. The smell of meat. Ahead of me, part of the forest is burning. I race towards it and there, on the side of the road, is the Mortons' boy with his back to me and a petrol canister in his hand, shouting excitedly to a group obscured by the undergrowth. 'Come on, come look. There's a fucking house on fire.'

I see the trees in the garden first, alight. And then the house. Flames dance through a hole in the roof and spews of smoke are pouring out of the windows. I stand, transfixed, able only to watch.

Already, a crowd is forming. Somebody holds up a mobile phone, aiming it at the house. In desperation I run towards the crowd but they back away. I see Eddie Tuck standing watching with his arms folded. 'What can we do?' I plead to him, but he shrugs his shoulders and will not look at me. 'Guess you should've got back sooner,' he says.

I move towards the building but the heat makes it impossible to get close. Parts of the roof are falling to the ground, setting the grass alight. A sound in the distance that I realize as it gets louder is a helicopter. I shut my eyes and will it onwards, imagine water cascading onto the flames, but when eventually the helicopter does arrive I open my eyes and see the television channel logo on its belly. It hovers above the forest a short distance away, filming, as I tumble to the warm ground and watch the house burn.

They did not want me to enter the building but I ignored them and they did not try to stop me. Small frazzled lumps of congealed wallpaper floated in pools of water left by the fire hoses. Parts of the ceiling had come down. The thick smoke caused me to cough as I came into the living room and my eyes were stinging so much that I could not see you at first. My feet crunched on the glass of a burnt photograph. I saw the melted case of the television and then, through the smoke, the image that never leaves me: our father, stretched across the armrest of his blackened chair, his face peeling and his scalp blistered and hairless. You on the ground beside him, your hand joined to his and your two bodies stiffened into that final position as you had tried to pull him free. ■

MARTIN AMIS
PAT BARKER
JULIAN BARNES
URSULA BENTLEY
WILLIAM BOYD
BUCHI EMECHETA
MAGGIE GEE
KAZUO ISHIGURO
ALAN JUDD
ADAM MARS-JONES

BEST OF YOUNG BRITISH NOVELISTS 1 (1983)

IAIN BANKS
LOUIS DE BERNIÈRES
ANNE BILLSON
TIBOR FISCHER
ESTHER FREUD
ALAN HOLLINGHURST
KAZUO ISHIGURO
A.L. KENNEDY
PHILIP KERR
HANIF KUREISHI

BEST OF YOUNG BRITISH NOVELISTS 2 (1993)

MONICA ALI
NICOLA BARKER
RACHEL CUSK
PETER HO DAVIES
SUSAN ELDERKIN
PHILIP HENSHER
A.L. KENNEDY
HARI KUNZRU
TOBY LITT
DAVID MITCHELL

BEST OF YOUNG BRITISH NOVELISTS 3 (2003)

IAN McEWAN

SHIVA NAIPAUL

PHILIP NORMAN

CHRISTOPHER PRIEST

SALMAN RUSHDIE

LISA ST AUBIN DE TERÁN

CLIVE SINCLAIR

GRAHAM SWIFT

ROSE TREMAIN

A.N. WILSON

ADAM LIVELY

ADAM MARS-JONES

CANDIA McWILLIAM

LAWRENCE NORFOLK

BEN OKRI

CARYL PHILLIPS

WILL SELF

NICHOLAS SHAKESPEARE

HELEN SIMPSON

JEANETTE WINTERSON

ANDREW O'HAGAN

DAVID PEACE

DAN RHODES

BEN RICE

RACHEL SEIFFERT

ZADIE SMITH

ADAM THIRLWELL

ALAN WARNER

SARAH WATERS

ROBERT McLIAM WILSON

GRANTA

SHERMAN ALEXIE

MADISON SMARTT BELL

ETHAN CANIN

EDWIDGE DANTICAT

TOM DRURY

TONY EARLEY

JEFFREY EUGENIDES

JONATHAN FRANZEN

DAVID GUTERSON

DAVID HAYNES

BEST OF YOUNG AMERICAN NOVELISTS I (1996)

DANIEL ALARCÓN

KEVIN BROCKMEIER

JUDY BUDNITZ

CHRISTOPHER COAKE

ANTHONY DOERR

JONATHAN SAFRAN FOER

NELL FREUDENBERGER

OLGA GRUSHIN

DARA HORN

GABE HUDSON

BEST OF YOUNG AMERICAN NOVELISTS 2 (2007)

ALLEN KURZWEIL

ELIZABETH McCRACKEN

LORRIE MOORE

FAE MYENNE NG

ROBERT O'CONNOR

CHRIS OFFUTT

STEWART O'NAN

MONA SIMPSON

MELANIE RAE THON

KATE WHEELER

UZODINMA IWEALA

NICOLE KRAUSS

RATTAWUT LAPCHAROENSAP

YIYUN LI

MAILE MELOY

ZZ PACKER

JESS ROW

KAREN RUSSELL

AKHIL SHARMA

GARY SHTEYNGART

JOHN WRAY

GRANTA

THE
BEST
OF
YOUNG
BRITISH NOVELISTS
WORLD TOUR

Starting on 16 April, *Granta* and the British Council invite you to join the Best Young British Novelists, from the new and previous lists, at events around the UK and across the globe.

LONDON

15 APRIL
The Announcement of the Best of Young British Novelists
The British Council (By invitation only)

16 APRIL
The London Launch
Waterstones Piccadilly

17 APRIL
The Best Young British Novelists Lit Crawl
In partnership with Foyles. Various Soho venues

UK April – May

Bath *in association with Bath Spa University, Topping and Company Booksellers*

Birmingham *Waterstones*

Brighton *Waterstones*

Cambridge *in association with Cambridge Wordfest, Heffers Bookshop*

Leeds *Waterstones*

Manchester *The International Anthony Burgess Foundation*

International Festivals

***Los Angeles Times* Festival of Books** *April*

PEN World Voices Festival *May*

London Literature Festival *May*

Worlds Literature Festival *Norwich, June*

York Festival of Ideas *June*

Edinburgh International Book Festival *August*

Hendrick's Carnival of Knowledge *Edinburgh, August*

Rest of World

Best of Young British Novelists will travel with the British Council to cities around the world for readings and discussion with their international peers, and to inspire a new generation of writers. Events will take place in countries including:

Brazil *São Paulo*
Canada *Toronto*
India *Ahmedabad, Bangalore, Chandigarh, Chennai, Hyderabad, Kolkata, Mumbai, New Delhi, Pune*
Italy *Milan*
Kenya *Nairobi*
Qatar *Doha*
Russia *Moscow*
Spain *Madrid*
USA *Los Angeles, New York*